PROFILES IN CRIME

HOW TO CATCH A KILLER

HUNTING AND CAPTURING THE WORLD'S MOST NOTORIOUS SERIAL KILLERS

KATHERINE RAMSLAND, PhD

STERLING
New York

STERLING
New York

An Imprint of Sterling Publishing Co., Inc.
1166 Avenue of the Americas
New York, NY 10036

ISBN 978-1-4549-3937-5
ISBN 978-1-4549-3941-2 (e-book)

Distributed in Canada by Sterling Publishing Co., Inc.
C/o Canadian Manda Group, 664 Annette Street
Toronto, Ontario M6S 2C8, Canada
Distributed in the United Kingdom by GMC Distribution Services
Castle Place, 166 High Street, Lewes, East Sussex BN7 1XU, England
Distributed in Australia by NewSouth Books
University of New South Wales, Sydney, NSW 2052, Australia

The text in this book contains graphic and disturbing depictions of murder.

For information about custom editions, special sales, and premium and corporate purchases,
please contact Sterling Special Sales at 800-805-5489 or specialsales@sterlingpublishing.com.

Manufactured in the United States

2 4 6 8 10 9 7 5 3 1

sterlingpublishing.com

Cover design by David Ter-Avanesyan
Interior design by Gavin Motnyk
Image Credits on page 295

For Josh Berman, my good friend and "Out West" Partner-in-Crime

CONTENTS

PART III: MISTAKES AND MISCALCULATIONS

PART IV: WITNESS REPORTS

PART V: SELF-SURRENDER

ACKNOWLEDGMENTS

I wish to thank those who have involved me in digging deep into the minds of serial killers, which helped me over the years to gain the expertise needed for this book. Marilyn Bardsley got me started, and several FBI profilers gave me access to their thinking about cases: John Douglas, Roy Hazelwood, Gregg McCrary, Bob Ressler, and Mark Safarik. Others who've helped me think through my work include Sally Keglovits, Dana DeVito, Rachael Bell, my "Dangerous Minds" students, Al Carlisle, Susan and Zachary Lysek, Dan Wisniewski, Bob Keppel, Bob Hare, and even Dennis "BTK" Rader, with whom I spent five years exploring his life story.

I'm also grateful to my long-time agent John Silbersack and my editors, John Meils and Stefan Dziemianowicz, who trusted my sense of this intense subject and encouraged my progress.

INTRODUCTION

The literature of serial murder is full of fascinating tales about how killers were caught. I once analyzed 300 cases for identification and arrest details—and identified more than a dozen distinct variables that played a key role in their capture. I learned that the largest number of successful resolutions (one in five) involved conscientious—even extraordinary—investigation. The killers' own errors mostly tripped them up after that, and a few even turned themselves in. The survey included different historic eras and countries (though mostly the U.S.), and I chose cases that offered clear details regarding identification and capture (so it was not a randomized sample). Still, it provided a lens through which I saw how incredibly difficult it can be for investigators to sort through evidence (or decry the lack of it) and identify productive leads.

And while there are many steps in any investigation, especially those that last for years, even decades, one or more specific but common factors usually lead to the key break in a case. These are:

1. Police investigation, including physical evidence/crime-scene behavior
2. Witness's description (including survivors)
3. Accomplice's betrayal
4. Associate's suspicions (friend, neighbor, relative)
5. Arrest during an unrelated police operation
6. Killed a victim that was easily linked to them
7. Killer's communication to press, victims, or police

8. Stored evidence (at home, on person, in computer, or in storage)

9. Error at a crime scene linked to other scenes associated with a suspect

10. Caught in the act

11. Turned themselves in

12. Recognized from published likeness

13. Common factor in multiple cases

14. Postmortem investigation (often after suicide)

From this list, I created five categories for this book:

1. Forensic Innovation

2. Police Procedure

3. Mistakes and Miscalculations

4. Witness Reports

5. Self-Surrender

The cases were then selected based on their notoriety, diversity, and teaching value. Those linked to a significant forensic contribution are probably the most instructive, since they revisit forensic history and could inspire future innovations. Still other cases were drawn from underrepresented populations, which might help to erode misconceptions about who commits serial murder. And a few are simply classic crime narratives. Although this collection is by no means exhaustive—thousands of serial-murder cases have been documented—it represents the variety of serial killers with which law enforcement must contend. Hopefully, these cases will also inspire some appreciation for the magnitude of their task and the lives they save when captures are made.

I should note that there are several myths associated with serial killers, thanks largely to misinformation or sensationalism from various media sources. Chief among them is the persistent notion that most serial killers wish to be caught. In fact, it's listed among the myths the FBI hoped to correct in their monograph from more than ten years ago, *Serial Murder: Multi-Disciplinary Perspectives for Investigators*. In my own survey, only 2.3 percent of serial killers turned themselves in (at times merely due to a lack of options). So while some criminologists believe that a subconscious desire to be caught leads to mistakes that end in arrest, only about 20 percent of serial killers in my study made such errors. Even if we stretch the notion to include as a "subconsciously motivated desire" being charged with another crime first, adding this 12.3 percent to overt mistake-makers (20.3 percent) and those who surrender on their own (2.3 percent) still equals just one in three who "want" to be caught. This myth appears to be built on the belief that we all have a conscience, but psychopathic predators have repeatedly shown that they experience little to no remorse. Even some who turned themselves in were not at all repentant about their murders.

This collection of cases demonstrates a historic arc from basic detective work to sophisticated forensic innovation. The phenomenon of serial murder weaves throughout the history of forensic science and psychology as the most challenging type of crime. However, improved resources over the past few decades help to identify these offenders more quickly. In addition, detectives now can return to former investigations with new tools, closing cases that had seemed unlikely to ever be solved. The stories told here affirm the positive evolution of serial-murder investigations and will hopefully inspire further forensic innovation.

PART I

FORENSIC INNOVATION

Some cases of serial murder inspired investigative innovation, while others benefited from it. Often, it took a meeting of the minds between scientists and investigators to recognize the possibilities, and some innovations significantly transformed crime-scene investigation.

THE MAD CARPENTER

THE CRIMES

Two young girls went missing in the small village of Lechtingen, Germany, in 1898. Hannelore Heidemann was seven, and her friend and neighbor Else Lanmeier was just a year older. They often walked home from school together, but neither arrived home on September 9. The worried mothers traveled together to the school to find them, only to learn that neither girl had arrived at school that day. A search of the local woods ensued. Neighbors pitched in. The girls' families were frantic. They asked everyone they knew, but no one recalled seeing either girl that day. And nothing turned up in the woods where the girls often played to indicate that they'd been there. It wasn't like either of them to skip school or worry their parents. As evening approached, it seemed possible that they would remain lost until morning, though several people kept looking.

Then a searcher deep in the woods spotted a light-colored object in some weeds. When he peered closer, he made out the bloodied arm of a child, seemingly torn from her body. Other limbs turned up nearby, along with a gutted torso and clothing that further confirmed foul play. Hannelore's mother identified her remains, but Else was nowhere to be found.

Darkness impeded the effort, but with evidence of one homicide, the villagers were determined to find the other child. They understood the implications for their own children. An hour later, Else's remains turned up under some thick bushes. She'd been torn apart as well. People wondered if wolves had attacked them—because surely no human would be this depraved.

Word spread through the village, and parents took special caution. The thought of a mad beast that could potentially charge from the woods at any moment put everyone on edge. Worse, it might be a person under the influence of supernatural power, a lycanthrope. At the end of the nineteenth century in Europe, such creatures were believed to exist.

By the 1500s in France and Germany, lycanthropy had become a diagnosable medical condition, with the uneducated often certain that such people had made a pact with the Devil. According to *The Book of Were-Wolves* by archaeologist and historian Sabine Baring-Gould, in some places lycanthropy was seemingly rampant, with hundreds of cases—even entire "wolfpacks" within families—being prosecuted for violent murders. Officials created and distributed pamphlets to demonstrate what happened to shape-shifters once caught, and to warn people against making such demonic deals.

The delusional form of lycanthropy supposedly compelled the sufferer to eat raw meat, attack others, grow their hair, and even lope around on all fours. During the nineteenth century, alienists studied such behavior, most notably Richard von Krafft-Ebing, director of the Feldhof Asylum near Graz and a professor of psychiatry in Strasbourg. In

A NINETEENTH-CENTURY ENGRAVING FEATURING A WEREWOLF ATTACKING A WOMAN.

1880, he published a standard diagnostic system for bizarre sexual disorders titled *A Textbook of Insanity*. Six years later, he added *Psychopathia Sexualis with Especial Reference to the Antipathic Sexual Instinct*. In it, he described the details of forty-five cases that focused largely on violent criminals with extraordinarily perverse practices. Among them were people who thought of themselves as vampires, cannibals, or werewolves. Some were described tearing into raw human flesh with their teeth.

As Krafft-Ebing studied the link between extreme erotic lust and homicidal tendencies, he developed a "vocabulary of perversion," as well as standards for case analysis and diagnosis. He was the first to try to study and categorize "lust murders" that included certain types of frenzied activity, the greatest percentage of them perpetrated by Caucasian males of all ages.

The residents of Lechtingen knew only that two young girls had been viciously ravaged. The small police force, with no experience in such investigations, questioned everyone in town to find out if a killer lived among them. A button was found near the remains that did not belong to the clothing of either girl. It could have been a random lost button, but police collected it in case it belonged to the killer. It was the only piece of possible physical evidence they had.

While canvassing, officers learned about a carpenter named Ludwig Tessnow. Someone had seen him come into the village from the woods that afternoon, his apron stained with dark splotches. The police went to Tessnow's residence to question him about his activities that day, and he told them he often got stains on his clothing from wood dye—that's all it was. He denied having seen the girls. However, the button from the crime scene appeared to match the buttons on Tessnow's jacket, which, notably, was missing one.

An officer searched Tessnow's workshop. When he found a can of wood-dye, he "accidentally" spilled some of it on Tessnow, to see if it looked like the stains on his apron. It did. With nothing more to implicate him, the police had to drop the investigation. What had happened to the two little girls would remain a mystery.

Tessnow was odd, but there were no further incidents during the remaining four months he lived there. When he left town, his neighbors were relieved. But a village about three hundred miles away would soon have cause for concern about his presence.

THE CAPTURE

Around the same time, scientists were working on reliable methods to analyze the behavior and composition of human blood. Among their goals was to develop a test that could distinguish whether blood came from an animal or a human. Criminals at the time often claimed that blood on their clothing came from animals, and there was no way to prove otherwise. A method had been proposed in 1841 where blood was heated with a chemical and sniffed for a specific odor, but it didn't really work.

During the next decade, a man named Ludwig Teichmann developed a technique of mixing blood with a solution of potassium chloride, iodide, and bromide in galactic acid to show that hemoglobin could be changed into hemin to enable an examination of the shape of the resulting crystals. It was a test to detect the presence of blood, and the method was used for half a century before another scientist added a more discriminating test.

As early as 1875, there was an understanding in some medical circles that there were different blood types. But it wasn't until 1901 that Dr. Karl Landsteiner at the Institute of Pathology and Anatomy in Austria was able to isolate the distinct types. He collected samples of blood from colleagues and, using a centrifuge, separated the blood's clear serum from its red cells. Landsteiner then placed the samples in different test tubes, mixing the blood of one participant with blood from the others. He found that sometimes the samples clumped together and sometimes they separated. He then identified three blood types, based on differences in a component called an antigen, which produced antibodies to fight infection. (In type A, antigen A and anti-B antibody were present, but antigen B was absent. In type B, antigen B was present but antigen A was absent. A third distinct reaction produced blood type C, in which both antigens A and B were absent; this type was later relabeled as type O.)

Two years later, Dr. Adriano Sturli discovered a type in which both antigens were present, so he called it AB. It was also clear that a person's blood type derived from genetic inheritance, which assisted with paternity tests.

In that same year, 1901, another German biologist was focusing on differences between animal and human blood. Paul Uhlenhuth, at the Institute of Hygiene in Griefswald, was working on a serum to cure hoof-and-mouth disease. During an experiment, he saw a visible reaction between antibody and antigen. When animals were injected to prevent infectious disease, the introduction of foreign substances caused the production of defensive substances. These "precipitins" could be utilized to distinguish different types of protein.

Uhlenhuth found that when he injected protein from a chicken egg into a rabbit, and then mixed serum from the rabbit with egg white, the egg proteins separated from the liquid to form a precipitin. He further discovered that each animal had its own characteristic blood-based protein.

And so did humans.

These discoveries led to a sea change for law enforcement. A coroner asked Uhlenhuth to test dried bloodstains from both animals and humans, and the results showed that the test was reliable. They could now eliminate suspects with blood type tests and determine if bloodstains on someone's clothing suggested murder. The police in Lechtingen could have benefited from such a test, but Tessnow would not get off so easily the next time. Had he moved farther away, his story might have ended differently.

On Sunday, July 1, 1901, two more children went missing on a resort island near the village of Göhren, a municipality in the Vorpommern-Rügen district. Six-year-old Peter Stubbe was out playing with his older brother Hermann. They ran into the woods. Hours passed, but no one was alarmed. It was a safe place. When the boys failed to return for supper, their parents started to grow concerned. They looked around but saw no sign of their sons, so they asked neighbors to help them search. By nightfall, the boys were still missing. Their parents would have to wait until morning to resume their search.

At dawn, a man came across both bodies in a clearing. The murdered boys lay together, their skulls crushed with a rock. As with the two girls in Lechtingen, their arms and legs had been torn off and scattered. The younger boy's neck was severed and his body was gutted, with his intestines hanging out. The older boy's pelvic section and legs were found in another area. The killer had taken the heart from one of the boys.

The crime seemed unthinkable. Not far away were crowds of tourists and pristine beaches. How could such a beast live in these woods?

Three weeks earlier, a farmer had claimed that someone had slaughtered seven of his sheep and left them in similar condition. He'd seen a stranger running away.

The local police interviewed everyone in the area. They found a fruit merchant who had noticed the boys with a reclusive carpenter named Ludwig Tessnow. A neighbor of Tessnow's reported that the carpenter had worn stained clothing on July 1.

Investigators went to Tessnow's home. He denied knowing anything about the boys and claimed they hadn't spoken to him. He offered a detailed account of his whereabouts on July 1. The officers searched his home and found freshly laundered clothing that showed some faint stains. Once again, Tessnow claimed the stains were from wood dye. The officers then brought Tessnow into town so the farmer with the mutilated sheep could have a look at him. He identified Tessnow as the man he'd seen running away from his farm. But it wasn't enough for the courts, since the farmer hadn't witnessed Tessnow actually kill any of his sheep. The officers decided to confiscate some of the carpenter's stained clothing and keep an eye on him. They knew they would have to catch him in the act, hopefully before he managed to kill again.

A local magistrate, Johann-Klaus Schmidt, remembered the case of the girls from Lechtingen. He contacted officials there and learned that Tessnow had been their key suspect. Stained clothing had also been the prime evidence. The coincidence was too significant to ignore. Schmidt discussed it with a prosecutor, Ernst Hubschmann, who'd read Uhlenhuth's recently published paper, "A Method for the Investigation of Different Types of Blood." The magistrate sent Tessnow's confiscated clothing and the rock believed to have been the murder weapon to Uhlenhuth, who dissolved numerous spots from the clothing in distilled water and applied his test. While some stains tested positive for wood dye, in seventeen stains Uhlenhuth detected traces of both animal (sheep) and human blood. He also found human blood on the rock.

When the results came back, Tessnow was held for trial. Uhlenhuth appeared as an expert witness to explain how his tests worked. Tessnow was found guilty and given a death sentence. The murders of the little girls appeared solved, but then Tessnow had an epileptic fit, which led to a psychiatric examination. Six medical experts declared him to be insane, but the findings failed to save him. With the conviction confirmed on appeal, Tessnow was reportedly executed. However, a strange footnote to the case involves a rumor suggesting that his sentence was secretly commuted, with word of his death spread anyway.

THE TAKEAWAY

Name: Ludwig Tessnow
Country: Germany
Born: February 15, 1872
Died: 1904
Killing Period: 1898–1901
Known Victims: 4
Date of Arrest: July 2, 1901

Tessnow appeared to suffer from the sort of bestial bloodlust that Krafft-Ebing documented in other sex murderers. Such killers develop deviant sexual motivations that become consuming fantasies. When they act out and find pleasure in murder, they seek more such opportunities. Bestial paraphilias that encourage savage attacks are obviously potentially dangerous. Their addictive nature often leads to mistakes on the part of the killer. Tessnow could not have anticipated the scientific breakthrough that led to his capture, but he knew he was under suspicion. Even with the scientific breakthrough, so new at the time and with so few people aware of it, it took the right crossing of paths at the right moment for forensic science to seal this momentous murder conviction.

2.

THE FOOTPAD KILLER

THE CRIMES

On November 21, 1983, fifteen-year-old Lynda Mann decided to go
see her friend, Karen. She felt safe in her little village of Narborough
in Leicestershire County, England. Leaving Karen's house around 7 P.M.,
Lynda went through the nearby village of Enderby before heading toward
a wooded shortcut, known as the Black Pad, back to her own village. The
path ran past the grounds of the local psychiatric hospital. As darkness
set in, Lynda might have seen the rising of a full moon before someone
grabbed her.

By 1:30 A.M., Lynda's stepfather, Eddie Eastwood, had notified the
police that she was long overdue. Eastwood went out himself to look for

her. He would later learn that he had walked right past her body without seeing it before he finally quit looking for the night.

At dawn, an employee of the psychiatric hospital on his way to work came across Lynda's partially nude body. The girl's jeans, shoes, and tights had been removed. A scarf covered her neck, but her jacket was pulled up and her nose had been bloodied.

Detective chief superintendent David Baker from the Criminal Investigation Division took over the investigation. A team arrived with bloodhounds, while other investigators searched for clues. It appeared that Lynda had been sexually violated before being killed. Her body was removed to the morgue for autopsy, which confirmed the rape. The cause of death was strangulation. Semen was recovered for antigen blood-type analysis, the best they had at the time. The rapist proved to have blood type A, which belonged to approximately one in ten adult males in the country.

Suspicion naturally fell on the nearby hospital inmates, but the facility's director assured the community that no one had left the building that night. Blood tests taken from all willing suspects turned up negative.

Two and a half years later, another local girl was accosted.

Ten Pound Lane, another wooded path half a mile from the Black Pad, ran from Enderby to Narborough. On July 31, 1986, Dawn Ashworth, fifteen, took it to visit friends. She did not come home that evening. The family went looking for her, walking along both the Black Pad and Ten Pound Lane. By late evening, Dawn's parents had phoned the police. The next morning, police searched the area with tracker dogs. Dawn's jacket turned up near Ten Pound Lane. On the second day of the search, they found her body.

Like Lynda Mann, Dawn had been stripped from the waist down. She lay on her left side, with her knees pulled up. Blood trickled from her vagina. The autopsy found that Dawn had been penetrated both vaginally and anally, and had died from manual strangulation. Semen showed the same blood type as Lynda's attacker. Since Dawn appeared to have struggled, police posted a notice in the newspaper asking residents to watch for a man with a fresh scratch.

A seventeen-year-old kitchen porter from the hospital, R. B., was seen loitering in the area of Ten Pound Lane. He watched the police activity with apparent interest. He even approached an officer to report that he'd seen the girl walking toward the gate. He appeared to know before the body was found that she was dead, so they arrested him.

Mentally slow for his age, R. B.'s answers to questions were inconsistent. He finally admitted that he'd talked with Dawn and accompanied her part of the way along the lane before going home. He liked to watch pornography, he admitted, and referred to girls as "slags," a cultural derogatory in England. Later, R. B. added another element: he claimed to have seen a man carrying a stick, following Dawn. Yet when the officers told him they suspected he was involved, R. B. admitted to killing her, claiming he'd been drunk at the time. He said he hadn't meant to hurt her, and thought he must have been in a trance because he couldn't remember doing it. Then, just as suddenly, he denied everything. His interrogators then got him to admit that he had seen Dawn's body and had sex with it.

Most of R. B.'s confession failed to match the facts, though he somehow knew things that had not been publicized. He also refused to confess to killing the first victim, Lynda Mann. The blood type from semen samples from each incident matched, which seemed to link them to a single offender. However, blood typing was too inclusive to identify R. B. and only R. B. as the local rapist-murderer. In fact, it was more likely that he'd be excluded, since his semen did not show the unique qualities evident in the crime samples, but he was the only suspect they had. Detectives needed a confession to both murders.

R. B.'s mother offered an alibi, but she was ignored after several young girls in the village claimed that R. B. had molested them. When

R. B.'s father read about the discovery of DNA testing for proving the father's identity in paternity suits in nearby Leicester, he told R. B.'s solicitor, who urged the case detectives to get a semen test for R. B. Chief Superintendent David Baker had read about this DNA testing discovery as well, and reached out to Dr. Alec Jeffreys, the scientist who'd made the breakthrough, to ask for his help. It would prove to be one of the most important connections in the history of crime investigation.

In 1984, Jeffreys, a molecular biologist, used DNA testing to solve an immigration dispute over a boy from Ghana who claimed he had a British mother and wanted to live with her. In his lab at the University of Leicester, Jeffreys and his colleagues looked for the small percentage of human DNA that shows individual variation, because it provided a marker for definitive identification far beyond what blood tests could achieve.

He later published his findings in *Nature*, where he and his team claimed that an individual's identifiable DNA pattern was unique and could not be found in any past, present, or future person. In 1985, Jeffreys gave an interview to a reporter for the Leicester newspaper, claiming "the new technique could mean a breakthrough in many areas, including the identification of criminals from a small sample of blood at the scene of the crime."

Jeffreys was also aware of the footpad murders. When Baker contacted him, he agreed to test the biological samples from the crime scenes. They were packaged and sent to his lab, along with R. B.'s blood sample. Although the sample from Lynda Mann was fairly degraded, Jeffreys put it through his process anyway.

After the analysis, the genetic profile of Lynda Mann's rapist was revealed. The semen removed from Dawn Ashworth was tested next and compared with the sample taken from Lynda Mann. Jeffreys reported to Baker that the semen came from the same person—but not R. B., who had falsely confessed and unwittingly become the first person in history to be exonerated by DNA testing.

Whoever had raped and killed the two fifteen-year-olds was still on the loose. Baker now had to find and capture a sexually motivated serial killer who might strike again. He also had a false confessor. When police asked R. B. why he'd lied, he said he'd felt pressured. Since he did know unpublished facts about the crime scene, detectives surmised that he had discovered the body before the police. It was also possible that the police had inadvertently shown or told R. B. things that he then used to relieve the pressure. (In subsequent decades, DNA testing would reveal that 15% to 20% of convictions involved false confessions.)

R. B. was released, sending investigators back to square one. But they had a new tool, a DNA test, so they decided to test every local man they could. It would represent the world's first DNA dragnet, a bold—and expensive—move. The police asked the men of Narborough and adjacent villages who were between fourteen and thirty-one years old to provide a blood sample. More than 4,500 men volunteered, most of whom were eliminated with conventional blood tests. But those samples with the blood type that matched the murdered women were sent for DNA analysis. Because it seemed unlikely that the killer would submit to a test that would prove his guilt, police watched for someone who would try to avoid getting tested. Instead of the needle in the haystack, they were looking for someone who refused to get near the hay at all.

The process for this "blooding," or taking blood samples for analysis, required showing ID and submitting to an interview. However, aside from the occasional passport or employment card, the ID cards bore no photos. Ultimately, this first-ever DNA dragnet resulted in no new suspects. Then, in September 1987, police learned of a suspicious incident.

THE CAPTURE

A woman overheard a baker named Ian Kelly say in a pub that he'd given his own blood sample to the police as a substitute for a friend, Colin Pitchfork. The twenty-eight-year-old Pitchfork was a known thief and a flasher, but he also had a wife and a child. To protect them from learning of his past, he'd asked other men to cover for him, and Kelly had obliged. When police arrested Kelly for perverting the course of justice, he admitted to assisting Pitchfork, which delayed the investigation by eight months. Pitchfork apparently told Kelly that he had already given his blood to cover for another man and would get into trouble if police figured it out. Pitchfork had also given Kelly a fake passport to use as ID.

The police then realized that they had already questioned Pitchfork after the Lynda Mann murder in 1983. He said at the time that his wife was at a class that evening, so he'd been watching their child. The claim had checked out, so Pitchfork had been eliminated as a suspect. Now he was back on the list.

When police arrested Pitchfork, he confessed. He said he'd been out driving with his baby in the car when he spotted Lynda Mann. He first decided to just flash her, but the excitement of the act aroused him so much that he chose to rape her in addition. She ran into the woods and Pitchfork followed her before realizing he would have to kill her to keep her from turning him in to the police. He then raped and strangled her. Upon returning to his car, he found his child still asleep, so he drove home to wash up before picking up his wife at school. Babysitting, it turned out, was a good alibi.

Pitchfork also admitted to killing Dawn Ashworth, but insisted he had not raped her anally. He also claimed to have not hidden her body where the police had found it, raising the possibility that R. B. or someone else had come across the body, had anal sex with it, and then hidden it anew.

Pitchfork confessed to another attempted rape of a sixteen-year-old woman who had not come forward, and also detailed his plan to silence Ian Kelly. During his confession, Pitchfork revealed his feelings of inadequacy since childhood. At age eleven, he'd begun flashing girls to experience a feeling of power. Eventually he'd been caught, but the humiliation had not stopped him. Even after he got married, he'd continued this deviance, setting the stage for behavioral escalation into something more dangerous. Most flashers do not become rapists or killers; but when such acts feed a deep-seated need that activates a satisfying fantasy life, it becomes addictive. And as with most addictions, the need for ever-greater stimulation occurs—and that stimulation can involve violence.

Police sent Pitchfork's blood for DNA testing to confirm his confession.

Jeffreys used "restriction fragment length polymorphism (RFLP) testing," a lengthy, expensive process that required an amount of biological material the size of a quarter. The results surprised no one. Pitchfork's genetic profile matched both semen samples.

THE TAKEAWAY
Name: Colin Pitchfork
Country: England
Born: March 23, 1960
Died: NA
Killing Period: 1983–1986
Known Victims: 2
Date of Arrest: September 7, 1987

Colin Pitchfork became the first person in history to be convicted of murder based on what was then called "genetic fingerprinting." On January 22, 1988, Pitchfork received double life sentences.

This case sparked headlines around the world and changed how crimes that involved biological evidence were investigated. Dr. Jeffreys was knighted for his contribution.

In the United States, DNA testing had to go through something called a "Frye hearing" before it could be used in court. DNA analysis had to prove itself to be scientifically sound in method, theory, and interpretation, and to have been positively reviewed by peers.

The hearing in the first U.S. case in 1987—involving Tommie Lee Andrews, a rapist—was complex, but finally the judge admitted the DNA methodology. However, the prosecutor overstated the odds of the samples coming only from the defendant, opening the door to legal challenges. This result motivated the scientific community to test and retest the approach. DNA analysis eventually gained increasing acceptance in the courts, though challenges were aimed at the way samples were interpreted, as well as at shoddy handling of specimen evidence. Without safeguards for proper scientific examination, the labs put prosecutors at a disadvantage because defense attorneys quickly learned of vulnerabilities in the system. Manhattan-based attorneys Barry Scheck and Peter Neufeld then co-founded the DNA Task Force of the National Association of Criminal Defense Attorneys to help create standards for forensic applications of DNA technology. Since many different things can occur between the collection of a sample and the final analysis, the courts were forced to review DNA testimony on a case-by-case basis. The FBI reported the first RFLP-processed case from its own lab in 1989, publishing guidelines to set standards for quality assurance.

The Pitchfork case demonstrated the power of DNA analysis to support both conviction and exoneration. Scheck and Neufeld founded the first Innocence Project to ensure that DNA assisted the innocent, too.

3.

THE CLEAN-CUT KILLER

THE CRIMES

Bill Jaeger, an autoworker in Michigan, took the month of June 1973 off from his job to take his wife Marietta, her parents, and their five children on a dream vacation out West. They made a three-day stop in Headwater State Park at Three Forks in southwestern Montana. On the night of June 24, their seven-year-old daughter Susie settled down, hugging her two favorite stuffed animals in the tent she shared with her twelve-year-old sister, Heidi. Bill and Marietta climbed into a camper truck a few feet away to prepare for bed themselves. The calming sound of the Missouri River could be heard nearby.

Early the next morning, Heidi felt a breeze and noticed a rip in the tent. She sat up, saw that Susie was gone, and woke her parents. Bill and Marietta thought Susie might have gone to the bathroom, but the rip in the tent told a very different, less innocent story. When they saw Susie's stuffed animals in the grass outside, Bill contacted the Gallatin County Sheriff's Department. Two deputies responded and, in the dew, noticed footprints that led to the empty parking lot. It seemed clear that the child had been taken.

The sheriff contacted the FBI. Special Agent Pete Dunbar, in Bozeman, took the case. He summoned helicopters and volunteers for a massive search effort. Some of the officers recalled an unsolved murder at that campground in 1968. Michael Raney, on a Boy Scout campout, had been beaten and stabbed in his tent during the night. For the current incident, investigators brought in local sex offenders for questioning. They were all given polygraphs and, based on the results, eliminated as suspects.

After five weeks of waiting in Montana, the Jaegers returned to Michigan. The FBI assured them they would continue the search and urged them to keep a recorder near the phone, though the lack of a demand for ransom money concerned them. The Jaegers offered a reward and posted flyers, but months passed with no information. At one point, when Marietta left the house briefly, the kidnapper called. The eldest son turned on a tape recorder and asked questions to keep him on the phone, but the man ended the call quickly. It was traced to a pay phone at a Wyoming diner, but the trail ended there.

Eight months later, in February, the sheriff's office received a report that nineteen-year-old Sandra Smallegan was missing from Manhattan, Montana. She lived about ten miles from Headwater State Park. No one had heard from her in days.

When a local deputy, Don Hauptman, drove near the abandoned Lockhart ranch in Horseshoe Hills, he saw fresh tire tracks—and a pair of women's panties in the dirt. Hauptman checked the barn, found the door nailed shut, and broke in. He lifted a tarp from a car parked inside that he recognized as Smallegan's missing vehicle. He also found a closet that appeared to have been repeatedly nailed closed, with traces of blood on it. Volunteers were brought in to search five square miles around the ranch. A fifty-five-gallon barrel produced charred wood and bone fragments. More than 1,200 bone pieces were collected, many of which a Smithsonian anthropologist would confirm as human. A few stray teeth would turn out to be Smallegan's.

As the area was searched, a local resident hung around, volunteering to help and asking questions about the case. His name was David Meirhofer, a twenty-three-year-old Vietnam vet. Meirhofer had been questioned already, based on an anonymous tip from someone who thought he was weird. Special Agent Dunbar questioned him again. Meirhofer admitted he'd gone out with Smallegan but said she'd declined a second date. Dunbar realized that Meirhofer was familiar with the area where Sandra's remains had been found, so he asked the young man to take a polygraph. Meirhofer agreed and passed. He denied knowing anything about the kidnapping or murder. He also agreed to be questioned under sodium amytal, at which time he repeated everything, without deviation, clearing him as a suspect. And the case stalled.

During spring 1974, Dunbar took an FBI-hosted criminology course with instructor Patrick Mullany, a member of the FBI's newly formed Behavioral Science Unit. The course was part of a new program that incorporated the psychological analysis of perpetrators. Special Agent Howard Teten had developed the course in 1970 while he was a police officer with the San Leandro Police Department in California, where he studied with two forensic psychiatrists. "By about 1960," Teten said, "I had developed a hypothesis that in certain types of homicides, you'd be able to determine the kind of person you were looking for by what you could see at the crime scene."

Teten believed that people committed crimes the way they lived. He became interested in hard-to-solve sexually related homicides, and had collected cases from local police agencies for an experiment. "When I received the crime-scene information, I would examine all the data and prepare a tentative description of the perpetrator. Then I would look at the individual found to have committed the crime and compare him to my description." Teten became skilled at accurately deducing detailed information on suspects from crime-scene details alone.

Teten included his unique approach in the Applied Criminology course he taught at the FBI. Mullany, with a graduate degree in psychology, joined him in 1972. Teten would describe the crime, while Mullany would supply the mental disorder. Applied Criminology became a core course for the newly formed Behavioral Science Unit, and was eventually renamed Psychological Profiling.

After the class ended, Dunbar asked Mullany to look at the kidnapping case. Dunbar had requested a full set of suspect interviews, crime-scene photos, and crime-investigation methods. Still, there wasn't much to work with. Another agent, Robert Ressler, joined the effort, as did Howard Teten.

"The Susan Jaeger case turned out to be the very first FBI case psychologically profiled," Mullany would later observe.

The three agents looked at the case separately, then pooled their ideas. They thought the kidnapper was a Caucasian male with military training, because he'd been so stealthy. He would have to be strong enough to carry a fifty-five-pound struggling girl. They also thought he would be an unmarried loner who had trouble with the opposite sex, because he grabbed a girl. He'd likely be intelligent and live near the campground, because he seemed to know the area. They thought it possible that he had a mental disorder like schizophrenia, so he could pass a lie-detector test. Or he might be a psychopath, with no guilt. He'd taken the girl for sexual reasons, not a ransom, and she was probably dead. He had likely committed crimes before and, as is typical with sex offenders, would do it again. Of the suspect pool, they thought Meirhofer was the best fit, but Dunbar insisted it couldn't be him.

"We met a lot of opposition from the FBI agent and the local police department," Mullany said. "The opposition was reasonable, because he [Meirhofer] had passed both truth tests." The local officers didn't think the polite, educated man was the type of person they were looking for. He'd been helpful in every way. But the profilers stood their ground.

Mullany and Teten believed that Meirhofer would make a phone call to the family on the anniversary of the kidnapping. "We thought that he was such an intimate killer," Mullany explained, "that he had become so personally involved in the killing and in the victim's life, and in the victim's family's lives[,] that he would celebrate this event like a normal person would celebrate an anniversary."

Marietta Jaeger gave an interview to a journalist to say that she felt sorry for the man. She wanted to talk to him. She hoped to flush him out and provoke the predicted call.

On June 25, 1974, the phone rang in the Jaeger household. Marietta answered. A man asked, "Is this Susie's mom?" He told her he was the one who'd taken Susie exactly one year ago "to the minute." He hung up. Marietta held her breath, hoping for more contact. Then he called again. Bill contacted the FBI to get a trace. Marietta kept the man on the phone. He bragged that he was smart and that Susie was having a good time with him, and that no one even suspected him. He claimed Susie liked being with him. Marietta said she was praying for him, which caused him to break down. The call had lasted an hour.

Unfortunately, the FBI's tracing system failed and they were unable to pinpoint the call. It was a tremendous disappointment to the family, seemingly their best shot at finding out what had happened to Susie. Mullany said the caller's arrogance suggested he was among the suspects who'd been cleared. The caller thought he'd been clever.

A month later, on his phone bill, a Montana rancher noticed an hour-long call to Michigan he hadn't made. The recipients were the Jaegers, so he called the sheriff. They found fresh tire tracks under the rancher's phone lines and evidence that someone had tapped into them. The rancher knew Meirhofer. He'd once hired him as a ranch hand. He also knew that Meirhofer had been a communications specialist in the military and would know how to tap the lines.

The FBI turned to a voice-print specialist to compare the recorded voice from the phone call against a recorded interview with Meirhofer. They matched. The agents devised a voice lineup and asked Marietta to listen to the voices. She picked Meirhofer as the man who had called her.

To strengthen the case, Mullany thought that Marietta should confront the suspect. This might throw him off his guard. They flew her back to Montana. Meirhofer came in, but he refused to admit to anything. She could tell he was mentally ill and told him she forgave him. "He was the one," she later said. "I knew he was the one, and I didn't want to let him out of my sight."

The deputies put him under surveillance. He wasn't fazed. One day, he slipped away and drove to Utah to place a call. It was a year since the first call, when Marietta had been out. She knew it was Meirhofer and told him so. He mentioned things that they'd discussed in Montana, incriminating himself. She reported it all to the agents. They traced the call to a Salt Lake City hotel room, but no one was in the room.

THE CAPTURE

When Meirhofer returned home, he was placed under arrest. The Jaegers' phone number was on a slip of paper in his pocket, along with the fake name he'd used to make the call from Utah. He also had stationery from the hotel where he'd stayed. To devise a search warrant, the sheriff used the profilers' advice that sex offenders kept trophies like jewelry or body parts. In Meirhofer's home, deputies found items in the freezer wrapped in butcher's paper. Among them was a human hand clutching two severed fingers with painted nails. When they showed this to Meirhofer's attorney, he vomited. Then he talked to his client before asking for a deal. Meirhofer was ready to confess. In exchange for a life sentence, he described four murders.

Meirhofer provided the horrific details without emotion. He'd committed the first murder in 1967, when he was a high school senior. Another student had picked a fight with him. One day, he saw the student's thirteen-year-old brother, Bernie Poelman, out fishing, so he shot and killed him in revenge. It was a high-risk act, but he got away with it. The next murder was Michael Raney, the Boy Scout at the Headwaters Campground. The local troop had kicked Meirhofer out, so he retaliated by stabbing one of its members. He'd intended to choke the boy but couldn't get in the right position. Susie Jaeger was next. He was watching the family and heard the girls in the tent. It was easy to cut through the tent and grab Susie. He took the child to the Lockhart ranch, sexually assaulted her, then strangled her. He dismembered the body afterwards, burning and scattering the remains, even cannibalizing some. He tossed her head into an outhouse. Sandra Smallegan's death, he said, was an accident. He'd broken into her apartment to abduct her but had covered her nose with duct tape, smothering her. He took her body to the ranch, dismembered it, and incinerated the remains, keeping some flesh in the freezer and spreading her bone fragments among Susie's.

Although Mullany predicted that the killer would be suicidal, a deputy gave him a towel and failed to keep him on suicide watch. Four hours after his confession, Meirhofer hanged himself in his cell.

THE TAKEAWAY

Name: David Gail Meirhofer
Country: United States
Date of Birth: June 8, 1949
Date of Death: September 29, 1974
Killing Period: 1967–1974
Known Victims: 4
Date of Arrest: September 27, 1974

This case demonstrated that profilers who had experience with a range of criminal types and behaviors applied a broader perspective on the type of person who would commit a child abduction than local investigators could. Teten and Mullany knew that so-called nice guys could also be remorseless killers. The deputies weren't trained to understand that rage can simmer into deadly long-term grudges.

For people like Meirhofer, humiliation runs deep, depriving them of self-esteem and a sense of control. The negative incidents feed their view of a hostile world that justifies payback. Surprisingly, there has been little research on this topic. Dr. Robert Hale published an article in 1994 about the role of humiliation in serial murder. Victims are symbolic, he stated. They trigger embarrassing internalized memories about being taunted, threatened, or abused that continue to enrage. The killer strikes out in an attempt to decrease the impact, but since the victim is not the offending party there is no resolution, so the murders continue. Further, the killer does not make the association between his past and what he's currently doing—he's just trying to feel empowered.

Serial killers, Hale added, do not progress through normal stages of development, in which one learns to distinguish between the things one can control and the things one cannot. They remain frustrated. Some develop an exaggerated sense of what they *must* control and feel ashamed when they cannot. When they use mastery as the basis of self-esteem, they set themselves up for a constant sense of inadequacy. They might mature in other areas—an ability to get a job and support a family, for example—but not in the social-sexual area. People did think Meirhofer, who seemed like a nice guy, was nevertheless strange.

Murder can also be a response to current frustrations, like job loss, conflict in a domestic situation, or other humiliating situations, so the killer wants to regain his or her sense of control. In other words, any disempowering or disruptive situation (as perceived by the killer) can trigger violence. If the end result feels better, mechanisms are in place, psychologically and biologically, to repeat the act as they try to restore their sense of self. For some killers, the perceived "wrong" becomes their justification for acting out against the targets. Meirhofer is a good fit for this pattern.

4.
THE VIENNA COURIER

THE CRIMES

On a mid-September morning in 1990, a woman's nude body was found in the woods just outside Prague, Czechoslovakia, on the bank of the Vltava River. The victim lay on her back, provocatively posed, with a pair of gray stockings tied around her neck and a gold ring still on her finger. She'd been strangled, stabbed, and beaten, but not raped. A layer of leaves covered her. An ID found separately said the victim was Blanka Bockova, a worker in a local butcher shop. Police learned that she'd been seen with a fortyish man at a bar before she vanished. No one questioned knew him.

Five weeks later in Graz, Austria, on October 26, Brunhilde Masser, a sex worker, went missing. Sex work was legal in Austria, and sex murders were rare. As with Bockova, there were no leads. On December 5, Heidemarie Hammerer, another sex worker, disappeared from Bregenz, an Austrian tourist city. Hikers came across her remains three weeks later. She lay on her back fully clothed. She appeared as if she'd been beaten, strangled with a pair of pantyhose, and then redressed. There were also bruises on her wrists, and she still wore her jewelry. Several red fibers inconsistent with her clothing were sent to the lab for analysis, as the Regional Office of the Austrian Federal Police opened an investigation.

Soon, Masser's skeletal remains were discovered in the woods north of Graz. The pathologist determined that Masser had been stabbed with a sharp weapon and possibly strangled with her pantyhose. She still had her jewelry, which helped police to identify the remains.

On March 7, 1991, sex worker Elfriede Schrempf vanished from her usual corner in Graz. A man called her relatives to harass them about her occupation. But the call provided no leads.

The police wondered if they had one killer who traveled, or two killers each of whose MO was similar to the other. The locations were just over six hours apart by car.

It was early October before hikers discovered Schrempf's skeletal remains in a forested area outside Graz. Like the other two victims, her remains were covered with leaves (though it was autumn, which could account for this factor).

Then, in less than a month, Silvia Zagler, Sabine Moitzi, Regina Prem, and Karin Eroglu all vanished from Vienna. All of these women were sex workers.

A team of Austrian investigators compared the cases and found dissimilarities. They decided they did not have a serial killer. However, Austria had no system at the time for a sophisticated behavioral analysis.

In May, the bodies of Moitzi and Eroglu were found in the woods outside Vienna. Both had been strangled with an article of their own clothing, and Eroglu had been savagely beaten. Aside from her jewelry, she was naked. Moitzi wore only a jersey, pulled up.

The press ignored the police and published articles about an international serial killer, dubbed "the Vienna Courier" and "the Vienna Woods Killer."

Former Inspector August Schenner, retired from the Criminal Investigation Department in Salzburg, was following the news coverage. The killer's MO reminded him of an inmate he'd interviewed in 1973 while investigating the murder of Marcia Horvath, who had been strangled with her stockings before being tossed into a lake. He knew about Jack Unterweger, who'd been convicted of killing Margret Schäfer, a friend of Barbara Scholz. Scholz had told police that Unterweger had lured Schäfer into a car, bound her, robbed her, beat her, and removed her clothes but left her jewelry on. In the woods, he had beaten her with a metal pipe before strangling her with her bra. He'd then covered the body with leaves. In court, he claimed he'd had an irresistible impulse: as he'd hit Schäfer, he'd envisioned his mother who had abandoned him as an infant.

When Schenner interviewed him in prison, Unterweger had denied being involved in any other murder besides Schäfer's. Now Schenner wondered if Unterweger had been paroled recently. He made inquiries and, when he discovered that Unterweger was indeed free, he urged investigators to keep their eye on him.

Since his release, Unterweger had become a celebrity among elite intellectuals. In prison, he'd taken writing courses and eventually produced poems and plays. His 1984 prison memoir, *Fegefeur* (*Purgatory*), was a best seller; and his rage-filled tale, *Endstation Zuchthaus* (*Terminus Prison*), won a literary prize. In his memoir, Unterweger claimed he'd been born to a young sex worker and had been forced to live with his abusive alcoholic grandfather. As a result, he got into trouble as a teenager. Now, he claimed, he knew better.

The Viennese literary community thought Unterweger's self-taught art appreciation had cured him. Prominent intellectuals urged politicians to grant him parole. He could support himself, they said, and help improve society.

Unterweger, forty, won his parole on May 23, 1990. He received a generous stipend and was invited to literary soirees and talk shows. He attended his own plays, often wearing white suits, silk shirts, and gold chains. He frequented Vienna's trendy champagne bars and nightclubs, where women flocked to him.

However, when a relative of Unterweger's named Charlotte Auer read *Fegefeur*, she was outraged. Unterweger's grandfather was her stepfather. Jack had lied. His mother had not been a sex worker. Yes, his grandfather had been an alcoholic, but *her* mother had been in the home throughout his early childhood, coddling him. Auer confronted Unterweger during a book tour, but backed off when he threatened her.

Meanwhile, a newspaper editor came up with the idea that Unterweger, the renowned writer and former murderer, should cover crime. Unterweger agreed and took on the recent string of murders of sex workers, wondering in print why investigators had not yet arrested anyone. Unterweger was playing a game.

On June 11, 1991, Unterweger left the country to write about prostitution and homelessness in Los Angeles, California. While he was away, there were no murders in Vienna similar to the string of unsolved killings.

On October 22, officials at the Criminal Investigation Bureau in Vienna brought Unterweger in for questioning, where he insisted that he knew none of the murder victims. However, he now realized that he was a suspect and encouraged his colleagues to take up the claim that he was being persecuted.

Early in 1992, in the mailbox of Regina Prem, who'd gone missing, her husband found five empty cigarette packs of her preferred brand rolled up. Among them was a passport photo of her son that Regina carried in her purse. By this time, it already seemed likely that she was dead.

Dr. Ernst Geiger, an official in the Austrian Federal Police, took charge of the investigation. Geiger took Schenner's warning seriously but could not accuse someone as popular as Unterweger without a solid case against him. Using credit card receipts, investigators then placed Unterweger in Graz when Masser had been murdered and again when Schrempf had disappeared. He'd also been in Bregenz when Hammerer was taken, and a witness said that Unterweger resembled the man with whom Hammerer had last been seen. He'd worn a red scarf.

Geiger also determined that Unterweger had been in Prague in September 1990. When he contacted the police there, he learned about Bockova. Finally, Unterweger had been in Vienna when the four women disappeared there. The evidence was building.

From interviews with Austrian sex workers, Geiger learned that Unterweger asked some to wear handcuffs during sex, which got rough. Geiger then found the BMW that Unterweger had bought upon his parole from prison, and then sold. Its new owner allowed the police to go through it. They found a hair fragment and sent it in for analysis. Manfred Hochmeister at the Institut für Rechtsmedizin in Berne, Switzerland, found sufficient skin on the root for a DNA test. It matched Blanka Bockova, placing her in Unterweger's car. The detectives were allowed to expand their search.

In Unterweger's Vienna apartment, they discovered a menu and receipts from a seafood restaurant in Malibu, California, as well as photographs of Unterweger posing with members of the Los Angeles Police Department. They also found a red knit scarf, which they confiscated. When the scarf's fibers proved to be consistent with those found on Hammerer, Geiger obtained an arrest warrant.

But Unterweger had gone on holiday with his eighteen-year-old girlfriend, Bianca Mrak. His friends alerted him to trouble, so he fled with Mrak to Miami, Florida, lying to U.S. customs agents about his criminal record. From Florida, Unterweger made calls to associates at Austrian papers to insist he was being framed. He claimed he had alibis for each of the murders and swore that he'd never spend another day in prison.

THE CAPTURE

Gert Schmidt, editor of *Success* magazine, offered to pay Unterweger for an exclusive interview. Unterweger provided his address in South Beach, a neighborhood of Miami Beach, for wiring the money. Schmidt passed the information along to Geiger. Soon, the U.S. Marshals Service had it, along with photos of the short, blondish man with dramatic prison tattoos. Three deputy marshals and an ATF agent put surveillance on a Western Union office.

Eventually, Unterweger and his girlfriend came down the street. Mrak entered the building to get the money while Unterweger waited outside. When Mrak returned, the marshals made their move. Unterweger, ever alert, took off running.

One agent went after Mrak, while the others followed Unterweger. He ran into a restaurant and out the back, but the agents cornered him in a parking structure, where he gave up. He was arrested and transported to Miami. On the way, the agents told Unterweger about the customs violation, which relieved him to the point of becoming jovial. Then they mentioned the murders in Austria, and Unterweger began to sob and claim he was being framed.

While he was awaiting extradition in custody, LAPD detectives Jim Harper and Fred Miller arrived to question him about the murders of three sex workers in Los Angeles during Unterweger's time there. All had been left out in the open, beaten, and strangled with their bras using an odd type of knot—the bras were cut in the same places, with the band stripped from the elastic on the left side and then tied in an identical complex manner. They knew that Unterweger had presented himself to the LAPD as a European journalist and requested a tour of the seedier parts of town. The credit-card statements from Geiger showed charges from a hotel near the murders.

With a warrant, the detectives drew Unterweger's blood and took hair samples and swabs of saliva. His DNA matched the semen from one of their victims. They mentioned California's death penalty. Unterweger thought he had a better chance in Austria, where he had supporters. He agreed to extradition. On May 28, 1992, Unterweger returned to Austria for trial. In interviews with the press, he claimed he was fully rehabilitated and would prove his innocence with alibis.

By April, the skeletal remains of Regina Prem had turned up in the woods. It had been a year since her disappearance, so her manner of death could not be determined.

Geiger knew he had little physical evidence. He'd heard of behavioral profiling, so he contacted the FBI and brought his evidence to Quantico, Virginia. Thomas Müller, Chief of the Criminal Psychology Service in the Federal Ministry of the Interior, accompanied him. They met with Special Agent Gregg McCrary and learned about Criminal Investigative Analysis, the method of interpreting crime-scene behavior. They did not need a profile, McCrary told them, but a signature analysis: behavior that would link the crimes to one another and collectively distinguish them from others. The more specific or exotic, the better.

Initially, McCrary examined only the crimes and crime-scene details. He entered data about all the victims into the Violent Crime Apprehension Program (ViCAP) database, using detailed forms that crystallized comparable factors. The database contained around 12,000 solved and unsolved homicide cases at the time. For the digital search, McCrary used fifteen cross-referenced criteria. When he looked at the results, he spotted a pattern in the victimology and manner of disposal.

The killer attacked sex workers, was organized, and planned his murders, usually binding and beating victims before he killed them.

Behavioral evidence linked all eleven victims, as well as one in California. However, the killer for this twelfth victim had been identified and convicted.

Then McCrary looked at Geiger's suspect data. When they placed Unterweger's timeline over that of the murders and compared his MO in the Margret Schäfer murder to the others, the linkage was solid on several key points. Supporting it was an analysis done at the Los Angeles Crime Lab by criminalist Lynn Herold on the killer's special ligature knot. Those from Los Angeles matched the knots tied in the pantyhose used on the Austrian victims.

The trial began in June 1994 in Graz. Detective Jim Harper came from the LAPD and Lynn Herold from the crime lab. McCrary was there to discuss the ViCAP system and the signature analysis—a first for Austrian courts, which prosecuted its citizens for crimes they committed anywhere. In addition, the prosecutor had a psychiatric report about Unterweger's sadistic criminal nature, Bockova's hair strand from Unterweger's car, red fibers from Masser's body consistent with Unterweger's red scarf, and negative character-witness testimony from former associates and girlfriends Unterweger had burned.

A confident Unterweger argued his own case. In a hurt tone, he asked the jury not to judge him by past deeds. His "higher sensibilities," developed through poetry and literature, had rehabilitated him.

The trial lasted two and a half months, during which opinions shifted among press opinion writers. Some who once had sided with Unterweger now viewed him as a con artist and a killer. Unterweger never presented the promised alibis and was found guilty of nine counts of murder: Bockova, all three Los Angeles victims, and five in Austria. (Two victims were too decomposed to determine cause of death.) Unterweger got a life sentence, again.

Defiant, he fulfilled one promise: when the guards weren't looking, Unterweger used the string from his prison jumpsuit, tied with his unique knot, to hang himself. He never spent another day in prison.

THE TAKEAWAY

Name: Johann "Jack" Unterweger
Country: Austria
Date of Birth: August 16, 1950
Date of Death: June 20, 1994
Killing Period: 1976, 1990–1991
Known Victims: 12
Date of Arrest: February 27, 1992

Unterweger's positive legacy was that Austria set up a system like the FBI's ViCAP program, with Geiger and Müller guiding its development. They were impressed with how such a searchable database improved law-enforcement investigations. The Unterweger case is one of ViCAP's success stories, proving the utility of data analytics. Unterweger also demonstrated that art does not cure psychopaths.

5.

BTK

THE CRIMES

Three children in Wichita, Kansas, waited in terror on January 15, 1974, as police responded to their call. Upon arrival, the police discovered their parents, Joseph and Julie Otero, strangled to death in their home. A plastic bag had been placed over their father's head. Carmen, thirteen, had tried to loosen the ligature around her mother's throat, while Danny, fourteen tried cutting the cords. Finding the phone line cut, they ran to a neighbor to seek help. They did not know that their younger brother and sister had also been murdered. Joey, Jr. was in his room with a bag over his head and Josephine hung from a pipe in the basement. The killer had used her for sexual gratification.

Fifteen-year-old Charlie Otero thought the mass murder was a hit by local organized crime, but no leads supported the allegation or led to any suspects. Then, ten months later in October, police arrested three men. Shortly thereafter, a call to a local reporter led to the discovery of a letter that would provide the details of the Otero quadruple homicide and prove that a lone offender had committed this crime. He was not among the three arrested. In the letter, he said he had studied other sexual criminals and had a "monster" in his brain that compelled him to kill. "The pressure is great and somt-times [sic] he run the game to his liking," he wrote.

Very little was known about serial killers in 1974, so no one knew what to make of the illness or possession to which the killer alluded. He indicated that this "monster" had "already chosen his next victim." It was a terrorizing threat, with an added "P.S." indicating "the code words for me will be bind them, torture them, kill them, B.T.K., you see he at it again. They will be on the next victim." The mystery correspondent did not take credit for the murder of twenty-one-year-old Kathryn Bright three months after the Oteros, which police had not linked to the Otero killings. The letter also gave no indication that after the Bright murder, the killer had gone home to greet his wife after work and start his murder journal.

No similar murders occurred again in Wichita until 1977. It was not that BTK—aka Dennis Rader—had stopped; he simply failed to find the right opportunity. He stalked potential targets, which he called "projects," but something always thwarted him. Years later, Rader would explain: "I think it can be that a man goes fishing and sometimes he's not very lucky. It may be some social issues. He's busy at home or work. I did not fit the normal profile of a serial killer. Why were there gaps of so many years? Bottom line, I was *always* on the prowl."

In 1977, two more women were strangled in their homes. Shirley Vian was home with her three children on March 17 when one of them opened the door to a man pretending to be looking for someone in the area. He locked the children in a bathroom while he tied Vian to her bed and strangled her. Eight months later, on December 8, he waited for Nancy Fox inside her home before killing her. When she expired from asphyxiation, he relieved himself in her clothing and left with her driver's license and other items. He considered her his perfect victim, because he had the time to do what he wanted.

In February 1978, BTK communicated again, sending a poorly written letter to KAKE-TV. This time he referenced the Bright murder without naming the victim, in hopes he'd be recognized as a serial killer of note. Four incidents with seven murders confirmed it. Rader included a drawing of the Fox murder scene and a list of other "elite" serial killers he considered his equal—H. H. Holmes, Jack the Ripper, "Ted of the West Coast" (aka Ted Bundy; see Chapter 17). He described how "Factor X" motivated all these killers, referring to the specific inner demon that lived in all of them. There was no cure, he said, and they could not stop. He also whined that he hadn't gotten the media attention that others had, and warned that he was already stalking victim number eight. "How many do I have to Kill," he asked, "before I get a name in the paper or some national attention? Do the cop [sic] think that all those deaths are not related?" Although he had already named himself BTK, he suggested other monikers such as "The Wichita Hangman" and "The Poet Strangler."

What no one knew yet was that BTK was a church-going married man with a job and family who was also taking courses in criminal justice at Wichita State University. Rader was ordinary, polite, controlling, and sometimes nasty, but he was no one's idea of a serial killer. He attributed his successful duplicity to "cubing," or an ability to act out many roles convincingly. Psychopaths have shallow emotional commitments, which allow them to switch in and out of false identities with ease. In his secret life, Rader was predatory. He watched and waited, learned his target victims' routines, and made notes to improve upon his "work" and avoid mistakes. He found employment as a security installer, which let him study the layout and security system of homes he targeted and calculate the best moment to attack.

Luck played a significant role in his success, as Rader was no mastermind. He made mistakes at each of his murder scenes that could have led to his capture: he left an item behind at the Oteros' house; Kathryn Bright's brother and Shirley Vian's kids had seen his face; and his voice was on record from calling in Nancy Fox's murder himself. Despite his motto of "leave nothing to chance," he'd been careless; he knew it and wanted to improve. He understood well how the mistakes of other serial murderers had led to their captures.

Yet Rader wanted to keep a record, so he started a journal in which he drew pictures from memory and jotted down details. "My brain is on fire," he stated after killing the Oteros, and began a list of "Projects," naming each with an identifier linked to a victim. One was "Project Waco," another "Project Lites Out." He hid the journals, along with items taken from his victims, in "hidey holes" around the house as he planned his next move.

Detectives debated what to do. Some believed that downplaying the incidents would prevent another murder, while others were sure that if this killer were ignored, he'd kill again. The authorities decided to let Wichita residents know that a local serial killer had murdered seven people and was a threat to murder more. No one knew where he'd strike next. Detectives noted that most of Rader's communications were photocopied and began tracking down the area copying machines to identify the signature of the one he used. The Xerox Corporation assisted, helping to pinpoint a machine at Wichita State University. Rader read this news item and changed his copy machine location. He began to make copies of copies, using different machines. This cat-and-mouse game appealed to him, giving him a sense of power.

As law enforcement marked the tenth anniversary of the unsolved Otero murders, detectives wondered if BTK had been arrested for something else, left the area, or died. He resurfaced once in the spring of 1979, apparently waiting in a house where his intended target did not come home before he had to leave. Afterward, he sent her a note, with a poem, to let her know she'd been his target. In 1984, a new task force went through the case files systematically to see if something had been missed.

Suspects were asked for blood samples and eliminated. An FBI special agent from the Behavioral Science Unit, Roy Hazelwood, offered a detailed portrait that yielded information already apparent: the killer was sadistic and controlling; he read detective magazines and pornography; he might enjoy S&M with a partner; and he liked to drive around. The profile moved the investigation no closer to an arrest.

At the time, Rader was busy with his home and church life, as well as volunteering with the Boy Scouts. In 1985, he decided to kill a neighbor, Marine Hedge. He made elaborate plans and carried them out on April 26, taking the body to his church to take photos of it before dumping it in a ditch outside. Rader figured he'd deviate from his profile, a common tactic for killers who follow the news about their own investigation. He sent no poems or letters this time, in part because he had broken his own rule to kill only those far away from his "regular" life. He didn't want police attention that might link his dead neighbor to him. To reassure his own family about a killing that had happened so close to their home, he tightened security on their windows and doors.

The following year, Rader targeted Vicki Wegerle. Pretending to be a telephone repairman, he persuaded her to let him in on September 16, 1986. Once he dropped the disguise, she fought valiantly but was no match for him. Rader strangled her, took Polaroid pictures for his collection, grabbed her driver's license, and stole her car. He sent no communications and was not publicly linked to the crime, leading Wegerle's husband to become the chief suspect.

With the development of DNA analysis for crime investigation that same year, and labs for testing DNA opening in the United States in 1987, investigators now had a method to match semen samples with a known suspect. However, with no viable suspects in the Wichita murders, the task force disbanded. Only Detective Ken Landwehr remained on the case.

Rader then apparently stopped killing again, for five years. He was in his mid-forties, still interested in looking for "projects," but losing confidence in his ability to get away with murder. He began to watch Dolores Davis, a sixty-two-year-old who lived alone in Park City, just north of Wichita. Again this was close to his home, but not that close. On January 19, Rader broke into Davis's home, strangled her, took photos, and dumped her body beneath a bridge. He used his volunteer work with a Boy Scout outing as cover.

Rader lost several jobs during this time, which often sent him looking for victims to help fend off feelings of helplessness. Eventually, he landed a job as a compliance officer enforcing Park City ordinances. He also got more involved in his church, becoming vice-president of the congregation. Law enforcement had yet to link Rader's final three murders to BTK. He reveled in being a modern-day Jack the Ripper or Zodiac Killer—the one who got away—and he might have, if it hadn't been for a news story that caught his eye in March 2004.

A reporter for the Wichita *Eagle* published a thirty-year retrospective of the unsolved BTK murders, including the news that a local author was writing a book on them. Rader bristled. He did not want to be forgotten, but he also did not want someone else writing his story, since it would surely fall short of crediting him for the ten murders he had committed. In order to correct this, he would have to break another of his rules—he would have to go public. Rader believed that if he'd gotten away with murder for this long, it was on account of being clever. "I never expected to get caught," he said. He became convinced that another cat-and-mouse game with the cops would get him more news attention, and greater respect for his skills, and deliver more terror to his city. Rader's desire for fame blinded him to the danger of exposure, particularly in the post-CSI era of innovative forensics. The "leave-nothing-to-chance" killer had not kept up with the technological times.

Rader sorted through his files and chose items that would prove to Wichita that the BTK Killer was still among them. He sent a letter to the *Eagle* from "Bill Thomas Killman" containing three photographs of a dead woman. She was posed, and a photocopy of her driver's license was included—it was Vicki Wegerle's. Clearly, BTK had killed her and taken trophies that he'd kept all these years. He'd used the unique BTK brand that he'd drawn as his signature, a sexualized design of the three letters that had never been publicized.

The police ran a DNA test on skin taken from under Wegerle's fingernails and compared it to thousands of offenders in a database, as well as to people who volunteered samples. It did not produce a viable suspect. A geographical profile indicated that BTK probably lived or worked not far from his known crime scenes, which were only four miles apart, and that he had some association with Wichita State University. Authorities were left to hope that whoever sent the Killman letter would communicate again.

And he soon did. A package showed up at KAKE-TV from "Thomas B. Kingman" on May 4 that contained a word puzzle, two handmade ID cards, and a piece of paper with chapter headings for *The BTK Story*, including "A Serial Killer is Born" and "Fantasy World."

Law enforcement deciphered the word puzzle, which was divided into three sections: MO, ID, and RUSE. They found words related to these items in each section. BTK seemed to be offering background information . . . maybe.

Then another package surfaced that detailed the Otero slaughter— Chapter One—and another that took credit for killing a young man who was likely a suicide victim. "BTK" suddenly got a lot of media attention, domestically and internationally, which thrilled Rader.

He was now fifty-nine. He thought he should make a big splash and went looking for another victim, identified one, and devised an elaborate murder plan. But he couldn't pull it off on his target date, so he postponed it until he could arrange his life again to support it.

In December, Rader placed another message in a cereal box and left it in a park. It contained Nancy Fox's driver's license, bound to the foot of a Barbie-like doll.

Police believed that BTK was familiar with law-enforcement techniques. They had a blurred photo from a surveillance camera of someone they believed was him driving a dark SUV in a Home Depot lot. They also began to suspect that BTK was behind the two unsolved murders in Park City. Yet despite more than 5,600 tips, they still could not identify him.

A Virginia company called EagleForce Associates used computer analysis to weigh the items of evidence for significance. They surmised that BTK was likely a white male around sixty years old with military experience and a connection to Wichita State University, who drove a black Jeep Cherokee.

The ever-careful Rader eventually got impatient and decided to short-cut his process of communicating with the press and police. He found the constant copying of photocopies too time-consuming. He knew that a computer would speed things along, so he asked Randy Stone, a cop in the Wichita PD's new Computer Crimes Unit, if an anonymous e-mail could be traced. He would later say that Stone told him it could not (but Stone refuted this). Convinced that using a computer would accelerate his game, Rader placed a message in an empty box of Special K cereal, asking Landwehr to confirm that he could communicate via floppy disk without being traced. He urged investigators to "be honest" and to run an ad in the *Eagle* to let him know. Landwehr ran the ad, hoping that this was the break they needed.

Rader used the computer at his church, Christ Lutheran. As the new president of the congregation, he had access to it for meeting notes.

He erased a floppy and prepared it with a "test" in rich text format that directed police to read the 3 x 5 card included in the package for details on how to communicate with him in the newspaper. The card said that all future communications would be assigned a number.

That was it. They had him.

THE CAPTURE

Stone got to work on the floppy disk. At the time, computer forensics, now called digital forensics, had become an important addition to investigations, mostly because so many offenders were using computers to commit crimes. On BTK's floppy, the police quickly found the name "Dennis." Then, by recreating data that had been overwritten, they were able to trace the disk to a computer at Christ Lutheran. They learned from a Google search that the president of the congregation was named Dennis Rader. Officers went to the church to question the pastor, who admitted that he'd shown Rader how to use the computer. Digital footprints showed up on the computer's hard drive indicating that the computer had been used to write a BTK message to a local media station. Perhaps more importantly, Rader fit the profile. He'd graduated from Wichita State University, and in his driveway in Park City was a black Jeep Cherokee (his son's). He worked in the compliance office and had served in the Air Force. A DNA sample subpoenaed from Rader's daughter's medical files clinched it. Rader, a family man, church leader, security specialist, and seemingly stable citizen, had bound, tortured, and killed at least eight people. His need for attention and control had been his Achilles' heel.

Landwehr directed the task force on how to approach him. Just as Rader had learned his victims' routines, the police learned his. They knew he went home every day at the same time for lunch. It would be easy to close in on him in his neighborhood.

On February 25, 2005, officers got into position and waited for the designated time. Rader drove by. Two detectives pulled him over, and the rest swarmed in to subdue and cuff him. They forced him to the ground. He seemed to know why they'd arrested him and asked the officers to tell his wife he would not be home for lunch. Getting into a car with Landwehr, Rader greeted him like they were friends. He'd developed a sense that Landwehr was in a game with him, enjoying it as much as he did. By greeting Landwehr by name, Rader sent a message that he was aware of him and on equal footing. Landwehr did not share this notion. For him, the "game" had been stressful, but he'd won.

During the post-arrest interview, Rader danced around his guilt for three hours, pretending to be a BTK wannabe who was just playing games. When Landwehr told him that they could match his DNA to the crimes and the floppy disk, Rader caved. He didn't realize that the police would preserve biological samples from his earlier crime scenes. He finally admitted that he was BTK. Rader believed he'd had a good thing going with Landwehr, who understood "the rules" for their cat-and-mouse contest. But Landwehr, he thought, had violated them, so Rader asked, "Why did you lie to me?"

"Because I wanted to catch you," Landwehr told him. He had his own set of rules, and they didn't include being truthful with a killer.

Rader would confess for many hours, adding Hedge and Davis to his list of victims. When relatives and friends waiting outside insisted that the police had the wrong man, they learned that he'd admitted everything.

Investigators persuaded Rader to give up his hiding places, so he drew a map to where they could find evidence. The search produced jewelry and photos of some of the victims, as well as Polaroid "selfies" of Rader in bondage. It was no surprise that he kept newspaper clippings about the incidents and copies of all his communications. The police confiscated his detailed journal, but Rader had thrown away many incriminating items, including Joseph Otero's watch and several of the victims' driver's licenses.

As part of his plea deal, Rader confessed to his crimes in court. He went meticulously over the details, describing each murder as if it were just business. He said he killed to satisfy his sexual fantasies, but then claimed that a demon had driven him to perform torture and murder (although he later dropped the claim). A two-day sentencing hearing showed his degree of depravity, and the DA recounted what Rader had done to his victims.

In several interviews, Rader was adamant that resurfacing in 2004 had not been an attempt to get caught. He made a mistake, which embarrassed him, but he certainly did not wish to spend the rest of his life in prison or embarrass his wife and children.

Rader received ten consecutive life sentences, to be served at the El Dorado Correctional Facility. The death penalty was off the table, since his murders had occurred before Kansas reinstated it. His horrified wife divorced him. In the end, Rader got the notoriety that he sought. Letters to him poured in from all over the world—and he would have plenty of time to read them.

THE TAKEAWAY

Name: Dennis Rader
Country: United States
Born: March 9, 1945
Died: NA
Killing Period: 1974–1991
Known Victims: 10
Date of Arrest: February 25, 2005

The BTK task force investigators realized that capturing Rader had relied on a carefully controlled media strategy, as the person they sought paid attention to the news. Rader needed to control how others perceived him and even viewed his cat-and-mouse game with police as a way to satisfy his "fan club." His narcissism and belief in his own cleverness, coupled with dogged police work, had been his downfall.

As a serial killer, Rader is unique in several ways. First, there is no known abuse in his background, so his development into a serial killer defies typical thinking on the subject. He had a few head injuries, but no neurological workup identified a causal influence. As a teenager, he'd admired serial killers like Harvey Glatman and H. H. Holmes, who seemed to share his penchant for binding and torturing females. He later copied other serial killers he admired.

Rader initially attributed his need to kill to a demon, citing a "Factor X," but he later dropped this notion. Still, he wasn't wrong about serial killers possessing motivating influences specific to their developmental trajectory. There is no single factor that sets up the causal conditions for individuals who become serial killers. Factor X refers to the multitude of influences in the individual's life. Rader applied the phrase to suggest a mystery, but it designates known psychological dynamics.

Among the most predatory of killers, the ability to live a double life is evident. They can pass as ordinary—even successful—people while also stalking and killing. Rader calls this skill "cubing," in reference to having many sides, any one of which is available to him at any time. Skillful killers can pivot to the person they need to be for any given situation because they have only a shallow commitment to a specific identity.

Rader demonstrates the psychological vulnerability of those killers who are motivated by the need for fame. As their cat-and-mouse game develops, they typically slip up and reveal something that leads to their capture.

6.

THE GOLDEN STATE KILLER

THE CRIMES

Between April 1974 and December 1975, more than a hundred homes were entered and ransacked in Visalia, California. Some items were vandalized, and women's underwear was scattered about. Only items of little value were taken, as if the burglar wanted only to get inside to prove something—or was rehearsing for something else. People in certain neighborhoods reported a strange man outside at night.

In February 1975, Claude Snelling saw a white male at his sixteen-year-old daughter's window and chased him away. Other prowling incidents occurred nearby, leaving shoeprints in dirt or grass matching those outside the Snelling home. Then in September, the prowler broke in and attempted to kidnap Snelling's daughter. He forced her outside, where Snelling confronted him. The intruder shot and killed Snelling before running away. The girl was frightened, but unhurt. She said she had woken up to find a stranger on top of her.

Other homes on that street were burglarized that night as well. The events seemed to end in December with no more violence, but with the "Visalia Ransacker" still out there.

Six months later and more than 200 miles to the north in towns around Sacramento, another series of crimes began that involved both burglary and rape. This "East Area Rapist" committed most of his crimes over the next three years around Carmichael, Rancho Cordova, Citrus Heights, and Sacramento. People often saw or heard someone on their property before an invasion, as if he were stalking them. A few received phone calls or hang-ups before or after an incident. Some calls were also made to the police, taunting them.

This masked intruder with an athletic build initially targeted women who lived alone, or teenage girls, which meant he studied neighborhoods and carefully planned his attacks. He also left little evidence behind, so he likely understood how law enforcement operated. However, during the 1970s and into the mid-1980s, there was barely a thought of using DNA to catch criminals.

In April 1977, the "East Area Rapist" adopted a darker tactic: he began to terrorize couples. Common to serial offenders for whom crime produces an erotic high, the East Area Rapist seemed to need a greater challenge, or perhaps he just wanted more people to suffer. Typically, he would enter during the night through a window or sliding glass door and wake the couple with a flashlight and threaten them with a gun. With ligatures he had already prepared, he'd force the woman to tie up the man before he tied her with a diamond knot. He would then make the man lie on the floor, facedown, and stack dishes on his back. If he moved, the intruder said, the dishes would make a noise. If that happened, everyone in the house would die. The man would then be forced to endure the sound of his companion as she was sexually assaulted. And for all he knew, they'd be killed anyway.

The assaults sometimes lasted for several hours. Then the rapist would ransack the home, eat food from the kitchen, make more threats, and often rape the woman again. If he took something, it was usually an object with personal value. It seemed clear that he was collecting keepsakes for reliving his crimes, rather than taking something of value to pawn. When he left, it would always be on foot or a bicycle. Wherever he may have parked a car, it was out of sight of the victims.

These attacks went on in Sacramento County until May 1977. They resumed in San Joaquin County to the south that June before returning to the Sacramento area in the fall. Rapes in several counties were attributed to the same perpetrator, by which time the East Area Rapist had become a killer.

On February 2, 1978, Brian and Katie Maggiore were walking their dog in an area of Rancho Cordova where five rapes had occurred. A man confronted them, and they tried to run, but he shot and killed them. A dark shoelace tied in a double loop found nearby implicated the rapist, but no definitive connection was made.

During 1978 and into 1979, rapes happened in Modesto, Davis, Concord, and the San Jose area to the east of Sacramento. Then in October 1979, a more dangerous intruder entered homes in southern California. His intent was to kill. He was not initially associated with the East Area Rapist, so media reports dubbed him the Night Stalker (later called the Original Night Stalker due to the name being applied during the 1980s to Richard Ramirez; see Chapter 24). His spate of crimes would terrorize this area for two years.

The first incident occurred in the town of Goleta in Santa Barbara County. The intruder entered a home on Queen Ann Lane and bound the couple that lived there. They overheard him mutter to himself that he would kill them. The woman screamed and the attacker fled on a bike. Their neighbor was an FBI agent. He pursued the man, who took a shot at him and then dropped his bike and fled on foot. His shoeprints were preserved, linking him to a double homicide in the same town nearly three months later.

KATIE AND BRIAN MAGGIORE, TWO VICTIMS OF THE GOLDEN STATE KILLER.

On December 30, 1979, Robert Offerman and Debra Alexander were fatally shot in Offerman's condo. They'd both been bound, but Offerman had broken loose and possibly tried to overpower the man.

The area then went quiet until March 1980, when Charlene and Lyman Smith were killed in their home after Charlene was raped. The killer bludgeoned them both with a log taken from their woodpile. A diamond knot was used to bind them with drapery cord—the same knot that the East Area Rapist favored. Some media outlets referred to the killer as the "Diamond Knot Killer," but this nickname didn't stick.

The next double homicide occurred five months later in a gated community in Dana Point. On August 19, Keith and Patrice Harrington, recently married, endured the now-common rape scene before the rapist bludgeoned them both to death.

In February 1981, the Night Stalker raped and killed Manuela Witthuhn in Irvine. Then he returned to Goleta in July, killing Cheri Domingo and Gregory Sanchez. Five years later, on May 4, 1986, Janelle Cruz was raped and bludgeoned to death in her home in Irvine.

Law-enforcement officials disagreed over whether the different crime sprees were connected. Hundreds of suspects were considered and discarded, with only a few arrested. One man associated with a victim was charged with two murders, but later cleared. Another suspect had died before Cruz was murdered and was therefore retroactively cleared. No solid suspects emerged, resulting in a dozen murders and nearly fifty rape cases going cold.

During the 1990s, cold-case squads formed in many police departments, dedicated to reopening older unsolved cases to try new technologies not in existence during the original investigations. The ability to link biological samples via DNA unique to a suspect became available in the United States in 1987, opening up new avenues to develop leads. It soon replaced fingerprinting as the gold standard for identification. And as DNA analysis evolved and matured, increasingly smaller samples yielded accurate results. It turned out that the East Area Rapist had left more evidence than anyone, including himself, realized.

In 2001, DNA analysis linked several rapes from Contra Costa County to seven of the Original Night Stalker murders. This proved that the East Area Rapist had become a serial killer. Detectives speculated that he was also the Visalia Ransacker. In another decade, two more murders were added. By this time, a writer and amateur sleuth named Michelle McNamara had renamed the offender the Golden State Killer. Like others, she was determined to identify him. It irked everyone—and embarrassed the law-enforcement authorities—that he seemed to have vanished into the darkness, getting away with so many crimes.

The FBI released composite sketches and crime details in the hope of jogging memories that would offer new leads. They posted a $50,000 reward for information that led to an arrest.

Lead detective Paul Holes, while working cold cases, was already exploring potential new threads. He'd pulled the case, with its complex array of incidents, from a dusty file cabinet. Over the years, investigators had used up most of the DNA from the Ventura County murder victim who was raped. Holes hoped his team would have enough DNA to continue their investigation. Then, they discovered that the pathologist had collected samples for a second sexual-assault kit, which provided a significant amount of DNA for more testing. The detectives submitted samples to an open-source genealogy website, GEDmatch, where people used their own DNA to learn about their family connections. The investigative team worked with a genealogist to construct family trees based on the rapist's DNA. The website identified ten to twenty distant relatives who shared the same great-great-great-grandparents. They eliminated one possibility after another with circumstantial information, such as location and age. Finally, they had two potential suspects, but quickly ruled out one of them. This left Joseph James DeAngelo, then seventy-two.

A Vietnam veteran who'd served in the Navy, DeAngelo had been married with three daughters. Since the 1970s, he'd lived in Citrus Heights, in the heart of where the East Area Rapist had initially operated. A former police officer with a B.A. in criminal justice, DeAngelo had been fired in 1979 from the Auburn Police Department for shoplifting dog repellent and a hammer. However, from 1973 to 1976 he'd served as a burglary unit officer in Exeter, near Visalia. Separated from his wife since 1991, he was living alone on Canyon Oak Drive. Aside from the shoplifting charge, he had no criminal record.

On April 18, 2018, detectives surreptitiously swabbed the door handle of DeAngelo's car to compare it to DNA from their crime scenes. They also collected tissues from his trash, once it had been put out for pickup. They put the samples into GEDmatch and saw what they expected: Joseph DeAngelo had committed the crimes attributed to the Golden State Killer. Other evidence led Holes to believe that DeAngelo was also the Visalia Ransacker. He had married in 1973, so he'd carried out a decade of burglaries, rapes, and murders while posing as a responsible family man. Shortly after his arrest in 2018, DeAngelo's wife, an attorney, ended their separation by filing for divorce.

THE CAPTURE

On April 24, 2018, officers from the Sacramento County Sheriff's Office went to DeAngelo's home. They'd been watching him for nearly a week. When he stepped outside that day, they placed him under arrest. He was surprised. One officer thought he appeared to be considering a plan he might have prepared for just such a moment, but police whisked him away before he could act on it.

They charged him with eight counts of first-degree murder with special circumstances. DeAngelo did not enter a plea at the time. His attorney said he was too fragile and depressed.

In May, the DA's office added four additional counts of first-degree murder. In August, he was also charged with Snelling's murder. Since the statute of limitations had run out for the rapes and burglaries, DeAngelo could not be charged with all the crimes of which he was suspected.

The arrest drew international attention, with media and the general public clamoring to understand his motives, but DeAngelo refused to talk. As details from his life were revealed, some speculated that he'd been warped by witnessing two men rape his seven-year-old sister. Others thought he was symbolically retaliating for rejection from a woman named Bonnie, who'd broken up with him in 1970. (Reportedly, he'd said, "I hate you, Bonnie" during one rape incident.) A few neighbors said he seemed perpetually angry.

Prosecutors from Sacramento, Orange, Santa Barbara, Tulare, Contra Costa, and Ventura counties are preparing for a long and complex trial (which has not occurred as of this writing). It will take place in Sacramento.

THE TAKEAWAY

Name: Joseph James DeAngelo
Country: United States
Date of Birth: November 8, 1945
Date of Death: NA
Killing Period: 1975, 1979–1986
Known Victims: 13, plus 45–50 rapes
Date of Arrest: April 24, 2018

DeAngelo had a talent for staying under the radar. He settled quietly into his community and passed as an ordinary family man, even as he likely devoted significant time to homicidal fantasies and intricate preparations. Like Dennis Rader (see Chapter 5), whose criminal culpability was also confirmed with DNA, DeAngelo seemed to take pride in getting away with murder for forty-four years (Rader managed the same thing for thirty years).

These two offenders were alike in many ways, particularly in their ability to pass as normal, to raise a family, and to carry on with steady employment while they were also committing a series of murders. Both liked to bind their victims, using their preferred knots. Both entered homes prepared, but also used items they found inside. Both took items from victims that had limited value. And both had preferences for house locations and escape routes. Finally, both were stalkers and voyeurs who learned their victims' routines and hid inside closets to wait and also used ruses to make their victims think their intent was not homicide. They also both taunted the police.

Implausibly, the two men were also both born in 1945 and had seemingly ordinary childhoods. Rader served in the Air Force, DeAngelo in the Navy, and each sought to be cops, with DeAngelo succeeding. Both also earned degrees in criminal justice and were burglars and thieves.

No one who knew them suspected either of murder. They were unremarkable men who strove to blend in. As home invaders bent on murder and psychological torment, they presented the most disturbing type of offender—killers who pose as normal citizens for whom the list of red flags for spotting serial killers can be entirely ineffective.

PART II
POLICE PROCEDURE

Sometimes a break in a case comes from diligent police work, but other times it's just a lucky break in the midst of an investigation. This section includes cases in which law enforcement's approach—usually involving a persistent investigator—brought a killer to justice.

7.

THE CANNIBAL KILLER

THE CRIMES

On June 3, 1928, ten-year-old Grace Budd went missing from 406 West 15th Street in New York City. A man in his fifties named Frank Howard had come to her home, posing as a potential employer for the Budd family's teenage son, Edward. When he saw Grace, he asked if he could take her to a birthday party for his niece. Wanting to please the man for Edward's sake, Albert and Delia Budd agreed to let her go. They waited all day, but Howard never brought her back.

Reports went to area police precincts describing the man as five-foot-six with gray hair, blue eyes, and a trimmed mustache. He had a bowlegged gait and was wearing a blue suit.

The Budds reported that Howard had first arrived six days earlier to interview Edward for a possible job on his chicken farm in Farmingdale, Long Island. He'd said he had six children, and he was quite open and friendly. He promised to pay Edward $15 a week, which was good money at that time. On his second visit, which he announced with a telegram, Howard arrived with strawberries and a decorative can of pot cheese.

When officers asked for the telegram, the Budds said Frank Howard had taken it back. But they had the address of the birthday party: 137th and Columbus Avenue in the Bronx.

The police learned that the address was fake. They recalled the unsolved case of another missing child a year before. On February 11, a thin elderly man with a mustache had grabbed four-year-old Billy Gaffney from Brooklyn. A friend playing with him had claimed "the boogieman" snatched him. Something similar had happened with eight-year-old Francis McDonnell on nearby Staten Island in July 1924. His mother reported seeing a stooped elderly man in the area. McDonnell's nearly naked body was later found beneath a pile of branches, assaulted and strangled to death.

Police searched in Farmingdale as well, but found no listing for a Frank Howard, nor was there one in Farmingdale, New Jersey. The Budds looked at photos in the police files to see if Howard was a convicted offender, but saw no mug shot that resembled him.

Detectives asked telegraph agencies to look for forms that Howard might have used on June 2. The Western Union office at Third Avenue and 103rd Street produced the original, which provided a sample of Howard's handwriting.

A pushcart peddler in East Harlem recognized an enameled can that Howard had left at the Budd home. The peddler ran his business from 104th Street and Third Avenue, close to the Western Union office, so police canvassed the area to find someone who might know him. This led nowhere, as did several other seemingly promising leads.

William F. King, a detective and lieutenant with the NYPD's Missing Persons Bureau, took over the Budd investigation. He chased down leads around the country, identifying suspects but none where he could make an arrest stick. King persisted. His preferred tool was journalist Walter Winchell's gossip column in the *Daily Mirror*, "On Broadway." He liked to feed Winchell information in the hope that the killer was reading it. On November 2, 1934, six years into the case, King asked Winchell to write that the Department of Missing Persons had a new informant and expected to crack the case soon. Winchell wrote that the case would be solved within four weeks. It was a ruse, but it worked.

On November 11, Delia Budd received a letter, sent via the Grand Central post office. She couldn't read, so Edward looked it over. Shocked, he took the letter straight to Detective King.

"My dear Mrs. Budd," the writer began. He went on to state that in 1894, he and a friend of his had shipped out as deckhands on the steamer *Tacoma* to Hong Kong. They got drunk while in port there and missed the boat's departure, so they were stranded in a foreign country suffering from famine and a lack of meat.

"So great was the suffering among the very poor that all children under 12 were sold for food in order to keep others from starving. A boy or girl under 14 was not safe in the street. You could go in any shop and ask for steak—chops—or stew meat. Part of the naked body of a boy or girl would be brought out and just what you wanted cut from it. A boy or girls [sic] behind which is the sweetest part of the body and sold as veal cutlet brought the highest price."

According to the letter, the writer's "friend" had acquired a taste for human flesh, and when he finally returned to New York, he kidnapped two young boys, bound them, and tortured them to make their "meat" tender. Then he killed and ate them.

"At that time," said the writer, "I was living at 409 E 100 St., near—right side. He told me so often how good Human flesh was I made up my mind to taste it. On Sunday June the 3—1928 I called on you at 406 W 15 St. Brought you pot cheese—strawberries. We had lunch. Grace sat in my lap and kissed me. I made up my mind to eat her. On the pretense of taking her to a party. You said Yes she could go. I took her to an empty house in Westchester I had already picked out. When we got there, I told her to remain outside. She picked wildflowers. I went upstairs and stripped all my clothes off. I knew if I did not I would get her blood on them. When all was ready I went to the window and called her. Then I hid in a closet until she was in the room. When she saw me all naked she began to cry and tried to run down the stairs. I grabbed her and she said she would tell her mamma. First I stripped her naked. How she did kick—bite and scratch. I choked her to death, then cut her in small pieces so I could take my meat to my rooms. Cook and eat it. How sweet and tender her little ass was roasted in the oven. It took me 9 days to eat her entire body. I did not fuck her tho I could of had I wished. She died a virgin."

The letter was unsigned, but the handwriting was similar to that on the Western Union form that King had saved from Howard's 1928 telegram. King examined the stationery and the envelope. He noticed an emblem over an address, obscured with scribbling. It bore the letters N.Y.P.C.B.A., or the New York Private Chauffeur's Benevolent Association, located in New York City at 627 Lexington Avenue. He called the president and asked for a meeting of the members. Then he assigned detectives to compare their handwriting to the letter. No one's matched.

King asked whether a nonmember might have taken the stationery. A part-time janitor, Lee Sicowski, admitted to taking a few sheets and envelopes. He gave King the address of his rooming house. This opened up an intriguing new lead. But when King investigated, he discovered that no one's writing on the register matched Howard's or the 1934 letter. He questioned Sicowski again and the janitor recalled that he'd stayed briefly at 200 East 52nd Street. He'd left some envelopes on a shelf in Room 7.

King asked the landlady there, Frieda Schneider, about Frank Howard, but she did not know the name. The man who'd rented the room after Sicowski, she said, was Albert H. Fish. King described Howard. She admitted that it sounded like Fish. King asked to see her register. Using the letter to Mrs. Budd, he saw that Fish's signature was a close match to the handwriting.

Although Schneider had no forwarding address for Fish, she said that Fish's son sent him regular checks from Georgia. Fish had told her he expected one more and would be back to pick it up. King could hardly believe he was finally so close to the man he thought was Grace Budd's abductor and murderer.

THE CAPTURE

King alerted postal inspectors to watch for Fish's letter and also set up surveillance at the boarding house. He then tracked down the address from the letter, 409 East 100th Street, and learned that an elderly man had boarded there temporarily in the summer of 1928. The pieces were falling into place.

King sensed that he was just steps behind this offender. Then, on December 4, he learned that the envelope he expected had arrived at the Grand Central post office, mailed from Georgia. It contained a check for $25.

But to King's disappointment, Fish did not show up. King worried that he'd sniffed out the surveillance. A week passed. Then on December 13, a short elderly man arrived at the boarding house. Mrs. Schneider called King. When King entered the boarding house, Fish attempted to defend himself with a razor blade, but he was no match for the burly detective.

During questioning, Fish resisted for a while, but finally confessed. Albert Fish, aka Frank Howard, stated that he had originally meant to kidnap Edward, but he thought the boy was too big. While at the Budd home the second time, he'd spotted Grace and decided to take her instead. He'd stashed his "implements of hell" (a saw, butcher knife, and cleaver) near a newsstand before going to the Budds', and he retrieved them with Grace in tow. Together they boarded a train bound to Westchester County, where Fish knew of an abandoned house called Wisteria Cottage.

Grace believed she was going to a party. She'd even run to fetch the canvas bag of tools when Fish accidentally left it on the train seat. Once they arrived at the dilapidated, eight-room house, he'd let her play in the yard while he undressed, then called her. In an upper-floor room he strangled her with his bare hands, which took about five minutes. Then he removed her head, draining the blood into a can. He'd tried to drink some, but it made him ill. He sawed the body in two and left the lower torso and legs behind the door. Taking the head outside, he covered it with paper. He also removed some of the flesh, which he wrapped to take home for the stew he described in the letter. He'd eaten it in a state of arousal that lasted over a week. Four days after the murder, he returned to the cottage to dispose of the decomposed torso, legs, and head, which he tossed into the woods behind a stone wall.

The Budds identified Fish as Frank Howard, clinching the case against him.

Fish agreed to take police to Worthington Woods to show them where he'd killed Grace and dumped her remains. Her skull was visible in the dirt behind the stone wall where a rusty cleaver, saw, and other bones were found. Dental records confirmed that the skull belonged to Grace Budd.

Once Fish was locked up, Detective King received a well-earned promotion.

Dr. Frederic Wertham, the senior psychiatrist at Bellevue Hospital in New York, examined Fish for over twelve hours to determine if he had any mitigating mental disorders. Fish claimed he had married four times (two of the women denied it), and after having six children with his first wife,

INVESTIGATORS CHECK ITEMS FOUND NEAR AN ABANDONED HOUSE CALL WISTERIA COTTAGE, WHERE ALBERT FISH MURDERED GRACE BUDD.

she'd run off with another man, leaving him to raise their children. The kids knew their father was eccentric, but they did not guess the extent of his depravity. Fish blamed his wife's betrayal for opening the floodgates of his sexual troubles. He had decided it no longer mattered what he did, so he allowed himself to fully explore and express his darkest desires.

Wertham counted eighteen different paraphilias, from cannibalism to vampirism to necrophilia. Fish's sexual needs focused on children, especially the buttocks. He seemed to prefer boys. He also loved pain, both giving and receiving. Finding things with which to hurt himself was uppermost in his mind, like inserting the stems of roses into his urethra and sticking needles into his testicles. In a 1935 letter from prison, Fish told a correspondent, "Strip Naked and annoy myself in every possible way stick stems of roses up my penis and behind." After he'd done that, he'd view his naked body for hours, then eat the rose petals.

To assault children, Fish would go naked under his painter's overalls so he could quickly remove his clothing and grab them. He'd chosen victims from the poorest classes, especially "colored children," because they seemed the least likely to raise a fuss or trigger an investigation. He'd also written obscene letters to strangers, seeking a kindred soul with whom to inflict and receive physical abuse.

Believing himself at times to be Christ or Abraham, and obsessed with sin and atonement, Fish had flagellated his naked body with spiked paddles and stuck lit cotton balls, soaked in alcohol, inside his anus. He'd once tried self-castration. He also believed he needed to kill children ("lambs") as a human sacrifice to please God and/or save their souls. He justified everything with Bible verses.

According to X-ray evidence, over two dozen needles were still in his groin and scrotum. He claimed he'd performed similar acts on some of his victims. He estimated that he had sexually abused over a hundred children in twenty-three states.

To Wertham's astonishment, Fish had been committed to Bellevue twice since the kidnapping, but no one viewed his demented predatory fantasies as dangerous. He'd been arrested in New York several times for the impairment of the morals of a minor, yet no one had connected him to the Grace Budd case. By Wertham's estimate, Fish had killed at least five children, perhaps more.

Fish entered a plea of not guilty by reason of insanity. The *Daily News* ran a five-part series that was purported to be Fish's memoir of depravity.

Just before his murder trial commenced in March 1935, Fish used a sharpened fish bone from his soup to cut his chest and abdomen. However, his injuries were not serious. Possibly he'd only been searching for a way to inflict pain.

During the prosecution's case, Grace's bones were brought into the courtroom, over defense attorney James Dempsey's vigorous objections, and Fish's full confession was read. King testified that Fish had admitted that he knew that what he did was wrong, and he had a letter from Fish to back it up.

Still, Fish had told Dr. Wertham that if a murder were not justified, an angel would stop him, as one had done in the Bible with Abraham before he slew his son, Isaac. Wertham testified that Fish had practiced "every known sexual abnormality," derived from a history of abnormal personalities in his family. His mental problems had developed over the past decade via an obsession with religion. With Grace, he'd supposedly had a premonition of a future outrage to her, so killing her had "saved" her. He also said that God had commanded him to sacrifice a virgin. Fish, Wertham said, had no rational control. He was dangerous but insane and should be institutionalized in a psychiatric facility. Fish's attorney insisted that he was a psychiatric phenomenon.

For the prosecution, Drs. Charles Lambert and James Vavasour found that Fish was legally sane. At the time of the crime, he had known that what he was doing was wrong. He had planned for the murder and chosen a place of concealment. The court accepted their recommendation.

The jury convicted Fish of murder. As he awaited his sentencing, he confessed to the murder of Billy Gaffney. He said he had drunk the boy's blood, cut his body into pieces, and roasted the buttocks with onions and carrots. He'd consumed the tender meat over the course of four days. He also admitted to the murder of the McDonnell boy on Staten Island. If he had not been interrupted, he said, he would have dismembered him too.

On June 17, 1935, Fish went to the electric chair at Sing Sing prison with his hands clasped in a prayerful pose. He offered no last words. At age sixty-five, Fish was the oldest man at that time to be executed in the electric chair.

THE TAKEAWAY

Name: Hamilton Howard "Albert" Fish
Country: United States
Date of Birth: May 19, 1870
Date of Death: January 16, 1936
Killing Period: 1924–1934
Known victims: 3+
Date of arrest: December 13, 1934

Fish presented himself as a kindly old man. Despite his many dark fantasies and habits, he knew how to manipulate expectations. Many people believe that a man his age is an unlikely serial killer—and, by probability estimates, this is correct. However, there is no age limit for sexual predators. The compulsion can remain strong into old age, and there have been a few serial killers in their fifties and beyond. Because they have more experience with people than younger killers, they often know better how to leverage a situation to their advantage.

While it is true that the Cannibal Killer had more documented sexual paraphilias than any other convicted serial killer, paraphilias do not rise to the level of psychosis. Even in abundance, they fail to qualify someone for an insanity acquittal.

A final takeaway is the value of investigative persistence. Sometimes the subtlest clue will break a case, and it can come years later. Observant detectives remain vigilant for such events. Many cold cases have been solved with something as simple as a lone fingerprint or drop of blood.

8.

THE KILLER CLOWN

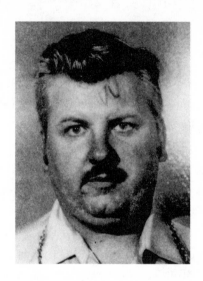

THE CRIMES

Rob Piest told his mother he'd be along soon for the party his family was planning for her birthday. First he wanted to speak to a local contractor who was offering a summer job that would pay nearly twice what the fifteen-year-old currently made at Nisson's Pharmacy. When Rob failed to come home that night, December 11, 1978, his frantic parents went to the police. The contractor that Rob had named was John Wayne Gacy; but when police questioned Gacy, he said he'd never talked with the boy.

The next day, detectives looked into Gacy's background. An officer learned that the thirty-seven-year-old businessman had an outstanding battery charge on a local man. More alarming, he'd been in prison for a sex crime in 1966 in Waterloo, Iowa, where Gacy had managed one of his father-in-law's Kentucky Fried Chicken franchises. He was married, had two children, and was active in the town's civic club, the Jaycees. But he had given underage boys alcohol as a way to leverage them for sexual favors. One of the boys, the son of a fellow Jaycee, told his father. Then another boy came forward with a similar story, and the police charged Gacy with assault. On May 10, 1968, he was indicted. A psychiatrist diagnosed him with antisocial personality disorder. Convicted of sodomy, Gacy received a ten-year sentence but was released after eighteen months on the condition that he go live with his mother in Chicago. He did so in June 1970, eventually purchasing a one-story ranch house at 8213 Summerdale Avenue in Norwood Park Township in Cook County, Illinois.

Gacy had become a prominent businessman with a thriving construction firm who gave to local charities and entertained sick kids dressed as Pogo the Clown. The cops knew they'd need strong evidence before they could charge him. On December 13, 1978, Lieutenant Joseph Kozenczak brought the case to Terry Sullivan, the Assistant State Attorney, who got a search warrant. Although Gacy passed a polygraph exam, he had skillfully dodged key questions.

A search of his house produced pills, sex toys, a board with handcuffs attached, male clothing too small for Gacy, and items belonging to others. He also had paintings of clowns and a collection of police badges. Nothing, however, supported a criminal charge, not even the smelly crawl space beneath his house. The searchers got the impression from the exotic books and videotapes found in Gacy's house that he was kinky. During the search, an officer picked up a photo receipt from Nisson's Pharmacy and bagged it as evidence.

Another team combed through uncleared missing-persons' reports of young men. Some had an association with Gacy, often as temporary employees for his construction company. A current employee was driving a car registered to one of these missing men, John Szyc. Another missing man had seemingly drowned in the river, and two others had abandoned their cars in the area before they vanished. Gacy's second ex-wife confirmed that she had divorced him because he was gay; and she also admitted seeing a man beat her husband, claiming that Gacy had raped him.

Assistant State Attorney Sullivan wondered who they might be dealing with. He didn't yet know that Gacy had killed two young men just the month before. The police put Gacy under surveillance.

Gacy was furious, insisting that their presence near his home would ruin his business. He had friends threaten the officers, and to one cop Gacy made the ominous statement, "Clowns can get away with murder."

A team of dog handlers went through a field where Gacy recently had gotten his vehicle stuck in the mud. They found nothing until they took the German shepherds to the police garage where Gacy's black Oldsmobile sat with its doors open. The dogs sniffed a boot that Rob Piest's parents had provided for this purpose. Then one approached Gacy's car, climbed into the passenger seat, and lay down—the signal that Piest's body had been there.

On December 18, Sullivan learned that several bodies of young men, sexually molested, had been recovered during the past six months from the Des Plaines River. He ordered a check on the pharmacy receipt found in Gacy's house. The number on it linked it to a friend of Piest's, who confirmed that she had put it in the pocket of a parka she'd once borrowed from him. It was the same coat Piest was wearing when he went to see Gacy. So, Rob Piest had been in Gacy's house. Another piece of potential evidence came from John Szyc's mother. She gave detectives some papers that included information about a TV her son owned. It was the same model the police had spotted in Gacy's bedroom.

The next day, Gacy invited two officers, Bob Shultz and Ron Robinson, into his house. The officers had previously plotted to distract Gacy while one of them got the serial number off his TV for comparison with Szyc's registration. Schultz went into the bathroom as the furnace kicked on. He smelled the distinct odor of decomposition. Something, he thought, was in that crawl space. But getting the TV serial number in the dark bedroom was a bust—Schultz had trouble seeing it clearly and didn't dare to turn on the light lest Gacy catch him.

The photo receipt was enough to get a second search warrant, along with authority to interview two of Gacy's employees, who described digging body-sized trenches in the crawl space before spreading bags of lime in them. One of the men said that Gacy had given strict instructions to dig nowhere else.

It all added up. As bizarre as it sounded, businessman and registered clown John Wayne Gacy was killing young men and burying them beneath his house. His attorneys filed a civil suit for police harassment, but Sullivan ignored them. He had almost all his ducks in a row.

THE CAPTURE

Late on December 20 Gacy's attorney, Sam Amirante, learned that Gacy wanted to speak to him and his law partner, Leroy Stevens. Amirante expected more discussion of the civil suit, but Gacy seemed oddly disheveled. He picked up a newspaper that featured a story about Rob Piest and said, "This boy is dead. He's in a river." As the stunned Amirante offered him a drink, Gacy told him, under attorney-client privilege, that he'd been "the judge, jury, and executioner of many people."

Amirante asked what Gacy meant. Gacy proceeded to tell him in detail about committing thirty-four murders. One incident involved three young men that he killed at the same time, tricking them into handcuffs before strangling them. He'd buried most of the bodies in his crawl space and thrown others off a bridge.

"He said he threw five in the Des Plaines River because he had run out of room in his house," Amirante would later tell reporters. "He was actually planning to build a second story on his house to keep the bodies in his house." (Only four bodies were recovered from the river, so if Gacy had dumped a fifth one, this would add up to his claimed total of thirty-four.) In reference to Rob Piest, Gacy said he'd strangled him by twisting a rope tight around his neck and then kept the body in bed with him the same night.

Amirante could barely process what Gacy, the seemingly ordinary entrepreneur, was saying. To his surprise, after hours of a rambling confession, Gacy fell asleep. While he slept, Amirante arranged a psychiatric appointment to prepare for an insanity defense, but Gacy woke up and left. He confessed to several more people, including his employees (who he later fingered as accomplices), and visited his father's grave. He knew his time was up.

The search warrant for Rob Piest's body was approved, but officers discovered that Gacy had turned off his sump pump to flood the crawl space. They spent hours draining it. An evidence technician made his way to the southwest area where reddish puddles containing thousands of tiny worms were visible. Digging into one, he found a human arm bone. He told cops they could charge Gacy with murder, adding, "I think this place is full of kids."

More help arrived. In fetid puddles, the crime-scene team found a nightmarish number of decomposing human remains. Another team dug up the backyard and looked in the garage. Graves seemed to be everywhere. Gacy had created his own private cemetery, right under the noses of his wife and neighbors.

On the afternoon of December 21, 1978, police placed Gacy under arrest. The next morning, he confessed to them, drawing a rough diagram of where specific victims were buried. He blamed the victims for bringing death on themselves and showed no remorse.

Gacy's typical victim was a Caucasian male in his teens or early twenties. He falsely claimed that all had come to his home voluntarily when he offered them drugs and alcohol, and that he had picked them up in places where male sex workers or runaways hung out. He changed his story many times, including recanting his various confessions, alluding to accomplices and saying that his employees had committed all the murders while he was away. Then he pretended to have an alternate personality, "Jack Hanley," who was responsible for the crimes. Jack supposedly took periodic control over Gacy.

The digging went on, making international headlines. Investigators recovered twenty-nine separate bodies of young men in all different states of decomposition, the parts of some intermingled with others. Three bodies were buried in the yard or garage, the others in the crawl space. Three more were dredged up from the river. Gacy thought that one body had landed on a barge when thrown off the bridge and would not be found. Rob Piest remained missing.

Since Gacy had piled some bodies on top of others, some three deep, the team's first task was to sort and separate individual sets of remains. Families offered photos, X-rays, dental records, driver's licenses, and other forms of identification. Some bodies were ID'd quickly, but others proved more difficult, possibly related to the news coverage of homosexual acts. Officials hired forensic anthropologists Charles P. Warren and Clyde C. Snow to assist, and they brought on forensic sculptress Betty Pat Gatliff to reconstruct badly deteriorated skulls into recognizable faces. Still, eight sets of remains went unclaimed. The two youngest victims had been fourteen when they died.

In April 1979, Gacy's house was demolished. That same month, Rob Piest's body was pulled from the river. He had suffocated from paper stuffed down his throat.

Once the forensic team completed its work, a chronology was constructed. Sixteen-year-old Timothy McCoy was Gacy's first victim, in 1972. Gacy picked him up at a bus terminal and claimed he'd killed the boy after McCoy threatened him with a knife. Gacy had apparently misunderstood the situation, but realized his mistake only after he'd stabbed

McCoy to death. He buried the body in his crawl space. During the murder, Gacy had experienced an orgasm. "That's when I realized," he said in an interview, "that death was the ultimate thrill."

It was two years before he killed again, but this time he planned it beforehand. Inspired by news reports about a Texas killer called "The Candy Man" (see Chapter 28) who tortured boys handcuffed to a board before slaughtering them, Gacy created his own sexual assault toys.

He buried his second victim in his back yard.

By 1975, Gacy was actively cruising areas like the three-acre Bughouse Square, looking for male sex workers, runaways, or drug addicts. Sometimes he posed as a cop to force a boy to accompany him, and sometimes he pretended to be a fun guy out looking for company. He also picked off a few of the high-school kids he hired during the summer. Gacy often tricked them into letting him put handcuffs on them (or got them high or drunk), and then he raped them. When he was ready to kill, usually after a considerable amount of torture, he'd apply "the rope trick," tightening a garrote around their necks to strangle them. He drowned or suffocated some victims (like Piest) with cloth or paper stuffed down their throats.

When Gacy's wife left him in 1976, he amped up his cruising. By 1978, he was killing one or two victims each month.

During a complex trial in 1980, Gacy's defense team developed an insanity defense based on an overwhelming compulsion to kill. Several psychologists and psychiatrists put Gacy through a battery of tests where he pretended to suffer from multiple-personality disorder. Some psychiatric experts bought the diagnosis, but the team as a whole was divided over it. The most striking claim was that Gacy had experienced an "irresistible impulse" when he killed each young man, an impulse where, thanks to alcohol, he'd either blacked out or blunted his inhibitions to such an extent that he was unable to control himself. This was in keeping with the phrasing of the insanity defense at the time in Illinois that allowed a person to know right from wrong and realize what he was doing but be unable to stop himself. No defense expert explained why Gacy hadn't sought help or understood the effect of alcohol well before he murdered so many people.

The prosecution, led by Terry Sullivan and William Kunkle, said that Gacy had known what he was doing when he assaulted and killed the young men, and had been in full control of his actions: his claimed disorder was fake. Gacy's ability to draw an accurate map for the police of where he'd placed each body proved his clear awareness. He had also shown evidence of planning to kill by having employees (who ultimately testified) dig trenches in advance. In addition, several young men who survived Gacy's abuse gave unnerving testimony about his treatment of them. (One of them vomited on the stand, and another nearly had a breakdown.) Kunkle also got testimony from Dr. Leonard Heston, the psychiatrist from Iowa who warned that Gacy's antisocial disorder was untreatable and dangerous. Kunkle underlined his closing argument with a dramatic display, tossing the head shots of twenty-two

A CRAWLSPACE BENEATH JOHN WAYNE GACY'S HOME. THE BODIES OF OVER TWO DOZEN YOUNG MALES WERE RECOVERED FROM IT.

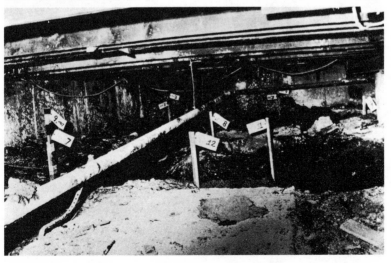

identified victims into the actual crawl-space trapdoor frame, brought from Gacy's house to the courtroom.

In a final ploy to avoid the death penalty, Amirante argued for Gacy to be committed to a psychiatric facility so he could be studied. Kunkle said there would be plenty of time for such research during appeals.

In less than two hours of jury deliberation, Gacy was convicted of multiple counts of sexual assault and first-degree murder. Then he was sentenced to death. In prison, he occupied himself by drawing and painting, including making portraits of himself as a clown. He claimed again that his associates had committed the murders, and he filed numerous appeals. None succeeded. At the age of fifty-two in May 1994, Gacy ate his last meal, which included a bucket of Kentucky Fried Chicken. Reportedly, his last words were, "Kiss my ass." After his execution by lethal injection on May 10, his brain was preserved for further study.

Six of Gacy's victims remain unidentified.

THE TAKEAWAY

Name: John Wayne Gacy
Country: United States
Born: March 17, 1942
Died: May 10, 1994
Killing Period: 1972–1978
Known Victims: 33
Date of Arrest: December 21, 1978

Twice in early 1978, young men abducted by Gacy reported extreme abuse at his hands (and one said that another man was present), but police believed Gacy's story that the rough sex had been consensual. By that time, Gacy had killed at least thirty young men. Finally, one abuse victim, Jeffrey Rignall, found his way back to Gacy's house and insisted on pressing charges. Gacy was arrested in July 1978 and released. His trial for battery was pending when he was arrested for murder. It was possible that Gacy was too well-connected into the local political system for accusations to be pursued without strong proof, and also possible that the police could do little with the conflicting "he-said, he-said" narratives. But there were occasions on which Gacy might have been stopped before his most active killing years.

Better training on cognitive issues in decision-making might improve police response for future cases. The notion that a businessman might be a sexually deviant serial killer was understandably foreign in 1978, but Gacy's case offers a valuable lesson. Though some officials failed to act, in the end it was the focused efforts of a law-enforcement team that followed the evidence to bring him down.

Sam Amirante authored procedures for the Missing Child Recovery Act of 1984. This effectively erased the law in Illinois that had forced police to wait 72 hours before acting on reports of a missing child. Other states across America adopted similar procedures, and a national network was formed to help locate missing kids. This network evolved into the Amber Alert system.

Amirante had argued that Gacy was such a rare type of criminal that he should be studied. Psychiatrist Helen Morrison, who served on Gacy's defense team, acquired Gacy's brain after his execution. Gacy set up conditions for his alleged amnesia by claiming he'd taken massive amounts of Valium. Morrison was certain she would find something about his brain that set him apart from normal people. To her dismay, a pathologist found nothing unusual. Although no structural differences were identified, neuroscience today might find functional differences.

But for that, they would need a living subject.

9.

THE *DATING GAME* KILLER

THE CRIMES

Cheryl Bradshaw walked onto the set of *The Dating Game* in September 1978 to choose from among three bachelors, each of whom was trying to get her to pick him for a date. She asked Bachelor #1 what his "best time" was.

"Nighttime," he responded. "It's the only time there is." Asked to elaborate, he said, "That's when it really gets good."

Bachelor #1, Rodney Alcala, who styled himself a skydiver and photographer, won the date. But when he greeted Bradshaw on the show, she felt uncomfortable. He dressed well and sported a fashionable longish style for his curly brown hair. But something seemed amiss to her. She declined to go out with him.

What no one watching the show knew at the time was that Alcala had already served several prison sentences, including one for the brutal sexual assault of a child. He'd also tortured and murdered several women.

His first known offense, on September 25, 1968, occurred when he lured eight-year-old Tali Shapiro into his car. A witness saw it, followed them, and called the police. They arrived at the address that the witness reported and interrupted a near-fatal sexual assault. Alcala fled. Although there were items in this house that identified Alcala, the investigation hit a dead end in finding him. An arrest warrant was issued, but Alcala had already fled the state.

He showed up in New York City, changed his name to John Berger, and enrolled in NYU's School of the Arts. When he worked at a summer camp, two girls saw his mug shot on an FBI "Most Wanted" poster in the post office. Notified, the FBI found Alcala and returned him to California to stand trial for kidnapping and child abuse. He pleaded guilty to child molestation, which came with a short sentence. He served less than three years.

In the meantime, a New York case went cold. Cornelia Crilley, twenty-three, had worked for Trans World Airlines and was moving into an apartment at 427 E. 83rd Street in Manhattan. On June 24, 1971, she suddenly stopped communicating. Her mother and boyfriend went to the apartment and found her body. A stocking was tied around Crilley's neck and her upper garments had been stripped off and stuffed into her mouth. She'd been beaten, raped, and bitten on the breast. Her killer was long gone.

Later, trolling for kids around Los Angeles, Alcala spotted thirteen-year-old "Julie J." He took her to an isolated spot to smoke dope and then got rough, but a park ranger intervened. Alcala got another short sentence and supervised parole. He charmed his parole officer into letting him take a trip to Manhattan during the summer of 1977.

While Alcala was in New York, heiress and socialite Ellen Jane Hover, twenty-three, disappeared. She reportedly met "Berger" or "Burgh," a photographer. Someone saw him knock on Hover's door on July 15, the day she was last seen. Ads and rewards to solicit information drew nothing. Hover appeared to have simply vanished.

Alcala returned to Los Angeles and found work as a typesetter with the *Los Angeles Times*. And he continued to kill.

On November 10, 1977, a pair of LAPD patrol officers responding to a call in the Hollywood Hills discovered the posed body of a young woman who'd been beaten and murdered. The mostly nude body, with a green sweater pulled up, was half-kneeling, half-squatting, positioned to cause the victim's buttocks to spread apart. The top of the woman's skull had been broken and her head touched the ground near one knee. Her right arm was folded under her body, the right hand placed under the vaginal area, its blood-drenched fingers curled upward. Her attacker had used three ligatures to strangle her and had bitten her right breast, nearly severing the nipple. Her name was Jill Barcomb, an eighteen-year-old sex worker who had recently arrived in LA from New York.

Drawing on his fine arts degree, Alcala persuaded numerous young people to pose for him. He took photos of nude teenage boys, underage girls in sexual positions, and himself having sex with some of his subjects.

By this time, police in New York had learned that John Berger was Rodney Alcala and contacted the LAPD regarding his whereabouts. When questioned, Alcala was casual. He said he knew Ellen Hover and had even been with her the day she disappeared, but had left her after their lunch at her place, alive. There was no other evidence to link him to her disappearance.

In December, the body of Georgia Wixted, twenty-seven, was found in her Malibu apartment, fatally beaten, strangled with pantyhose, and left naked on the floor, posed with her legs spread. A bloodstained clawhammer that matched her head wounds lay near the body. She'd been raped vaginally and anally. It seemed like a completely random murder.

Within six months, there was another one.

The family of Charlotte Lamb, thirty-two, reported her missing in June. Her body was discovered in the laundry room of a large apartment complex in El Segundo, naked and posed with her legs spread open. No one who lived there knew her. Lamb's arms were bent under her back to prop her up and exaggerate her breasts, and she'd been strangled with a shoelace, bitten, and sexually violated.

Around the same time, police located the skeletal remains of Ellen Hover on the wooded Rockefeller estate in North Tarrytown, New York. A woman came forward to say she had once posed for "Berger" near the spot where the remains were discovered. The information was circumstantial, but Alcala was now a firm suspect. That September, he went on *The Dating Game*.

On February 13, 1979, fifteen-year-old Monique Hoyt got into Alcala's car. He raped her and fled. From a police six-pack of photos that substituted for a live line-up, Hoyt identified Alcala. He had no alibi when questioned, so he was placed under arrest. His mother posted his bail. The following month, Alcala left his job at the *Times*, possibly to prevent anyone from learning about the trial he faced in September.

On June 13, 1979, Alcala entered the second-floor Burbank apartment of twenty-one-year-old Jill Parenteau by cutting a screen. After brutally beating, raping, and strangling her, he placed a pillow under her to pose her, face-up, and spread her legs wide. He left a bite mark on her right nipple.

Then he got careless. At Huntington Beach that month, Alcala spent time taking pictures. He approached several young girls. Twelve-year-old Robin Samsoe's blond hair and blue eyes caught Alcala's attention. He approached her and a friend, then waited until she was alone. He grabbed Samsoe as she rode her bike to a new job.

THE CAPTURE

Robin's family called the police and made a concerted effort to find her. A woman who'd seen Alcala approach the girls gave detectives a description. It resembled Alcala's mug shot. During the investigation, one of the detectives happened to see a rerun of *The Dating Game* from nine months earlier. The team homed in on him. Six people who'd been on the beach when Samsoe went missing identified Alcala as the photographer. After two weeks, Samsoe's remains turned up in the woods. Newspapers covered the discovery.

Alcala prepared to flee. He stashed items in a storage locker and told his girlfriend he was moving to Texas, but was arrested before he got away. Police taped a conversation between Alcala and his sister about items in a storage locker he had in Seattle that he asked her to remove. Detectives had a receipt for a Seattle storage locker that they'd found during a search of Alcala's home. They got there before the sister and found a large cache of photos.

The case against Alcala for the murder of Robin Samsoe was mostly circumstantial, but items from Alcala's storage locker turned up a surprise. Samsoe's mother identified a set of gold ball post earrings in Alcala's recovered cache that she herself had modified, which made them unique. There were also photos of young girls, including one that proved Alcala had been on or near the beach on the day in question.

Alcala pleaded not guilty. He was convicted in 1980 and given a death sentence. The conviction was overturned because the California Supreme Court decided that jurors had been improperly informed about Alcala's prior sex offenses, and he was retried in 1986. Convicted again, with another death sentence, Alcala fought it. The Ninth Circuit Court of Appeals nullified the second conviction for several reasons, including not allowing a psychologist to testify for the defense. In 2001, the State of California forced Alcala to provide a biological sample for DNA analysis. This led to links between Alcala and the murders of Parenteau, Lamb, Wixted, and Barcomb.

In 2003, prosecutors from two jurisdictions requested that the five cases be joined in a single trial. Alcala's attorney fought the move, but a judge granted it in 2006. Alcala decided to represent himself, and in January 2010 the case finally came to court. No one was prepared for how bizarre the proceedings would get. Alcala questioned himself for hours, tried to get a coroner to confirm that he had a large penis based on the injuries to his victims, and played his segment from *The Dating Game* to show himself wearing the gold post earrings that were germane to the Samsoe case (that apparently only he could see, as they were not visible on the screen). His focus on minutiae was tedious, and he completely ignored the strongest evidence against himself, the DNA results.

For the third time, Alcala was convicted of Robin Samsoe's death, along with convictions for the other four murders.

During the sentencing phase, psychiatrist Richard Rappaport, testifying on Alcala's behalf, claimed that he suffered from borderline personality disorder with psychotic episodes. Alcala's condition, Rappaport said, had partially erased his memory each time he committed a murder. Rappaport further claimed that Alcala had been shocked by what he'd done, and had developed a defense mechanism that blocked the incidents from his memory. On cross-examination, Rappaport struggled to describe anything from Alcala's early life that supported his evaluation.

Mental-health professionals evaluated Alcala many times throughout his adulthood. Although he had grown up in an outwardly normal family, had a high IQ, and seemed polished, skilled, and ambitious, he deteriorated during his military stint. Two years after enlisting in the Navy, Alcala went AWOL several times. Eventually, he showed up at his family's home. His mother persuaded him to turn himself in to military officials. Those who examined him in the Naval hospital ward where he was detained deemed him unable to perform his duties in the foreseeable future, diagnosing him with a chronic antisocial personality disorder.

A 1963 psychiatric report detailed Alcala's issues. His initial diagnosis from the U.S. Naval Hospital at Camp Pendleton was "schizophrenic reaction, latent type," which meant he had prepsychotic instability in thought and affect. He could function, but he might adjust poorly to his circumstances. But the psychiatrist at the receiving hospital disagreed, finding merely an immature, impulsive, antisocial attitude. Still, the medical staff found Alcala's basic personality structure problematic enough to prohibit further military duty, as he had serious conflicts with authority. Alcala apparently understood the difference between right and wrong, but had no concern for social rules.

The naval doctors discovered nothing in Alcala's background to explain his issues. He had lived in San Antonio, Texas, until he was nine years old. The Alcala family, practicing Catholics, moved to Mexico, and at some point his father, Raul, abandoned the family. They stayed in Mexico for three more years and then moved to Los Angeles. Once discharged from the military in 1964, Alcala took college courses that helped him to transfer to UCLA for a Bachelor of Fine Arts degree in photography.

Alcala was evaluated again almost ten years later, in August 1972, and was found to have a schizoid personality disorder with passive-aggressive tendencies. In addition, he had homosexual tendencies, which was considered a psychosexual disorder at the time. Also, he was found to have incestuous tendencies, pedophilia, sadism, and exhibitionism. Other reports from his various assessments noted his "chameleon-like personality." He could be personable and charming when it served his objectives, but he used his skills and intelligence to lure victims into vulnerable situations. He was considered to have a "sick" and "twisted" sexual pathology, and he presented "an absolute threat to any and all young boys and girls, and to any and all adult females."

Investigators did not know about these psychological records, especially the detectives in New York. Cops working the Crilley case had removed saliva from the bite mark on her body. DNA testing linked it to

Alcala. So did the impression and a fingerprint on an envelope removed from under her body. Then there was the Hover case, with the strong circumstantial evidence. In 2011, a grand jury indicted Alcala for both murders. In June 2012, he was extradited to Manhattan. Former FBI profiler Mark Safarik devised a behavioral analysis to determine similarities between the New York murders and those for which Alcala had already been convicted.

Safarik evaluated the offender's MO, rituals, signature, and possible evidence of staging. He considered body location and treatment, incident time frames, victim and offender risk levels, crime-scene dynamics for both parties, and degree of planning evident versus impulsive choice, as well as postmortem activity. The victims were all white females. From those for whom determinations could be made, except for one, there was sexual assault. There was blunt-force trauma on all. Some were manually strangled, but most were strangled with a ligature or some other item. Hover was a difficult case, because her body was skeletonized when found. Samsoe's remains posed similar challenges. Multiple knots had been tied in the ligatures of five victims, including Crilley. This was unusual and became part of a behavioral signature. There were bite marks on the breasts of five, including Crilley. Posing was evident in most of the cases. Safarik was able to link the Crilley homicide to the California cases, but not Hover.

On the day before Safarik was ready to provide his report in 2012, Alcala pleaded guilty to both New York murders, which added a 25-years-to-life sentence onto his current sentence. It was the first time that Alcala ever admitted to murder.

Investigators published 120 of the photos found in Alcala's storage unit, hoping to match some to cold cases of missing persons or Jane Doe murders. More than 900 other photos were considered too sexually explicit to show to the public. Some women, still alive, came forward to identify themselves as the subjects in question. One photo closed a cold case in Wyoming. In September 2016, Alcala was charged with the murder of twenty-eight-year-old Christine Ruth Thornton, who'd disappeared in 1977. A relative recognized her in one of Alcala's photos. Her body had been discovered in Sweetwater County in 1982, and she was identified in 2015 when DNA matched relatives' tissue samples from her remains.

There are others. In 2010 in Seattle, Alcala had also been named a "person of interest" in the unsolved murders of Antoinette Wittaker, thirteen, in July 1977, and Joyce Gaunt, seventeen, in February 1978. In March 2011, investigators in Marin County, California, announced that Alcala was likely the person who had killed Pamela Jean Lambson, nineteen, in 1977.

THE TAKEAWAY

Name: Rodrigo Jacques Alcala Buquor
Country: United States
Date of Birth: August 23, 1943
Date of Death: NA
Killing Period: 1968–1979
Known Victims: 8+
Date of Arrest: July 24, 1979

Smart, careful predators like Alcala pose the greatest challenge to law enforcement. They study investigations, leave little evidence, move around a lot, exploit holes in investigative strategies, and act quickly. They've often studied criminal investigation or law. When caught, they use charm to get reduced sentences or special treatment. Generally, only a mistake on their part will bring them down. For Alcala, the alteration to Samsoe's earrings was too subtle for him to realize that they could be traced to a victim. This discovery started the chain of events that linked him with other murders. Given his cross-country travels, he might have many more victims than are currently attributed to him.

10.

THE SLAVE MASTER

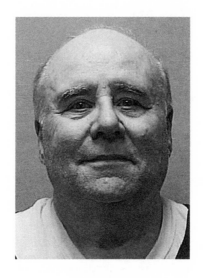

THE CRIMES

Paula Godfrey, eighteen, disappeared from her family's home in Overland Park, Kansas, a suburb of Kansas City, in 1984. She had told her family she was going to a training session in Texas to be a sales rep for a company run by John Robinson. When her worried father hadn't heard from her, he contacted Robinson, who denied knowing where she was. Soon, a disturbing note arrived from Paula to her family. In it, she told her father that she had left and did not want to see him anymore. It didn't sound like her at all: she'd had a good relationship with her family. The police declined to investigate. Paula was an adult, they said, and could make up her own mind.

Just across the Missouri River in Kansas City, Missouri, and a year later, nineteen-year-old Lisa Stasi met a man named John Osborne when a social worker referred him to her. He said he offered job training to unwed mothers. Living in a temporary shelter for battered women with her four-month-old daughter, Tiffany, Stasi was pleased to get the job. She'd recently left her abusive husband and had no means of support. All she had to do to get the job, she learned, was to sign four pieces of blank stationery and list the names and addresses of her relatives. This upset her enough to call a relative, but then she hung up because "they" were coming. No one ever heard from her again.

Soon after that, John Robinson told his brother and sister-in-law, Donald and Helen Robinson, who were looking to adopt, that he'd found a Caucasian baby for them. He told them the child's mother had committed suicide in a Chicago hotel room. He collected a legal fee of $5,500 from them and, unknown to them, forged the adoption papers. Lisa Stasi appeared to have vanished.

So did a mid-twenties woman named Catherine Clampitt when she arrived for a job with Robinson's company in Kansas City in 1987.

That year, Robinson was convicted of multiple counts of illegal fraud. He was sentenced to serve time at the Western Missouri Correctional Facility. There, he sweet-talked prison librarian Beverly Bonner, forty-nine, who left her husband and children in 1993 to go with Robinson upon his release. He diverted her $1,000-a-month alimony checks to a Kansas post office box before she disappeared. When her letters to relatives ceased in 1997, suspicious family members contacted police, who found no trace of her.

In prison, Robinson had learned how to use computers. He recognized the emerging Internet as a fertile place for uninvestigated fraud and anonymous hook-ups. Setting up five computers in his home, he adopted several aliases. Chat groups formed for people with similar interests, and some of these groups involved kinky sexual practices like bondage and discipline or sadomasochism, or both (BDSM). Robinson posed as the "Slave Master."

Sheila Faith fell into his trap. She had a disabled teenage daughter who needed care (which meant to Robinson that she received disability checks), so Faith went online to meet men. She entered bondage chat rooms because she sought a dominant partner. In 1994, she spoke with "John," a wealthy executive who invited her to Missouri. He told her he would pay to put her daughter in a private school. Faith went to meet him. Around Christmastime, relatives received letters from her, in which she said she was living a great life in Europe with a man named Jim. However, her Social Security checks, along with benefit checks for her daughter, went to a Kansas address.

In those early days of the emerging public use of the Internet, law enforcement barely understood it. When they learned about criminal enterprises online, they were usually many steps behind. There were few resources for setting up digital labs and few training opportunities for learning the tools. For a period of time, criminals enjoyed the perfect outlaw playground.

In a BDSM chat area, the "Slave Master" met Izabela Lewicka, a twenty-one-year-old student from Poland studying at Purdue University. He invited her to move to Kansas City to immerse herself in the master/slave relationship, and he offered her a job. Izabela worked with Robinson for a while, pretending to be his niece or his wife; but in the late summer of 1999, communications between her and her relatives fell off. Robinson told some people that Lewicka had been deported.

Izabela's parents looked for her, but she sent angry letters telling them to leave her alone. They couldn't understand how she'd changed so dramatically, but they were helpless to do anything.

The Slave Master next approached Suzette Trouten, a twenty-eight-year-old nurse's aide who posted a personal ad for a master. As "John Rob," he invited her to come to Kansas and take care of his elderly father.

The job paid well. When she arrived in February 2000 with her two dogs, Robinson gave her a slave contract, which required not just sex but also the passwords to her e-mail accounts. Robinson also insisted that she address a number of envelopes to her friends and family. On March 2, 2000, he told her they were going together to California to pick up his yacht and sail to Hawaii, but they'd stop first in La Cygne, Kansas. She called her mother to let her know.

Later that day, Robinson collected the dogs from the kennel, then called the police to pick up some strays. He was alone. A housekeeper at the hotel where Trouten had stayed noticed blood on the towels. She also saw Robinson packing items from the room into his car.

Suzette's mother was quite close to her daughter and knew something was wrong. After March 2, there were no more calls. The e-mails she received sounded nothing like Suzette. The writer spelled her dogs' names wrong and signed off with a nickname that Suzette would never have used. When the Trouten family contacted John Rob, he said Suzette had left with another man. Her mother knew this could not be true. She wanted to contact authorities, but Robinson tried to dissuade her. The family received more odd letters.

The Troutens took their concerns to the police in Overland Park, Kansas. Law enforcement there knew about John Robinson, with his criminal record for fraud, and put him under light surveillance.

Soon, psychologist Vickie Neufeld entered a police station and filed a complaint against Robinson for theft and sexual assault. She had moved to Kansas City in April 2000 to pursue a relationship with Robinson, but things went badly. Robinson allegedly had misrepresented himself and forced her to have rough sex. He'd also stolen her bag of sex toys, valued at $700. She admitted that she'd agreed to participate in a master–slave relationship with him, but he'd taken it too far. The more time they spent together, the more she saw how angry he was. She didn't like the things he was trying to get her to do, so she finally decided to report him.

Aware of Robinson's association with several missing women, a multi-jurisdictional task force was formed to look more deeply into him. Robinson lived with his wife, Nancy, who managed his business, in a trailer park in Olathe, Kansas, near Overland Park. They had four kids together, and Nancy knew of some of her husband's infidelities but believed they were fleeting. Officers tapped Robinson's cell phone and confiscated his trash. They found items that suggested he had storage lockers in Raymore, Missouri, near Kansas City. With digital analysis, they also learned that emails sent to Suzette Trouten's family had come from Robinson's home.

When another woman reported that Robinson had hit her and tried to lure her to a farm, detectives had enough to get warrants to search his various properties. On June 2, 2000, they placed Robinson under arrest.

THE CAPTURE

At Robinson's residence, police found items belonging to six of the missing women, including Social Security cards, passports, jewelry, bank statements, and driver's licenses. They also found fake credit cards and books on how to create a false identity.

Robinson owned a vacant property in Linn County, Kansas, about sixty miles south of Kansas City. A team of detectives and some cadaver-dog handlers set out to explore it. The dogs hit on a yellow metal barrel. The stench suggested that it held something nasty. An officer moved it, tipping it, and a stream of red fluid emerged and immediately attracted flies. They pried open the barrel and saw the decomposing form of a nude woman, blindfolded. She'd been bludgeoned in the head. They opened a second barrel and found another female corpse, bludgeoned. The first one turned out to be Suzette Trouten, the other Izabela Lewicka. The Kansas team notified officers in Missouri of their discovery.

On Monday, June 5, detectives and a crime-scene unit opened Robinson's two rental lockers at Stor-Mor-For-Less in Raymore,

Missouri. They'd been leased under Beverly Bonner's name. Inside were three barrels labeled "Rendered Pork Fat." All three contained decomposing human remains: Beverly Bonner, Sheila Faith, and her daughter. Fingerprints confirmed that Robinson had handled the barrels. He was charged with multiple counts of first-degree murder in both states (the Kansas charges included those for murdering Lisa Stasi). Even though Stasi was still missing, fingerprints and DNA testing proved that the baby Robinson had arranged for his brother to adopt was Stasi's daughter, Tiffany. The circumstances strongly suggested that Stasi was dead.

Missouri and Kansas prosecutors argued over who should try Robinson first. Both states had the death penalty. Since the Kansas task force had undertaken most of the investigation and made the first discovery, Robinson was tried there first. He pleaded not guilty to the murders of Izabela Lewicka, Suzette Trouten, and Lisa Stasi.

The jury was seated on October 4, 2002. The prosecution team presented Robinson as an S&M practitioner and predator who killed women for his own gain. By the end of the month, Robinson was found guilty of the Kansas murders. He received two death sentences and one life sentence. He also received sentences for "interfering with the parental custody" of Stasi's baby and for kidnapping Trouten.

To avoid the death penalty in Missouri, Robinson acknowledged that prosecutors had enough evidence for five murder charges (Bonner, Godfrey, Clampitt, and the Faiths), though he would not plead guilty. He was fifty-nine, one of the oldest serial killers ever convicted at the time.

In 2006, the body of a young woman was found in a barrel in Iowa, where Robinson had once had business dealings. She was too decomposed for identification, so he was not charged.

That same year, Heather Robinson (formerly Tiffany Stasi) filed a civil suit against the social worker who had referred Robinson to her mother without checking him out, and against the Truman Medical Center in Kansas City. She received a settlement. In 2007, she won a judgment that prevented Robinson from profiting from book or film sales. She founded "The Lisa Stasi Effect" to try to find out what had happened to her mother's remains, so she can claim and bury them. Donald Robinson and his wife Helen legally adopted her.

THE TAKEAWAY
Name: John Edward Robinson, Sr.
Country: United States
Date of Birth: December 27, 1943
Date of Death: NA
Killing Period: 1984–1999
Known Victims: 8
Date of Arrest: June 2, 2000

Robinson is the first convicted serial killer who exploited the Internet's anonymity to seek victims. His case brought attention to the dangers of meeting cyber acquaintances offline, especially for sexual practices like S&M. People who feel marginalized due to their sexual proclivities might be willing to put themselves at risk in order to find community or partnerships. Robinson knew this and carried out a double life, using aliases and secret rentals to shield his dark activities from his wife.

An offender who started with white-collar crimes, Robinson went on to use his knowledge of technology to commit significant fraud and multiple murders. He used the women sexually at times, but he was more interested in taking over their income. In the case of his brother Donald, Robinson spotted an opportunity to make money off the couple's desperation.

Robinson had grown up in a blue-collar, two-parent home with no evidence of abuse or neglect. He became an Eagle Scout, sang in front of the Queen of England, and was accepted into a Preparatory Seminary but declined to pursue the priesthood. In 1964, he married Nancy Jo Lynch.

Robinson then moved to Kansas City and used forged documents to get a job. He was arrested for embezzlement and sentenced to probation, which encouraged him only to get savvier with his crimes.

Predatory deviance and con artistry like Robinson's are practiced in secret. Yet such offenders might give off signals through certain patterns of behavior, which can help targeted victims spot the danger. People who understand the various Internet tools these offenders use to "groom" potential victims are better prepared to resist them.

Robinson's case is a cautionary tale. He knew how to target vulnerable women, how to make them trust him, and how to reduce their resources so he could control them. He bought or rented disposal sites so he could get rid of bodies once he had what he wanted. Despite his S&M practices, he killed not for sexual gratification but from greed.

11.

THE ABC KILLER

THE CRIMES

Between July and October 1994, the bodies of a dozen young adult black women were discovered in remote areas of South Africa, around the Pretoria-Johannesburg suburb of Cleveland. Most were found close to a mine-dumping site. Decomposition indicated that some had been there for several months. All had been raped and strangled, and all were openly displayed. The killer had removed personal items that could have identified the victims. He had manually strangled some, and used items of underwear to strangle others.

Those that were identified from missing-persons reports yielded more information. Most of the victims were unemployed or commuters, and some were well dressed. Money was taken from some victims' bank accounts after they were killed.

Police offered rewards and appealed to the killer to turn himself in. They decided that media coverage would just pressure him to change his dumpsite area, so staking it out offered little advantage. With Interpol's help, they extradited David Selepe from Mozambique for interrogation. Blood in his car and a collection of newspaper clippings about the murders implicated him. "The Cleveland Strangler" confessed to killing fifteen women and offered to show police where he had dumped the bodies. When they arrived at the first site, Selepe grabbed a tree branch to attack his escort. An officer fatally shot him. Although he would never be tried, police announced that Selepe was linked to thirteen killings. It appeared as though the cases would be closed because the killer had been stopped.

Then, in the suburb of Atteridgeville, about forty miles north, more female bodies started turning up. As far as everyone knew, the Cleveland Strangler was dead. But *somebody* had been killing women since then. The first one, severely decomposed, was found in a field on January 4. About a month later, a nude female corpse was discovered with her clothes folded and some rocks placed on her chest. Another month went by before construction workers digging a ditch saw a nude body protruding from the soil. The fourth body turned up on April 12, her hands tied behind her back with a bra.

From May through June, more bodies were found, some of them women who had recently vanished. A dead two-year-old boy was among a group of corpses, presumably the child of one. Of those identified, most were unemployed. The dead boy's mother, it turned out, had been responding to a job offer. The theory was either that Selepe had had an associate who was still killing, or there was another serial killer in the area with a similar approach. The tally for the so-called "Atteridgeville Strangler" was fifteen.

On July 17, a man in the Boksburg suburb, ten miles east of Cleveland, watched a couple walk into a field. They were trespassing, so he called out to them, but the male said he knew the area. Sometime later, the man emerged alone, looking around furtively before he ran. The witness from the earlier encounter investigated and found the woman raped and murdered, with a belt around her neck. But when police questioned him, the witness could not recall the killer's features well enough to help. The victim was Josephine Mantsali Mlangeni, twenty-five, a mother of four. She had told associates that she was meeting a man about a job offer.

A task force was formed; but as they looked over the cases, they discovered so many differences among the incidents that it was a hindrance to developing a clear profile. The killer then returned to the Cleveland area, where yet another body was reported on September 12.

Four days later, a rabbit hunter discovered a dead woman at the Van Dyk mine near Boksburg. Upon investigation, a mass grave was discovered. Forensic experts recovered ten female bodies in varying degrees of decomposition. The victims, aged twenty to forty-three, had been raped, strangled, and left naked and exposed. Some believed it was no coincidence that Boksburg Prison was only three miles away.

The victim total had reached forty. Police believed they were looking for separate killers, but journalists speculated that there was only one and that Selepe had possibly been wrongly accused. Because of the three clusters where the bodies had been found, the murders were dubbed the ABC killings—for Atteridgeville, Boksburg, and Cleveland—although accounts of the chronological order differ.

President Nelson Mandela visited the Boksburg site to plead with residents for information. Killings, rapes, and robberies had reached epidemic proportions in the country since the end of apartheid. Mandela feared that the people of South Africa had become desensitized to violence. He also knew they mistrusted the police.

Micki Pistorius, a former journalist training to be a psychologist, volunteered with the South African police service. Pistorius was writing her doctoral dissertation on serial killers and had already contributed to the "Station Strangler" case in Cape Town, where she'd joined the task force and provided a profile. For the present series of unsolved murders, she urged the investigative team to contact former FBI Special Agent Robert Ressler, who had helped to develop the FBI's famed Behavioral Science Unit in the 1970s and '80s. At the FBI, Ressler had initiated a program of interviews with incarcerated serial killers that led to a database where insights about extreme offenders could be drawn. Officials sent a request for Ressler to consult, and he arrived on September 23, 1995.

As part of the task force, Ressler visited the crime scenes (now clear of bodies) to ponder the killer's behavior. He also viewed them from the air, to get a sense of the geography. Then he spent time with the evidence in the forensic lab.

Ressler thought the killer or killers had returned to the bodies. There were more similarities in the modus operandi in the three clusters than differences, but he acknowledged that the evidence against Selepe was convincing. He deduced that the active offender was familiar with all three areas, had done prior surveillance, and viewed himself as immune to capture. He was probably luring victims, perhaps with promises of money or employment, rather than attacking them by surprise.

Ressler's behavioral profile, developed from Pistorius's early effort, was detailed. He thought the offender was black, owned an expensive vehicle, was financially secure, wore flashy clothing and jewelry, was in his late twenties or early thirties, and had a strong sex drive with aggressive fantasies. He was intelligent, sophisticated, streetwise, and nonthreatening. He'd be self-employed and speak several languages. He might be engaged in fraud. An extrovert, he'd seem charming to women. He might be married, knew a lot about other serial killers, and was likely following news about the investigation. Contemptuous of women, he likely savored the killings, which were related to a negative experience with a woman who he believed had wronged him. There would be physical similarities between that woman and those whom he targeted.

Ressler thought there could be two killers operating together, with one of them dominant and controlling. He saw evidence of escalation in the number of killings and of rising sophistication in the torture of the victims. In Cleveland, the killer had manually strangled the victims, but he (or they) had used ligatures made from the victims' clothing at the other two sites. At Boksburg, he'd progressed to a cloth-and-stick garrote ligature, and four recent victims had been hog-tied. Ressler thought the killer might have taken victims alive to the sites to show them the bodies of other victims for added mental torture.

Body placement also showed some differences. In Cleveland, they were scattered over a large area, but were more concentrated in the other two places. He thought the killer wanted them to be found so he could get a thrill from the community's shock.

Ressler further offered investigative strategies. First, he thought the crime scenes should be preserved and guarded. He also urged police to place mobile phones in the humbler neighborhoods, so tips could be called in. He thought soil samples should be taken from the dump sites, in case they found soil in a suspect's vehicle, and he recommended a psychological consultant for interrogating suspects. He predicted that the offender, who liked attention, would soon contact the police or newspapers.

Two weeks later, an anonymous telephone call came to *The Star* newspaper. The caller claimed to be "the man that is so highly wanted." He said he'd committed the murders in revenge against a woman who'd falsely accused him of rape, and that he'd picked victims who resembled her. He then claimed to have been abused and tortured in prison, and while he was incarcerated, his parents and sister had died. "I force a woman to go where I want," he said, "and when I go there I tell them 'Do you know what? I was hurt, so I'm doing it now.' Then I kill them."

He said Ressler's profile was wrong because he did not have a car, hadn't committed the Cleveland killings, and did not kill a child.

He claimed to have killed seventy-six women so far, and gave directions to a body that police had yet to discover. He called two more times. Police traced the call to a public phone, but just missed catching him. They did, however, get another lead.

Investigators discovered that one of the identified victims, Amelia Rapodile, was seen prior to disappearing with a thirty-one-year-old man named Moses Sithole, a youth counselor with a prison record for rape. Rapodile had told relatives that she had an appointment with Sithole on September 7 for a job. A second victim had a similar connection, so Sithole was now a common factor. Police went to see him, but he proved difficult to locate. They guessed he knew he was a person of interest.

On October 3, the body of another young woman was found raped and strangled near Benoni, thirteen miles northeast of Boksburg.

Police uncovered more information on Sithole. He'd used several false names and operated a fake company that supposedly provided services to youth in need. He looked like a viable suspect, especially in light of Ressler's profile—Sithole was the right age and had experienced a so-called "precipitating incident" in his youth.

Sithole was born into poverty in 1964 near Boksburg. His father had died, negatively impacting the family's financial situation, leading his mother to abandon him and his four siblings at a police station. Sithole then suffered abuse in an orphanage for three years until he ran away. In his twenties, he began raping women. Buyiswa Doris Swakamisa filed a police report against him in 1989, which resulted in a conviction and prison time, despite his claim that he was falsely accused. He was released early in 1993 from Boksburg Prison, not far from the third dumping ground.

The police made a photo of Sithole public, with a request for tips and information. Officers intercepted communication between him and a relative with whom he was trying to hide. Clearly, he sensed law enforcement closing in. On October 18, a tip about where Sithole was heading to acquire a gun led police to a slum area of Benoni. Sithole was there.

THE CAPTURE

As officers approached in the driving rain to make an arrest, Sithole advanced with a hatchet, wounding one officer in the arm. Another shot Sithole in the foot and stomach. Sithole was taken to a hospital and ultimately recovered. While there, he was diagnosed as HIV-positive.

Several people who saw Sithole's photo provided police with information about how he'd posed variously as a youth counselor and a wealthy man who could offer employment or a paid trip to a displaced woman's homeland. Sithole's sister said he'd used her phone to field inquiries from women until she pressed him about his business. She said she did not know he was killing these women.

When police finally interrogated Sithole, he confessed to murdering many of the women who'd been found as part of the investigation. The police were secretly recording him as he chewed on an apple and smoked a cigarette, talking casually about murder. Repeating his call to the newspaper, he blamed Buyiswa Doris Swakamisa, the woman who'd accused him of rape. Because of what he called her false accusation, Sithole said he'd been subjected to abuse and torture in prison. Upon release, he'd selected women to rape and kill who looked like Swakamisa so he could fully vent his anger. Charming, attractive, and confident, it had been easy for him to attract them into isolated areas with promises of employment. He would tell them he owned a factory and wanted to show it to them. On some of the bodies, he'd written "bitch." Sithole denied having an accomplice and said he'd never met Selepe, but he thought there was a copycat killer because he said he'd never killed a child.

On October 23, 1995, Sithole was charged with twenty-nine murders. He went back to Boksburg Prison to await trial while investigators analyzed the evidence.

A year passed before the trial began on October 21, 1996. By then, the charges against Sithole had increased to thirty-eight counts of murder (including the toddler), forty counts of rape, and six counts of robbery. Sithole pleaded not guilty.

The prosecutor's trial strategy involved testimony from Sithole's rape victims before presenting his connection to many of the identified murder victims. This helped to demonstrate his modus operandi of luring women with false promises. The prosecutor also introduced the hour-long video of Sithole's incriminating interview. However, because it had been recorded illegally, the proceedings were delayed for six months before the judge finally admitted it into evidence. The prosecution closed its case on August 15, 1997.

Sithole's defense team then put him on the stand, but his testimony was rambling and difficult to follow. The defendant did himself no favors, quickly demonstrating the folly of his arrogance with no alibi evidence, forcing his defense to rely primarily on his denial, which rang hollow in the light of his recorded admissions.

The jury found Sithole guilty of all charges. Since the death penalty had been declared unconstitutional in 1995, the judge sentenced Sithole to 2,410 years in prison, a life sentence. Ironically, Sithole received better medical care for his HIV infection in prison than he would've gotten otherwise, likely extending his life.

THE TAKEAWAY

Name: Moses Sithole
Country: South Africa
Born: November 17, 1964
Died: NA
Killing Period: 1994–1995
Date of Arrest: October 18, 1995

Sithole was one of several South African serial killers who engaged in violence after the repressive policies of apartheid were undone in 1992. A generation of men who had endured state-sponsored racism, poverty, and family separations during their childhood were free to act on their deep-rooted resentment. As police departments transitioned and retrained, crime rates soared.

Journalist Philip von Nekerk reported that there were 11,750 murders in South Africa in 1989, and by 1995 there were 25,782. Rape and robbery had similarly escalated, but the reformed post-apartheid law-enforcement system was "ill-trained and ill-equipped" to investigate or fight crime, especially crimes in which the victims did not know their attackers.

The "Cape Town Strangler" tortured and killed at least twenty sex workers, while "Donnybrook Serial Killer" Christopher Mhlengwa Zikode murdered eighteen people and attempted to kill another eleven. "Kranskop Rapist-Killer" Samuel Bongani Mfeka confessed to raping and strangling six women, and Sipho Agmatir Thwala was convicted of murdering sixteen as the "Phoenix Strangler." David Mmbengwa, the "Lover's Lane Murderer," believed he was on a divine mission each time he murdered a couple he found making love. He was charged with eight deaths, while the "Station Strangler," suspected of sodomizing and strangling twenty-one boys at train stations, turned out to be Norman Avzal Simon, who could speak seven languages.

By 2004, fifty South African serial killers had been recorded over two decades, with an increase of 900 percent annually between 1990 and 1996. The country had the highest incidence of cross-ethnic offenses of any country. Most of the killers had been exposed to trauma, neglect, and isolation, highlighting the relationship between social environment and serial murder. People who become serial killers are often psychologically sensitive to cultural tensions, and the form that their murders take tends to express this influence.

12.

THE HANGING PRO

THE CRIMES

A website called GroupSuicide.net is one of dozens that offered advice, company, and even assistance with ending life. Those who gravitate to this community want help to die. Often they're young and just hurting from a break-up or feeling bereft of purpose. Some want partners. "Is there anyone," a young woman pleaded, "who will die together with me?"

A growing number of Japanese people have formed suicide groups. Most are composed of strangers who met online, and many are young adults. Some pass out detailed instructions. Once an individual agrees to a pact, it can be difficult to pull out. Group suicides are twice as common in Japan as in other industrialized countries. But dramatic as they are, the pacts represent a mere two percent of all the suicides in Japan, a country with one of the highest per-capita suicide rates in the industrialized world. Among the most common ways to do it are jumping in front of high-speed trains, burning charcoal in a sealed space, and using household chemicals to concoct lethal gas. Some prefer going to a well-known suicide shrine, Aokigahara, or "Suicide Forest," near Mount Fuji.

Hiroshi Maeue was aware of these websites. It seemed to him a solution to exercising his violent compulsions without legal consequences. He'd already been arrested for assaulting male associates and trying to strangle two women, for which he'd spent time in prison. But prison hadn't cured him. Once free, he'd tried to strangle a young boy, who survived, which resulted in Maeue going back to prison. He grew craftier after being released in 2005, targeting people who *wanted* to die. Their messages on these suicide websites were proof.

Maeue joined an online suicide club. Over a period of four months, whenever someone asked for others to enter a group suicide pact, Maeue would volunteer. He'd lure his prey to an isolated spot with the promise of a charcoal-induced death together. Then he'd manually strangle or smother them. Two of his victims were adults, and one was a fourteen-year-old boy. He filmed the murders so he could relive them for his personal gratification. "I wanted to watch a face in agony," he'd later say. He then dumped the bodies in wilderness areas. Police ultimately caught him through his chain of enticing emails to a missing woman.

When he was arrested in 2005, the thirty-six-year-old claimed he'd been aroused by descriptions of strangulation in a novel he'd read as a boy. Upon conviction, he was hanged in 2009. But Maeue's devious modus operandi inspired someone else with a death compulsion.

Several young women vanished from different areas around Zama in Japan's Kanagawa Prefecture *after* Maeue's execution. All the women had Twitter accounts on which they expressed dark feelings. Kureha Ishihara, from Ora, in the Gunma Prefecture, was only fifteen years old; two other missing girls were seventeen. One couple vanished together, and another missing woman was married with children.

Aiko Tamura was twenty-three and lived in the Tokyo suburb of Hachioji. She vanished in October 2017. She had expressed feelings of sadness and regret on a suicide site and asked if anyone would join her in a suicide pact. A man named Takahiro Shiraishi communicated with her. The twenty-seven-year-old had a suspended sentence for scouting for a prostitution ring.

Tamura's brother reported her disappearance to the police, but also launched his own online investigation. He hacked into his sister's Twitter account and used it to ask around. A woman on the social media site who knew Shiraishi told him about Shiraishi's invitations to women. In cooperation with the police investigation, she agreed to make an appointment with Shiraishi for assistance with ending her life. He gave her the address to his apartment in Zama, twenty miles southwest of Tokyo. But she didn't show up. Instead, two investigators arrived to question Shiraishi about Aiko Tamura.

THE CAPTURE

Shiraishi did not seem surprised when the police arrived. He pointed to a food cooler near the door when he heard Tamura's name and said, "In there."

He had dismembered Tamura and stored the parts.

Shiraishi's studio apartment was cramped, with a ladder to a loft over the tiny kitchen and bathroom. The living area was filled with food coolers and storage boxes. The officers recognized the foul smell. This place was an abattoir. They opened the cooler nearest to the front door. In it, they found decomposing heads, arms, and legs. They called for additional police resources.

By the end of the day, the body parts of nine people that Shiraishi had killed and dismembered were discovered throughout his apartment, including two severed heads. The scene was on a par with America's Jeffrey Dahmer (see Chapter 26) or Britain's Dennis Nilsen, both of whom kept bodies and body parts in their confined living spaces. And similarly to those cases, neighbors in this twelve-unit apartment building had complained about the smell but hadn't gone to the police. One neighbor noted that Shiraishi's bathroom ventilation fan was on at all times. The body parts showed multiple cuts and some had been reduced via defleshing to bone. Shiraishi admitted to disposing of internal organs and fleshy parts, along with victims' personal items, in the trash. He kept the bones for fear of being caught. Eight of the victims were women; the other was a man.

An investigation turned up witnesses who had seen missing women or girls with Shiraishi around the time of their disappearance. There was also CCTV footage of him with his final victim. He said that he found the deaths arousing. The victims were vulnerable, and Shiraishi had manipulated their vulnerabilities to first sexually assault them before killing them, usually with a rope.

According to a former girlfriend, Shiraishi was obsessed with death. Another friend described the choking games they used to play as boys. Upon serving his prison sentence after the arrest for his role in the prostitution ring, Shiraishi had moved in with his father, complaining that he had no sense of purpose. His state of mind indicated that he had nothing to lose by acting out his fantasies, even if it led to his arrest.

Exploring the same places on the Internet that he had used to lure girls into the sex trade, Shiraishi had set up two Twitter accounts. On one, "Professional Hangman," he offered his services "@hangingpro" to women who expressed suicidal thoughts. His profile featured a Manga image of a man with scars on his neck and wrists, with the words "I want to help people who are really in pain." He'd Tweet things like "I want to spread my knowledge of hanging" and "I really want to become the source of strength for everyone who is in pain."

On the other Twitter account, "I Want to Die," he posed as a forlorn person seeking company. He urged those who were at a "dead-end" to consult him for guidance and assistance. He posted his own fake suicidal thoughts as bait. If they wanted a suicide pact, Shiraishi offered to die with them. He knew they couldn't do much about his reneging once they were dead. Sometimes he used "suicide recruitment" hashtags. As long as he appeared compassionate and sincere, he found it easy to lure his victims. Once someone expressed interest, he'd meet them at a train station and then take them to his apartment. He killed one in August 2017, four in September that year, and four in October. Four of them were teenagers.

But Shiraishi had to dispose of the bodies. So he dismembered the victims, defleshed some in his bathroom, and chose places around his apartment to store them. He kept some body parts in coolers and some in storage boxes filled with cat litter. He put bones in toolboxes. But these hiding spots did not diminish the putrid smell as the body parts decomposed. Shiraishi knew he couldn't keep up his behavior for long, but he managed to kill under the radar for two months.

Police found a saw, bindings, scissors, knives, and a gimlet they believed he used for dismemberment. All bore traces of blood. Shiraishi hadn't bothered to clean things up.

Questions were raised about the lone male victim, Shogo Nishinaka. This twenty-year-old had not been suicidal. He'd accompanied a depressed friend to Shiraishi's place when she went there to discuss her own arrangements. Nishinaka left, but when the girl vanished—she was Shiraishi's first victim—the young man returned to find her. He confronted Shiraishi, who realized Shogo knew too much and invited him inside so he could kill him. (Some accounts say that Shiraishi instead went out looking for Nishinaka.)

The investigation turned up near-victims as well. One young woman who talked with Shiraishi on the phone heard a female groaning in the background. She told reporters, "He had given me two options. One was that he makes me unconscious by putting sleep drug in my drink and then [he] strangles me with a rope. The other was that he strangles me with a rope from behind while I'm watching TV or something. If I had met with him, I may [sic] have been dismembered like other victims. I may be lucky, but I'm rather scared now."

The media labeled Shiraishi's apartment a "house of horrors." Previously, he'd lived with his father. He told his father he'd met someone he loved and wanted to get his own place. His father acted as a guarantor on the $227 monthly lease. Shiraishi moved in on August 22, and began killing soon thereafter. Although he learned that those who claimed they wanted to die merely wanted someone to talk to, he killed them anyway, usually the same day he met them. "I had no intention of killing myself at all," he told detectives. "None [of the victims] wanted to die actually."

He'd usually give them alcohol or sleeping pills before strangling them. Then he would hang them. It took him three days to reduce his first victim to body parts that he could store, but he said he got more efficient over time. Stealing thousands of dollars from the victims' purses and bank accounts, he used the money to support himself.

A SCREEN-CAPTURE OF SERIAL KILLER TAKAHIRO SHIRAISHI'S TWITTER PROFILE IN WHICH HE BOASTS OF HIS KNOWLEDGE OF HANGING.

By all reports, Shiraishi had been a quiet, conscientious boy who played baseball, got average grades, and ran on the track team in school. When he was a teenager, his parents had divorced. His mother and younger sister had moved out. With no aspirations for a career, Shiraishi did various odd jobs, including at a supermarket, before he became a scout for an illegal prostitution ring. He spent a lot of time online.

Given the decomposed and defleshed state of the mingled remains, the police struggled to identify the victims and locate their families. Some personal items Shiraishi had kept, including cell phones, helped police track down relatives. As families were notified, DNA matches were made, and investigators were able to piece together how the victims had met their killer online.

THE TAKEAWAY

Name: Takahiro Shiraishi
Country: Japan
Born: No DOB; 27 years old on arrest
Died: NA
Killing Period: August–October 2017
Known Victims: 9
Date of Arrest: October 30, 2017

A 2003 comparison of 82 Japanese serial killers to 402 American serial killers over a span of 200 years indicates that Americans are more likely to be sexually motivated, while Japanese offenders tend to kill for financial gain, have accomplices, and have adult male victims. In Japan, serial murder rates have gradually increased. The killers often travel, and their victims are typically between twenty-six and forty. They tend to have sexual or mood disorders, with victim mutilation the most common post-mortem activity.

The research confirms that motivations of serial killers derive from covert social values that encourage violence as power and control, exacerbated by social tensions. A review of how such killers have behaved throughout history indicates that they represent an aspect of the human condition that emerges under pressure and times of social transition or dissonance. Some people with low impulse control and poor coping skills might internalize the stress of this disparity and play it out in aggression.

The fact that both suicide-pact serial killers in Japan deviated from typical past motivations in their culture to cite sexual compulsion as their trigger suggests a shift in the culture at large. Both used social media to look for victims. They might have been exposed to the abundance of graphic sexuality available online. Even apart from the Internet, Japan itself seems to have changed. Criminologist Eric Hickey noted the recent increase there of sexually explicit materials and industries; he suggests that greater exposure to sexual content has spawned more sexually motivated serial killers today than in the past.

In addition, the Internet has created greater opportunities for predators to find and lure vulnerable people. A study in Britain found that 20 percent of young adults with a history of suicidal self-harm had visited sites containing information on how to commit suicide. There are numerous websites as well, where suicide-prone people discuss their desire to die. In response to serial killers exploiting these websites, a senior member of the Japanese government instructed ministers to improve their oversight: "The use of Twitter—a social networking site that is difficult to keep an eye on—to exploit the cries for help by victims who wrote about committing suicide is despicable," one Japanese official said. "We will get to the bottom of this crime, and work toward preventing its reoccurrence." The government now offers more official resources for counseling for those with suicidal thoughts.

13.

THE GRUDGE COLLECTOR

THE CRIMES

November 6, 2003 seemed like another ordinary day at the Superbike Motorsports shop in Chesnee, South Carolina. That afternoon, a customer named Kelly Sisk was looking at go-karts when he noticed a man asking about motorcycles. Not long after Sisk left, another man named Noel Lee arrived to talk with the bike shop's thirty-year-old owner, Scott Ponder. Lee saw store manager Brian Lucas lying in the doorway, in a pool of blood. Then he spotted Ponder on the ground near his mother's car. Both had been shot. Just inside the showroom was the body of Ponder's mother, Beverly Guy, who kept the books. Lee called the police. When they arrived, they added a victim from the back of the shop:

twenty-six-year-old mechanic Chris Sherbert. All four had been shot multiple times.

Guy had not yet made the day's deposit, so thousands of dollars remained in the store, along with valuable merchandise. Clearly, the crime had not been a botched robbery. Looking into the victims' backgrounds, police dug up rumors about drugs, but found nothing that rose to the level of such violent payback. Lee was a suspect, but he was soon cleared. A mistake in the crime-scene sample collection threw suspicion on Ponder's pregnant wife, but this too was eventually cleared up.

Sisk offered a description of the man he'd seen: a stocky white guy, about six foot, 180 to 200 pounds, with feathered dark brown hair. He was wearing a leather coat too warm for the weather. Sisk thought the resulting police sketch looked nothing like the man he described. A list of customers was generated to highlight people who'd been difficult in the past, but the police failed to use it for leads. A year went by before investigators invited former FBI profiler John Douglas to work up a profile of the kind of person who would commit such a horrific act. Douglas suggested that the killer had carried a grudge against the shop rather than against any particular person. Among the files given to him to review, none included the list of disgruntled customers, despite his suggestion that this was who they should be looking for.

The case went cold, and the victims' families and friends had to live with the painful questions.

Twelve years later, on December 22, 2015, Meagan McCraw Coxie, twenty-six, and her twenty-nine-year-old husband, Johnny Coxie, told relatives they were on their way to clean a house for a real estate agent in Spartanburg, South Carolina, about fifteen miles from Chesnee. Then they vanished.

Relatives went to the police, but officers thought the couple had simply run away to avoid the consequences of their petty crimes. Meagan had recently been released from jail on a charge of child neglect, but told her mother just before she vanished that she intended to turn her life around. Police had a cell phone number for Meagan that they could have pinged for her location, but they declined to do so. The fate of the Coxies remained a mystery.

A woman named Kala Brown and her boyfriend, Charlie Carver, went missing on Labor Day weekend in 2016. They left a friend's home on August 30. That was the last time they were seen, although another friend received a text on August 31. When she answered, there was no response. Kala and Charlie's beloved dog was discovered at home alone, without food or water, which was unlike them. Their friends and family searched frantically, posting numerous flyers, but heard nothing and found no traces. Odd items kept popping up on Carver's Facebook page suggesting that he and Kala were all right, but the posts seemed off, as if someone else were writing them. Carver claimed they'd gotten married and bought a house, but that seemed unlikely since he was not yet divorced from his first wife.

This time, the police investigated. A tip pointed to Todd Kohlhepp, a realtor in Spartanburg, who'd hired Brown and Carver around the time they'd disappeared to remove brush from his 95-acre property in Woodruff, about twenty miles south. A ping to Brown's cell phone indicated that she'd arrived at the property at the end of August or early September, but there was no activity after that. On November 3, with search warrants in hand, a team of detectives went to talk with Kohlhepp, while another team searched his property in Woodruff.

Nothing about Kohlhepp raised alarms. He was a successful businessman with a pilot's license, a BMW, and a college degree. People who knew him seemed to like him. When the detectives arrived, Kohlhepp was startled. He remained calm as officers went through his house. Detective Tom Clark told him about Kala Brown's cell-phone records at the end of August, and Kohlhepp confirmed that the couple had been at his Woodruff property that day for about an hour. He said he knew

Brown from Facebook and had hired her before. Yet the phone record indicated that she'd been on the property all day. Kohlhepp had been the last person to see the couple alive; he had just lied.

At the same time, investigators explored the Woodruff property. Ninety-five heavily wooded acres was a lot to search, but they started with an area that was already cleared. As they neared a 30-foot green metal Conex shipping container, they heard banging. Someone inside was calling for help. It sounded like a woman.

They brought tools to force open the container and found a young woman inside at the back, with a heavy chain around her neck. It was Kala Brown. Her rescuers could hardly believe they'd found her alive. Scared but alert, she told them that Kohlhepp had shot her boyfriend three times, wrapped his body in a blue tarp, and placed it in the bucket of an excavator shovel, to bury later.

Once free, Brown told the officers that Kohlhepp had driven Charlie and her to his property and taken them to a two-story garage. He pretended to need a certain area clipped, but then went into the garage and fetched a gun. As he came back out the door, he lifted it and shot Charlie three times in the chest. Brown had been stunned: there had been no provocation. Kohlhepp then grabbed her in a headlock and forced her into the dark container.

"He was prepared," she said. She did what he wanted, including letting him rape her. "He told me it was easier to control someone if you took someone they loved," she said.

Kohlhepp told Brown he had killed others. At one point, he'd shown her three graves. If she tried to escape, he'd assured her that he'd kill and bury her too. For more than two months he kept her chained up, using her sexually. She believed he'd eventually kill her. Kohlhepp brought paper and pens for her to write letters to him, which he collected when he brought food. Brown complied with all his demands, too scared to do anything else.

THE CAPTURE

The searchers conveyed their discovery to Clark, alerting him to the dangerous man he was questioning. When Clark told Kohlhepp "We have Kala," the realtor said, "Excuse me?" Clark could tell that Kohlhepp understood that it was over. The officers placed him under arrest. He told them he could close some cases for them, but first he wanted to talk to his mother, to give her a photo and transfer money to a college fund for a friend's kid. Since he seemed cooperative, they allowed it. On a recorded call, Kohlhepp told his mother, Regina Tague, that he had killed some people.

Shocked, she asked, "How many?"

"You don't have enough fingers," he told her. "They're going to keep pulling bodies off my land."

This grandiosity would become a theme with him. He seemed to want others to believe he was a serial killer with a high body count. Some killers exaggerate their crimes to enhance their notoriety or to launch an intimidating reputation before entering the prison environment.

Kohlhepp told the detectives he'd killed seven people in three separate incidents: four men in a motorcycle shop where he tried out a bike; Charlie Carver; and another couple.

They figured the other couple was the Coxies. He said he'd killed the male when he pulled a knife. Then he'd kept the woman in his shipping container for a week before killing her. He'd buried both on his property. "The land was supposed to be my sanctuary," he whined, "not my killing field." He insisted that he had not raped Kala Brown, that she had wanted the sex. At one point, he said, "It turned into *50 Shades of Gray* with bodies."

Searchers found Carver's vehicle in a ravine and his body, wrapped in a tarp, buried across from the shipping container. One report said that his feet were missing. But they hadn't been chewed off by animals or damaged by machinery—they'd been surgically removed. On November 6, Kohlhepp led authorities to the Coxie graves. Their feet were similarly missing. Kohlhepp did not explain. He also had twenty illegally acquired weapons on the property.

On May 26, 2017, Kohlhepp pleaded guilty to the seven murders, along with multiple rape and kidnapping charges, and was eventually sent to Broad River Correctional Facility in Columbia, South Carolina, to serve his life sentences.

In December, Kohlhepp wrote to the *Spartanburg Herald-Journal* to claim there were more bodies. He told the same thing to detectives. He said the media had only ten percent of the story, that he'd killed two people before the Superbike slaughter, while he was living at the Hunt Club Apartments in Spartanburg County. He claimed some residents there had harassed him. One had supposedly pulled a knife on him and another had come at him with a hammer, so he'd stabbed them and buried them at a dead-end road off Interstate 26 between Spartanburg and Columbia.

Producer Maria Awes explored Kohlhepp's new claims in a three-part documentary for the ID network, *Serial Killer: Devil Unchained*. She included Gary Garrett, Kohlhepp's chosen biographer, and former FBI profiler John Douglas.

Kohlhepp was interested in helping. He agreed to fill out the FBI's 57-page criminal-profiling interview form. Douglas was surprised that not only did he answer the questions, "he answered *way* beyond anything I'd ever experienced. He actually added pages, additional sheets of paper, where he wanted to fully describe the cases and his motivation. He wanted to learn why—what made him be this type of killer."

To prepare for understanding him, they looked into his background.

Kohlhepp was born Todd Christopher Sampsell on March 7, 1971 in Fort Lauderdale, Florida. He was young when his parents divorced, and he stayed with his mother, Regina. She had a second failed marriage and sent him to live with his allegedly abusive grandparents. As he got older, he took delight in harassing other kids and seemed preoccupied with sexual content. At the age of nine, Kohlhepp was sent for counseling and ended up in a psychiatric hospital for three months. "Behaviorally," states one of his juvenile records, "he is demanding, self-centered and likely attempts to force others to do what he wants in order to meet his own needs." Some officials thought he was smart but incorrigible. A probation officer described his sense of entitlement. He seemed to be a budding psychopath.

When he was twelve, Kohlhepp insisted on moving in with his biological father, William Sampsell, in Tempe, Arizona. His mother resisted the move because she'd just purchased new furniture for him, so he picked up a hammer and smashed it all. She let him go. But although he picked up Sampsell's gun hobby, things did not get better. He claimed that his father neglected him. Awes asked Sampsell about Kohlhepp's accusation, and he said he had tried to create a stable home life for Todd, adding that Todd lied a lot. He also said that the only emotion his son seemed to feel was anger. Sampsell thought his son was sick.

Kohlhepp certainly misbehaved. One evening when he was fifteen, he lured a fourteen-year-old neighbor, Kristie G., from the house where she was watching her younger brother and sister. He would later say that it was his inability to express love that got him into trouble, but the Kristie situation went far beyond clumsy immaturity.

With a gun, he forced her toward his father's house. When she turned and resisted him, he pulled the trigger while aiming at her face. The gun misfired, but it scared her enough to comply. He flashed a knife and ordered her to remove her clothes. He then applied duct tape to her mouth and tied her up. He tried sodomizing her first, before raping her. Police lights next door interrupted them. Kristie's family must have called the cops. Kohlhepp told Kristie that he would now have to kill her, but she convinced him that she'd say nothing about what he had done. He warned her that if she did, he'd kill her whole family. When she went home, she told her father. Kohlhepp was arrested and sent to adult prison for fifteen years. His only concern was what would happen to him. When he got out, he had to register as a sex offender. He went to live with his mother in South Carolina.

At that point, Kohlhepp seemed to have cleaned up his act. He went to college and earned bachelor's degrees in computer science and business. He also got a pilot's license. With an IQ of 118, he was bright. In 2006, he studied to become a real estate agent and lied about his sex-offender status so he could get a license. He started his own real estate company, TKA, and did well enough to hire a dozen agents and to purchase several large properties.

Awes and Garrett took a hard look at the killer and his victims. Garrett began to doubt that Kohlhepp had committed the Superbike murders, because when he described them, he got key facts wrong. However, Brown told police that Kohlhepp had claimed to be the Superbike killer even before they ever arrested him. He apparently enjoyed bragging that he was both a mass murderer and a serial killer.

Awes had some doubts about Brown's story when she uncovered social media messages that suggested that she'd been having an affair with Kohlhepp before she ever stepped on his property. He said they'd been hooking up for about a year. He showed Awes the warm letters Kala had written to him while she was a captive (insisting that it had not been captivity, but protection). The truth about this aspect of the case remained unresolved in the documentary, but Brown denied having anything to do with Kohlhepp beyond a business relationship. She'd cleaned five other properties for him without any signs of trouble, and she had planned on marrying Charlie.

The documentary team got involved in the search for the other two alleged murder victims. They brought in K-9 handlers from South Carolina Foothills Search and Rescue. The dogs turned up some animal bones, but no human remains.

Kohlhepp continued to hint that he had more victims. "Like a loose string on a sweater, once you start pulling you never know what it unravels," he wrote in a letter to Awes. At first, he told her he had "considerably" more victims, but then reduced his number to just two more. Garrett thought he was trying to puff himself up.

Kohlhepp's mother gave an interview on *48 Hours* to defend her son. "He did some bad things," Tague admitted, "but a monster? No." The murders, she said, were reactive, not something he enjoyed. Supposedly, someone at the shop had teased her son, whose new motorcycle had been stolen, so he shot them all. When he didn't get his way, his mother admitted, he acted out, often harming others. "He was doing it because he was mad and he was hurt." She blamed Carver for having a "smart mouth." To her mind, if they hadn't treated her son badly, no one would have been hurt. She insisted he had not molested Brown. "He would have told me," she claimed.

Tague described Kohlhepp as smart, kind, and generous, but someone who shouldn't have been provoked. "They embarrassed him," she said, as if this justified murder. "No one wants to be embarrassed." Since a lot of time had passed between the mass murder and the other killings, Tague didn't think her son was as bad as the media were saying. "It wasn't like he went out daily and killed people. . . . He wasn't a serial killer."

KALA BROWN WAS CHAINED INSIDE A METAL SHIPPING CONTAINER BY KOHLEPP ON HIS PROPERTY FOR ABOUT TWO MONTHS BEFORE BEING RESCUED BY SOUTH CAROLINA AUTHORITIES ON NOVEMBER 3, 2016.

Kohlhepp also claimed to have shot someone in Arizona, though this has not been confirmed. He became a suspect in a triple homicide in Greer, South Carolina, in 2003, but that incident involved a bank robbery. It did not match his MO. Kohlhepp also told Awes that he'd been part of a "hunt club," where he flew to Juarez, Mexico, to shoot "undesirables" for sport. When asked what it was like to kill, he shrugged and described it as "mechanical."

THE TAKEAWAY

Name: Todd Christopher Kohlhepp
Country: United States
Date of Birth: March 7, 1971
Date of Death: NA
Killing Period: 2003–2016 (possibly longer)
Known victims: 7
Date of arrest: November 3, 2016

As a society, we've grown used to the idea that sexual compulsion motivates serial killers, and we know that mass killers generally strike out of anger, but we don't often hear about the blend of these types in the angry killer who fatally retaliates on separate unrelated occasions. These cases exist, but they defy the stereotype. Kohlhepp is also unusual, but not unique, in that he committed both mass and serial murder. About 2.8 percent of other serial killers have included a mass murder in their series.

For people like Kohlhepp, who have a strong streak of entitled narcissism, humiliation threatens self-esteem and a sense of control. They don't get past it. Instead, the incidents fester, feeding their view of a hostile world that justifies payback. Few researchers have studied this motivator in serial killers, but the Kohlhepp case shows a need for more attention to it.

14.

THE CHOKE-AND-STROKE KILLER

THE CRIMES

On August 13, 1989, the half-naked body of Audrey Nelson, thirty-five, was found in a dumpster behind a Chinese restaurant in the Central Avenue–Alameda Street corridor of South Central Los Angeles. She had been beaten and strangled. Less than three weeks later in the same area, a nine-year-old boy peeked into an abandoned garage and saw the body of Guadalupe Apodaca, forty-six. She was nude except for a sex-stained yellow shirt. She had been strangled; her killer was long gone. The cases were soon forgotten. Both women were sex workers who lived difficult, high-risk lives where they were willing to be alone with potentially dangerous men to make a little money. They became mere statistics in a high-crime area until the cases were revisited twenty-three years later, in 2012.

LAPD homicide detectives Mitzi Roberts and Rodrigo Amador screened DNA results from cold cases they'd been assigned to from South Central LA. The results connected the murders of Nelson and Apodaca to a man named Sam Little, whose DNA went into the database when he pleaded guilty to an assault in San Diego. Skin cells from under Nelson's nails and semen from Apodaca's shirt were a match to Little. Since the victims had been sex workers and Little may have been a customer, the detectives looked for more evidence.

They contacted analysts at the FBI's Violent Criminal Apprehension Program (ViCAP), a national network used to link crimes with similar signatures and MO, to identify John Does who died violently, and to connect offenders with victims. Funded in 1985 as part of the National Center for the Analysis of Violent Crime, the process of successful linkage requires collaboration among investigators, computer programmers, computer analysts, and major-case specialists. Analyst Christie Palazzolo looked up Little's records, eventually teaming up with Angela Williamson, a Department of Justice policy adviser and ViCAP liaison. It turned out that Sam Little was quite the slippery career criminal.

In 1961, he had been busted in Ohio for breaking into a furniture store; he had served three years. By 1975, he'd been arrested for a variety of crimes, from theft to armed robbery to assault, in eleven states. Suspected in two murders, he escaped punishment. He returned to prison in California when a twenty-two-year-old woman accused him of trying to strangle her; he was also caught red-handed with another unconscious woman. He served just over two years in total for both offenses. Little got break after break, gliding through the system like an eel.

The detectives were astonished at how many crimes Sam Little had committed. They knew, in part, that this was due to lax investigation.

They linked another South Central case to him, the strangulation murder in 1987 of Carol Elford, forty-one. It became imperative to find this serial killer.

Little left a barely discernible trail. He had no address, no credit cards, and no work documents; only a prepaid Walmart card offered a lead. Through it, he collected Social Security payments, which showed that he'd recently been in Louisville, Kentucky.

Roberts and Amador contacted officials at the U.S. Marshals Fugitive Task Force. They found seventy-two-year-old Sam Little at a homeless shelter.

THE CAPTURE

On September 5, 2012, authorities arrested Little on a minor drug charge. He was extradited to Los Angeles to face the three murder charges. He fought every step of the way, claiming he'd just been at the wrong place at the wrong time and with the wrong people. "I didn't do it!" he repeatedly yelled.

He soon became a suspect in dozens of other murders. Palazzolo and Williamson turned Little's detailed criminal history into a 150-page timeline. Their next step was to look for unsolved homicides that overlapped. They identified a few in California and sent them to Roberts. They also contacted authorities in Odessa, Texas, about the 1994 murder of Denise Brothers. The mother of two, Brothers was a heroin addict. Her body lay in a vacant lot for three weeks after she was strangled. The responding detective fed the details into the ViCAP database, hoping they'd help identify the killer one day.

ViCAP issued a national alert to agencies around the country, urging them to check their unsolved strangulation murders against what they knew about Little. The case against him began to grow.

Roberts contacted the survivor of an assault by Little in California who had turned him in. She described Little's approach as one of enticement—he'd offer money and a bit of sweet talk to charm women into his car. Then he'd use his fist to knock them out. A six-foot-two former boxer with large hands, Little could deliver a powerful punch.

But he wasn't talking. Little insisted he was innocent. With the DNA matches and the help of two survivors who testified against him, Little was convicted of the three Los Angeles homicides in 2014. He got three life sentences. Little thought he'd been set up and ranted against the LAPD, refusing to tell them anything about his other crimes. Roberts worried that Little's health was such that he might die before giving a full account of his acts—he had diabetes and heart problems, and he needed a wheelchair.

Then came a break from an unexpected source.

In 2017, a Texas Ranger named James Holland heard about Little. Holland had a talent for interviewing psychopaths and a passion for solving cold cases. Given how mobile this killer had been and the type of victims he targeted, Holland knew Little's toll could be high. He went to visit him and quickly noticed the size of his hands.

At the same time, journalist Jillian Lauren was exchanging letters with Little, hoping to get a confession to more crimes. She met Detective Roberts, who told her that she believed Sam Little had killed a lot of women around the United States. Roberts had hoped that other police agencies would open investigations, but it hadn't happened. She thought it was because Little had targeted the "less dead"—those who didn't count much in society.

To get him talking, Holland and Lauren both brought Little things he liked: pizza, soda, M&Ms, and milkshakes. Both indulged his rants against the LAPD and his musings about insignificant things.

Eventually, Holland got him to break. He knew how to make Little feel big: he told Little he was smart, talented, and important. He asked Little to describe the places where he had traveled, and he complimented his artwork. The baiting tactics worked. When Little mentioned Odessa,

Holland knew it was a breadcrumb. Little even said, "Hookers is all you're gonna find."

Little finally described the Denise Brothers murder. He had brought heroin to her pimp, and she then left her with him. Little told her he loved her and that she was beautiful, and she warmed up to him. Then he strangled her with one hand while he masturbated with the other. Then he brought her back and did it again, drawing out his pleasure as long as possible. Little liked the conflict between their respective goals—she fought for her life, while he fought for his pleasure. When she was dead, he felt as if he owned her. It was how he felt with all his victims, he said. They were his "babies." He often depicted them later in drawings, to keep the murders present in his mind so he could relive his power over his victims.

Soon, Little was offering details about more murders. When the ViCAP database came back with no information (because a murder was unreported), the analysts turned to Google and got results from local news articles. Nothing Little said was proven false, though not everything to which he confessed was corroborated. The list of victims included many Jane Does.

Holland wanted to move Little closer to his base so they could meet daily. But Texas had the death penalty. Holland asked the district attorney in Odessa to take the death penalty off the table for the Odessa murder, citing the greater good in solving a number of other cases, and the DA agreed. Holland got Little transferred temporarily to a Texas facility. Over the course of seven hundred hours, Holland learned about sixty-five murders in nineteen states. Most of these happened in Miami and Los Angeles. Holland gave Little some art supplies, and the killer produced fifty sketches in color, including details such as buck teeth, curly hair, eye color, and dentures. He said he'd stopped counting after eighty-four, but he knew there were more. Little finally estimated that he'd killed ninety-three women in thirty-five years (though he waffled on the number). All were sex workers or drug addicts—women without resources. He thought they wanted to die and he was their angel, their mercy killer. (This was a lie, as he killed a woman who had just gotten divorced and was celebrating. She even told him before she expired that she was too young to die.) Very few women whom Little targeted got away. His last murder had been in 2005 in Mississippi. (ViCAP linked this assertion to Nancy Carol Stevens, forty-six, in Tupelo.)

Now that he was facing mortality as he neared eighty, Little wanted to get it all out. He also hoped to exonerate anyone convicted for his crimes (and there were some). His ability to get away with his crimes was directly related to his level of mobility and his victim selection—he intentionally targeted people who wouldn't inspire much investigation.

Confirming Little's claims proved more difficult than getting his confession. (Most investigators know that some serial killers inflate their numbers for their own reasons, such as greater notoriety, playing games with law enforcement, or enhancing their reputation in prison for being dangerous.) The effort called on a network of FBI agents and local law enforcement across numerous states. Little grew up in Lorain, Ohio, raised by a grandmother after his teenage mother abandoned him. His career in boxing hadn't gone the distance, but he was briefly known as "the Machine Gun" for his hand speed.

Little had learned to draw while serving time. He also had a photographic memory for the circumstances of his crimes and the appearance of his victims, even if his memory was less reliable on dates and locations. Some called him the "Van Gogh Killer" for his talent for drawing his victims. The FBI sent out his sketches, which quickly linked Little to a cold-case homicide in New Orleans.

Holland fed out information to jurisdictions from Florida to California, assisted by ViCAP records. When investigators came to talk with Little, he drew them pictures. Most were impressed with his memory.

Little's first murder involved a blond sex worker in Miami during New Year's in 1969–1970. She had touched her neck, which triggered thoughts of violence in Little. He'd first experienced this when a teacher of his touched her neck, arousing him. Then a grade-school girl classmate made the same gesture. And the neck became Little's fetish point. At fifteen, he saw a photo in a true-crime magazine of a strangled woman and saved it, because "she had a beautiful neck."

In May 2018, Little began a long string of confessions and guilty pleas, which were followed by indictments and some convictions (four in Ohio). He strangled most of his victims, then either left their bodies in places no one frequented or dumped them elsewhere. He threw one off a cliff. When Little failed to recall the year or location of a murder, Holland used cues like the type of car he had been driving, which often unlocked more information.

By November, the FBI's ViCAP team confirmed thirty-four of Little's murders. In many of them there was no DNA evidence, often because so little effort had been put into an investigation at the time of a murder. Little was typically tied to a "Jane Doe" whose identity remained unknown. The ViCAP analysts could only work with what they had, and that meant that crimes which were recorded only in Little's memory didn't really exist in terms of tracking them down so much later. The FBI continues to provide the sketches (each marked by Little with a possible city and year), hoping for public assistance in identifying victims who have yet to be named.

THE TAKEAWAY

Name: Sam (Little) McDowell
Country: United States
Born: June 7, 1940
Died: NA
Killing Years: 1970–2005
Number of Victims: 8 convictions; 50–60 confirmed victims (accounts differ); 93 claimed
Date of Arrest: September 5, 2012

If Little is definitively linked to all the murders he has claimed, he will be the most prolific serial killer in U.S. history, surpassing "Green River Killer" Gary Ridgway, who confessed to forty-nine (but said there were at least twenty more).

Some predators learn that certain types of victims not only accept bodily risk for money, but are also devalued by law enforcement. Little figured out that sex workers and drug addicts were the easiest prey. Even when they survive a violent assault, authorities can be slow to respond to them. However, cold-case units have had a dramatic impact on identifying victims, often using innovative methods. Despite evading justice for more than forty years, Little was finally caught.

But there might be others like him who haven't been.

"The biggest lesson in this case," said ViCAP Supervisory Crime Analyst Kevin Fitzsimmons, "is the power of information sharing. These connections all started in our database of violent crime."

These databases assembled over the past decade that collect criminal behavior show another surprising fact—although it's a common notion that serial killers are predominantly Caucasian, since 1900 only 51.7 percent have been white. About 40 percent have been black, and it appears that that percentage is increasing.

Additionally, murder by men over age fifty-five accounts for 0.5 percent of sexually driven homicides. For these offenders, victims tended to be over forty, with a third over fifty-five. Little killed older victims while in his thirties, but his homicidal assaults decreased as he got into his fifties and sixties. His last murder occurred when he was sixty-five.

PART III

MISTAKES AND MISCALCULATIONS

Despite the solid police work that was undertaken in most of the following cases, the killers assisted in their captures by making significant errors. Often, they think they're smarter than the police. When they get away with murder, they grow more confident and sometimes get sloppy. Some of these errors seem too stupid to be true, but we can't underestimate the power of narcissism to make a killer feel invincible.

15.

THE CHICAGO SCAMMER

THE CRIMES

In Philadelphia, Pennsylvania, on September 3, 1894, a man looking for a patent dealer on Callowhill Street went to the dealer's second-floor office. A stench filled the air. When the caller spotted a decomposing corpse with a blackened face on the floor, he summoned the police.

The victim's head, chest, and right arm were badly burned, and a spent match and broken bottle of chloroform lay nearby. It appeared to police that he had accidentally struck a match near an explosive solvent.

The victim was Benjamin F. Pitezel. When his wife, Carrie, was notified, she requested the life insurance payment from Fidelity Mutual of $10,000. An imprisoned convict who'd been an accomplice informed the insurance company that the Pitezel death was a scam, with a body substitution, but his warning came too late. A man named H. H. Holmes had already brought Pitezel's daughter, Alice, to identify the body and settle the claim. The insurance settlement had been paid.

Fidelity officials hired the Pinkerton National Detective Agency to go after Holmes. The agents followed his trail around the country, gathering information about his numerous frauds and thefts and his seductions of victims over the years. Holmes's real name was Herman Mudgett, and he was one of the most successful swindlers they'd ever seen.

Holmes had lived in Chicago during the 1880s, when the city was preparing for its world's fair, the Great Columbian Exposition, of 1893. Some 27 million people went through the exposition during its six-month run, and there were ample opportunities for a clever man to commit fraud. Holmes was among those who took advantage. He'd foreseen the need for lodging close to the fair, knowing that some travelers would be single, naïve women who would easily succumb to the charms of a successful and charming "doctor." He presented himself to the public as a graduate of a prestigious medical school.

In fact, Holmes's first Chicago employment was as a prescription clerk at a pharmacy at 63rd and South Wallace Streets, but he soon took over the business from the owner, Mrs. E. S. Holton, who then "went to California" with her daughter. No one ever heard from them again, but Holmes now owned the shop. He'd then purchased property across the road with the aim to build a hundred-room "castle," as he referred to it.

The first floor of the building consisted of shops and offices; but when detectives investigated its second floor and cellar, they discovered things that exceeded their worst expectations. Holmes's castle included soundproof sleeping chambers with peepholes, asbestos-padded walls, gas pipes, sliding walls, and vents that Holmes could control from another room. Some rooms had trapdoors, with ladders leading to smaller rooms below. One asbestos-lined room appeared to be capable of incinerating its occupant alive. There were greased chutes that emptied into a two-level cellar, in which Holmes had installed a large furnace, and there was an asbestos-lined chamber with gas pipes and evidence of something having been burned inside. It seemed that Holmes had placed his chosen victims into special chambers into which he then pumped lethal gas. In the cellar, he had set up an "elasticity determinator," an elongated bed with straps. From reconstructions based on the findings, it seemed that Holmes had tortured and murdered many women on the premises, disposing of their corpses by defleshing them and selling the skeletons to medical schools. Investigators discovered several complete skeletons and numerous incinerated bone fragments, including the pelvis of a fourteen-year-old child.

The most pressing task, however, was to find Holmes. Three of the Pitezel children were in his custody; if he had killed their father, it seemed possible that he would kill them as well.

THE CAPTURE

The agents tracked Holmes's trail to Boston and nabbed him on November 16, 1894, as he seemed poised to flee the country. The Pitezel children were not with him. He said he'd sent them on ahead in the company of a woman named Minnie Williams. When confronted about Pitezel, Holmes admitted only to fraud, saying that Pitezel was in South America.

Holmes was sent to prison in Philadelphia to await trial. Further investigation over the next few months revealed that Pitezel was indeed the victim whose body had been found in the second-floor office. Investigators surmised that Holmes had persuaded Pitezel to get insured and use his family to collect the money after his "death." But Holmes then killed Pitezel to take the funds for himself. "Minnie Williams" could not be found, and Carrie Pitezel was frantic with worry, so Holmes was presented to District Attorney George S. Graham for further questioning.

Graham told Holmes that authorities suspected he had murdered the missing children. Holmes played games with them and adjusted his strategy to whatever seemed necessary to defend himself. He was deeply offended, he said, by the accusation.

Detective Frank Geyer believed that there were kernels of truth within the story Holmes told. Holmes admitted to having had Alice Pitezel, fifteen, in his custody. He had also picked up Howard, eight, and Nellie, eleven, telling Carrie where to meet him to reunite with her husband. Alice and Nellie had written letters to her, documenting their daily journey, but Holmes had never mailed them. The arresting officers had confiscated them, and Geyer thought they would offer clues as to where the children had been. Holmes tried to direct him to England; but Geyer knew there was no Minnie Williams, and the street in London that Holmes gave as her address did not exist.

On June 26, 1895, Geyer set out by train, carrying photos of Holmes and each of the children, along with an inventory of items and clothing associated with them. He also had photographs of three travel trunks they'd taken.

Arriving in Cincinnati, he joined with Detective John Schnooks and began asking around in hotels for anyone who might have seen Holmes or the children. He found a hotel clerk who remembered them. On September 28, 1894, Holmes had checked them into a cheap hotel under the name Alex E. Cook. That clerk pointed Geyer in another direction, and he soon found the next hotel at which they'd stayed.

Geyer and Schnooks also talked with realtors. Geyer followed numerous clues that eventually led him to Indianapolis, and then Chicago (where he visited Holmes's "castle") and Detroit. From this location, Alice had written something to her mother that made Geyer's blood run cold: "*Howard is not with us now.*"

Moving on to Toronto, where the last letters from the girls had originated, Geyer located a house that someone using the name Holmes had

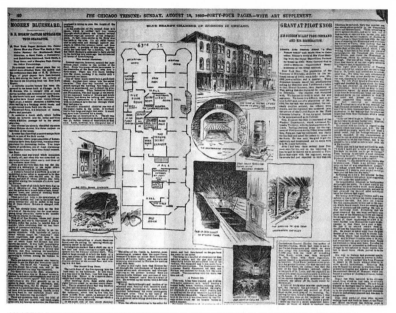

AN ARTICLE IN *THE CHICAGO TRIBUNE* (AUGUST 18, 1895) CALLED H. H. HOLMES' CASTLE "A TOMB."

rented. Inside, Geyer discovered a trapdoor that led to a cellar. Down there, he found evidence of digging in the soft dirt floor; and when he dug, he smelled decomposition. After digging three feet, he turned up a small bone that looked as though it had been part of a child's arm, so he called the local police inspector and employed a local undertaker to take charge. After much more digging, they slowly exhumed the unclothed corpses of two girls, which Geyer believed to be Nellie and Alice Pitezel. The cause of death for both was suffocation.

"Alice was found lying on her side with her hand to the west," Geyer wrote. "Nellie was found lying on her face, with her head to the south, her plaited hair hanging neatly down her back." He sent a telegram to Philadelphia about the day's events, and later concluded in his memoir, "Thus it was proved that little children cannot be murdered in this day and generation, beyond the possibility of discovery."

Carrie Pitezel traveled to Toronto and identified her children at once. She now knew that Holmes had lied to her and killed her children.

Five weeks later, after a great deal of intricate sleuthing, Geyer located young Howard's remains in the chimney of a house in Indianapolis. It was now August 27, fully two months after he'd left on this journey. He had proved that Holmes was a serial killer.

On September 12, 1895, in Philadelphia, Holmes was indicted by a grand jury for the murder of Benjamin Pitezel. He entered a plea of not guilty, and his trial date was scheduled. Even as he adopted a pretense for the court, people were learning much more about what he'd done in Chicago. Estimates of his victim total rose.

Holmes insisted that he had nothing to do with any murders. Those people had either taken their own lives, he claimed, or someone else had killed them. Nevertheless, the *Chicago Tribune* announced that "The Castle is a Tomb!" and *The Philadelphia Inquirer* described many bones removed from the "charnel house."

Holmes, now thirty-four, penned *Holmes' Own Story, in which the Alleged Multimurderer and Arch Conspirator Tells of the Twenty-two Tragic Deaths and Disappearances in which he is Said to be Implicated.* He claimed to have experienced an ordinary life, with an ordinary set of parents and a normal schoolboy routine, in Gilmanton Academy, New Hampshire, where he grew up as Herman Webster Mudgett. He'd received a medical school diploma from the University of Michigan. Then he'd changed his name to H. H. Holmes and posed as a pharmacist in Chicago.

The trial commenced on October 28, 1895, and lasted five days. Judge Michael Arnold allowed Holmes to serve as his own defense counsel, so Holmes himself questioned the prospective jury members, at which point his appointed attorneys left the courtroom. He demonstrated the coolness with which he handled stress when he tried to reject each prospective juror who said he had read the newspapers, but the judge pointed out that this was not a legitimate cause for challenge.

The prosecutor described how Pitezel had died and how Holmes had injected chloroform into the corpse's stomach to make his death appear a suicide. Holmes often deflected the questioning with forays into minutiae and frequently squabbled with the prosecutor. Although he handled his questioning in a professional manner, he failed to score any points to support his claim of innocence.

Holmes asked that the court allow his two defense attorneys to re-enter the case, and with that he relinquished his role as a criminal lawyer. He got up only once to examine another witness—his third wife, who testified against him. Holmes pretended to be stricken by her betrayal, but he failed to persuade her to change her testimony about his behavior on the day that Pitezel was allegedly murdered.

Noted phrenologist John L. Capen took notes on the trial for the *New York World*. Phrenology, a pseudoscience, maintained that practitioners could "read" the shape of a person's skull to discern thirty-five different personality traits. A bump might be felt over an area of the brain when a trait was especially strong, and a depression when it was absent. Holmes's expression, Capen said, was cruel and inhuman, and his twisted ears clearly stamped him as a criminal. He described how Holmes's ear rose to a point, like a demon's. The top of his head was flat, save for one bump "rising suddenly and sharply," and the back of the skull was also "abnormally shaped."

The jury convicted Holmes of Benjamin Pitezel's murder and the judge sentenced him to death by hanging.

Holmes made another confession, prompted by a $10,000 fee from the Hearst newspaper syndicate and published in the *Philadelphia Inquirer*. Hoping to become infamous, he claimed that he had killed over a hundred people. Then he reduced the count to twenty-seven, including Pitezel and his children. "I was born with the Evil One as my sponsor beside the bed where I was ushered into the world," he lamented. As he admitted to the murders, he said he was "branding myself as the most detestable criminal of modern times." He thought his countenance was changing. "I have become afflicted with that dread disease, rare but terrible . . . a malformation. . . . My head and face are gradually assuming an elongated shape. I believe fully that I am growing to resemble the devil—that the similitude is almost completed."

Then he turned his attention to Pitezel, indicating that from the first hour after they had met, he knew he would kill the man. Everything he did for Pitezel that seemed to be a kindness had been merely a ploy to gain his confidence. Holmes had needed him to perpetrate his many frauds, but Pitezel had figured things out and so he had to die. Holmes had forged letters from Pitezel's wife to depress him and make him turn to liquor. One time when Pitezel was drunk, Holmes bound him, saturated his clothes with benzene, and lit a match. "I left the house," he wrote, "without the slightest feeling of remorse for my terrible acts."

This narrative was published in newspapers on April 12, 1896. But then Holmes recanted it, and some of his purported "victims" turned out to still be alive. When told by police that his tale was inconsistent with the known facts, he supposedly said, "Of course it is not true, but the newspapers want a sensation and they got it."

On May 7, 1896, Holmes was hanged in Moyamensing Prison, Philadelphia, having just changed his victim toll to only two. He tried to say more, but at 10:13 A.M. the trapdoor opened, and he died soon after. Holmes had paid his attorneys to get him buried in a coffin filled with cement. No stone was erected to mark where it was buried.

In 2017, Holmes's remains were exhumed to determine whether he had substituted someone else's body and gotten away, as some rumors held. He hadn't. Under an empty pine box and all that concrete, his skeleton, with brain preserved, was there.

THE TAKEAWAY

Name: Herman Webster Mudgett, aka H. H. Holmes
Country: United States
Date of Birth: May 16, 1861
Date of Death: May 7, 1896
Killing Period: 1891–1894
Known Victims: 9+
Date of Arrest: November 17, 1894

So many people who'd rented rooms from Holmes during the Great Columbian Exposition had actually gone missing that sensational estimates of his victims reached around two hundred, and some people cite this unsubstantiated toll even today. We might not be able to accurately gauge the victim toll, but we do know that Holmes was among the cleverest serial killers, then and now. Our inability to document his crimes fully attests to how well he exploited those chaotic times and their lack of record-keeping to cover his tracks.

Neuroscience may soon demonstrate that psychopaths, the most persistently dangerous of all offenders, experience no emotional connection or remorse because their brains are just *different*. They have a reduced incentive to be prosocial. This leaves them self-centered, with a tendency toward exploitation. Reduced brain matter in key areas appears to be implicated in their pervasive indifference.

Neuroscience has not yet proven the absence of free will, however, or a lack of responsibility. An impaired ability to read emotional clues does not translate into an inability to understand that an act is illegal or immoral. Even if Holmes had allowed scientists to confiscate and preserve his brain so we could study it today, and even if that brain showed the deficits typical of a psychopath, we don't yet have reason to believe that he did not know that what he was doing was wrong.

16.

THE MOORS MURDERERS

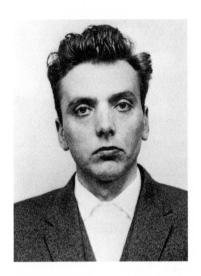

THE CRIMES

In 1961, when she was eighteen years old, Myra Hindley found a job as a typist at Millwards Merchandising, Ltd., in Manchester, England. She hoped to find her way out of this dead-end employment as soon as possible. Among the other employees, she spotted a tall, blue-eyed stock clerk, often clothed in black, who seemed intellectual. She felt an immediate attraction.

Ian Brady, however, barely noticed her.

Determined to get his attention, Hindley showed up in places where she knew he'd be and sometimes carried books to appear to be on his level. *They* were special, she believed. They would connect.

At an office Christmas party, Brady finally approached her. They soon became intimate.

According to Hindley's diary, Brady began reforming her way of thinking on religion, politics, and sex. Brady's favorite authors were the Marquis de Sade and Friedrich Nietzsche, and he also read sexual classics like those by Henry Miller. When he persuaded Hindley to experiment, to see how far she'd go, things grew darker. Brady made Hindley take out *Sexual Murders* from the library in her name. He was testing her capacity for wickedness.

One afternoon in 1963, as they picnicked on a blanket near the heathered crags of Saddleworth Moor outside town, Brady raised the idea of "switching on the dark," and committing crimes together like Bonnie and Clyde. He told Hindley about Nathan Leopold and Richard Loeb, who had tried to commit the perfect murder in Chicago in 1924 by bludgeoning and smothering fourteen-year-old Bobby Franks. They were caught, but what intrigued Brady was their desire to use murder to prove their moral superiority. Brady thought he could do the same thing and get away with it.

He wanted to have sex with children and then kill them. He had a plan: Hindley, he said, would act as bait. As a female, she could more easily lure a child than he could. Brady would then rape, kill, and bury the victim on Hollin Brown Knoll. Hindley didn't like this idea, but she didn't want to lose the man who she considered the great love of her life. She borrowed a Ford Prefect van, and they rehearsed.

The next step was to find a victim.

Hindley's younger sister, Maureen, had a friend named Pauline Reade. Pretty, slender, and sixteen, Pauline had dark hair and blue eyes. On Friday evening, July 12, 1963, she prepared to go to her first dance. She set out on foot, alone, wearing a pink dress, blue duster, and white shoes. Around the same time, Hindley began trolling for a victim; Brady followed the van on his Tiger Cub motorbike.

Hindley turned onto Gorton Lane and saw a girl who appeared to be around eight years old. Brady blinked his headlamp to signal his approval, but Hindley did not stop. She steered onto another street and saw an older girl. Again, Brady flashed the light. Nervous, Hindley slowed down near the girl. "Excuse me," she called out. "Can you spare a minute?"

Pauline turned, and Hindley recognized her. She realized that getting someone who knew her into the van would be easier than luring a stranger inside, so she beckoned her over. Eager for a ride, Pauline got in. Hindley asked if she would go out to the moors to help her look for a glove that she'd dropped and promised her a nice reward. Pauline agreed.

Hindley drove out to Hollin Brown Knoll. Brady passed her on his motorbike to arrive first. Hindley dropped Pauline off with him. She later claimed she never witnessed the sexual assault or murder, although Brady said she was an active participant. However, assaulting children was *Brady's* fantasy, not Hindley's. The truth probably lies somewhere between their claims. After the rape, Brady sliced Pauline's throat so deeply that she was nearly beheaded. He buried the body and brought the spade back to the van, wrapping it in plastic to keep blood off the carpet. As they drove into town, they saw Pauline's parents out searching. For Brady, this was an added thrill.

At home, Brady and Hindley erased all evidence linking them to the incident. During their subsequent lovemaking, they used the theme from *The Legion's Last Patrol* as their "code" for what they'd done to Pauline. Brady thought that having a song to go along with murder made "turning on the dark" more fun.

Brady soon wanted to kill again. John Kilbride, their next victim, was twelve. He disappeared on November 23 from Ashton-under-Lyne. Brady strangled the boy and buried him near Pauline, selecting *24 Hours from Tulsa* as Kilbride's song.

With this second murder, Hindley thought she'd changed into someone she did not recognize. She knew there would be more murders, and considering her participation thus far, she couldn't just quit and walk away. She was now a dark soul with her demon lover.

As Brady read news articles of Kilbride's disappearance, he viewed them as "critical reviews" of his "performance." On New Year's Eve, 1963, he and Hindley drove out to the moors to drink a champagne toast to the dead boy.

In June, Brady was ready again. For the theme song, he'd already picked Roy Orbison's *It's Over*. He and Hindley drove in a Mini-Traveller to find another child.

Keith Bennett had just turned twelve. He was walking with his pregnant mother, Winnie, to his grandmother's house. Diverging from Winnie's path, though, he turned down a street, out of her sight. Hindley drove up. Keith agreed to assist her in her request to move some boxes. Winnie arrived where she thought her son would be, but he was gone. She would never see him again.

Hindley and Brady took the boy to a different area of the moors. Brady raped Bennett and strangled him with a cord, burying the spade he'd used to dig the grave near the body. He took a photo that showed the blurred image of a boy on the ground with his pants down.

On December 26, 1964, the killing couple prepared to go out again. Sandi Shaw's hit song, *Girl Don't Come*, was their code as they drove out to Silcock's Wonder Fair. They figured there would be many easy marks where kids congregated—Lesley Ann Downey, for example. Her brother and friends had already gone home, but the sounds and lights of the fair mesmerized her. Hindley and Brady approached her together and pretended to need help with boxes of groceries they were carrying. Hindley offered Lesley a reward for going with them. The girl didn't have to be asked twice.

This time, they took her to their house on Wardle Brook Avenue. Brady attempted to undress Lesley for some photos, and she screamed. Brady turned on a tape recorder to preserve the sound of the girl's terror. Then he raped and strangled her. He took her body into the bathroom to wash it. (Brady would later claim that Hindley had strangled the girl—had even insisted on doing so.)

They bundled Downey's body into a sheet and carried it to the car. However, snow made the roads impassable, so they had to return home. The following day, despite poor weather conditions, they drove to their killing field on the moors and Brady buried their latest victim near Higher Wildcat Lowe.

THE CAPTURE

In August 1964, Hindley's sister Maureen married David Smith. Brady wanted to bring in another partner, so he took a keen interest in Smith. He'd spotted Smith's insecurity and knew he'd already committed some petty crimes, so he thought the grooming would be easy. Brady began by inviting the newlyweds for drinks, paying for the liquor, and initiating frequent social contact. He knew this process would take time, but he foresaw an inevitable criminal enterprise.

During the summer of the following year, Brady decided it was time to draw Smith into their "party." He'd already lured him into a few robberies and discussed the topic of murder. The grooming was over. Smith, he believed, was ready.

On October 6, Brady and Hindley spotted seventeen-year-old Edward Evans at the train station. Brady invited him home. Hindley went to fetch Smith.

When he entered their house, Smith heard a high-pitched scream. Hindley shouted that Brady needed help, so he rushed toward the sound. In the living room, he saw a young man, his head and shoulders on the couch, faceup, and his legs on the floor. Brady stood over him with a bloody hatchet. Smith was stunned when Brady brought it down hard on the young man's head, hitting him over and over as he tried to fend off the blows. Finally, the victim gave up and went still. Brady got a cord and strangled him. Smith remained frozen in place. The scene was surreal, especially when Brady commented that this was "the messiest yet," and Hindley began to clean up the room. When Smith saw Hindley pick up clumps of hair and brain matter, he knew she'd seen murder before.

Brady instructed Smith to assist. Smith realized that if he didn't comply, they'd kill him too. Cringing, he helped to carry the blood-spattered body up the steps and into a bedroom. Caught between the two killers, Smith kept his panic in check and tried not to think about what he was doing.

Finally, Smith said he should leave so that Maureen wouldn't wonder where he was. With each step he took toward the door, he worried that he'd feel the hatchet buried in his skull. Once he was out of Brady's view, he ran the few blocks home. There, he vomited repeatedly and tried to describe to Maureen what he'd witnessed. Grabbing a knife for protection, the Smiths ran with their dog to a telephone box to phone the police.

Smith recalled that Brady had admitted to killing people, but he'd dismissed it as an idle brag. Brady had also inquired of Smith whether he thought *he* could kill someone. Now it all made sense. Smith warned the responding officers that Brady was armed.

When the police entered Brady and Hindley's house on Wardle Brook Avenue, Brady's guns were out of reach. They found the victim's body in an upstairs room. The officers placed Brady under arrest; Hindley accompanied her lover to the station, prepared to defend him.

Brady claimed that Evans' death was accidental, the result of a "rowe," but as police discovered more items in Brady's home, his story rang false. Photographs and the tape recording resolved the mystery of what had happened to Lesley Ann Downey, and John Kilbride's name turned up on a list that Brady had made. When police heard Hindley's voice on the Downey tape and lifted her fingerprints from the photos, they charged her as an accomplice.

Photographs that the couple had taken of the moors suggested burial locations. On October 16, police exhumed the remains of Lesley Ann

Downey. Less than 400 yards away, diggers found the remains of John Kilbride. Not long afterward, Brady confessed to killing Kilbride, Downey, and Evans. He refused to discuss the other two missing children.

The trial for both defendants started on April 19, 1966, focusing on the three murders Brady had confessed to. Hindley insisted that she had not participated in any murders, and Brady backed her up. She hoped for a conviction for merely harboring a criminal and a relatively light sentence.

It took the jury less than three hours to return verdicts. The Moors Murderers stood up, side by side, to hear their fates. Brady was found guilty in all three murders, while Hindley was convicted in the murders of Edward Evans and Lesley Ann Downey. In the John Kilbride case, she was found guilty of harboring and assisting Brady. Both received life sentences.

When police escorted Brady from the courtroom, he didn't even look at his former partner in crime. However, Hindley was still in love. She felt bereft. They wrote to each other regularly from their separate prisons until their bond began to weaken. Hindley found solace in her former Catholic faith, along with a series of affairs with female inmates. Seeking a chance for parole, she said she'd been under a predator's influence. She botched an attempted prison break and wrote a self-exonerating document that was leaked to the press.

Brady saw Hindley's document and decided that payback was in order. He recanted his statement from the trial and now implicated Hindley in all the murders. Just as Hindley received a recommendation for parole in May 1985, Brady delivered the blow: he confessed to the murders of Pauline Reade and Keith Bennett, with Hindley as an equal partner in them.

Police took Hindley to the moors to assist with further searching, but she failed to help. In 1987, she admitted her part in the abductions and murders of Keith and Pauline, but she claimed that she'd been forced with threats to her life.

That July, someone noticed a change in the vegetation in one particular area on Hollin Brown Knoll. Police went there and exhumed the well-preserved body of Pauline Reade. The location of Keith Bennett's body remained a mystery.

As Hindley neared sixty in 2002, her health failed. Late in the afternoon on November 15, after a priest delivered the Last Rites, she died from bronchial pneumonia.

Brady outlived Hindley by nearly fifteen years, during which he tried to starve himself to death with a hunger strike that resulted in his being force-fed. He finally died in 2017, never revealing where he'd buried Keith Bennett. Some correspondents thought he'd left clues to the location in certain letters, but no one could decipher their "code." In 1991, Brady had sent a letter to Keith's brother to say that instructions for finding the gravesite were in his will. However, by the time of this writing in 2019, the court was still denying access to locked briefcases with effects that Brady had left behind.

THE TAKEAWAY

Name: Ian Brady and Myra Hindley
Country: England
Born: January 2, 1938 and July 23, 1942
Died: May 11, 2017 and November 15, 2002
Killing Period: July 12, 1963–October 6, 1965
Known Victims: 5
Dates of Arrest: October 7, 1965 and October 11, 1965

Around 20 percent of serial killers operate as teams, and a third of these are male/female couples. Criminologist Eric W. Hickey, who analyzed trends for over five hundred such team offenders, has said that each couple featured one person who psychologically maintained control, usually the male. The dominant partners sought followers among those who were insecure, young, needy, mentally ill, or intellectually challenged, because they proved easier to manipulate.

"I'm always amazed at how these people vector in on each other," says former FBI profiler Gregg McCrary. "There's radar, gaydar, and maybe mur-dar. It's like when normal people meet. You decide whether you're going to get along, but with these couples it takes a dark turn. They sense the excitement of a kindred spirit."

Janet Warren and Robert Hazelwood studied twenty middle-class female accomplices in sexual assault and murder and identified the male as the person responsible for a process of gradual reshaping of the female's sexual norms. The males targeted females with low self-esteem, then isolated them and gradually reformed their thinking. The male's fantasy had organized the couple's subsequent criminal behavior. We see this pattern in the Moors Murderers killings, although Hindley appears to have been more eager than most to be involved in Bonnie-and-Clyde–style escapades.

Although followers might initially resist being groomed by their partners, their fear of being abandoned helps them to rationalize the depravity and decrease the discomfort. Hindley came to believe that the compartmentalizing ability that she developed while growing up in an abusive home had prepared her for Brady. Love had pushed her the rest of the way.

In his book *The Gates of Janus*, written while he was in prison, Brady described this shared delusion as a *foile a deux*, an intellectual form of persuasion by one person to convert another. It can occur, he said, only if the target person is "fertile soil." Thus, he implicated Hindley as a willing rather than compliant accomplice.

At their trial, the judge described the Moors Murderers as "two sadistic killers of the utmost depravity." Their crimes illustrate the twisted dynamics of dominance and submission in the context of violent fantasies that the dominant partner wants to act out.

17.

THE CROSS-COUNTRY CHAMELEON

THE CRIMES

Officer Roy Dickey sat in his patrol car in Tallahassee, Florida, late on February 10, 1978. It was nearing 11:00 P.M. and the streets were quiet. Bored, he watched a thin male wearing jeans, a blue cap, and a red quilted vest walk away from the Florida State University stadium area. The man seemed ordinary.

The officer on the next shift, Leon County Deputy Keith Daws, saw him too, around 2:00 A.M. Three weeks earlier, two girls had been murdered and two others bludgeoned at the Chi Omega sorority house on the Florida State campus. The crimes, which were possibly linked to the assault of another woman nearby that same night who'd barely survived, were as yet unsolved.

Daws noted the man doing something to the door of a Toyota, so he stopped to question him. The man said he was looking for a book. When Daws saw a tag for another car inside the Toyota, he went to his patrol vehicle to look it up. To his surprise, the thin man sprinted away too fast for Daws to follow. That same night, a white Dodge van was reported missing from Florida State University—possibly the van with the flat tire that Daws had seen parked near the Toyota. He'd later learn that he'd just missed catching a notorious fugitive who was wanted in five states. The day before, this man had abducted and killed a twelve-year-old girl.

The fugitive, Theodore Robert Bundy, knew his time was running out. When he'd been convicted in February 1977 for an attempted abduction in Utah, detectives from Washington, Utah, and Colorado had pooled their information about unsolved murders of young women. They realized that Bundy might be a cross-country killer who had murdered at least fifteen victims. When he was taken to Aspen, Colorado, to face charges for the 1975 murder of Caryn Campbell, he escaped by jumping from a courthouse window, but was recaptured six days later. On December 30, 1977, he exploited a weakness he'd spotted in the Garwood County jail where he was confined and escaped again, making it as far as Tallahassee.

Although the actual start of Bundy's criminal career is uncertain, he came to the attention of law enforcement as "Ted" in the summer of 1974. By then, several young women had been assaulted or had disappeared in Oregon and Washington. When two had suddenly vanished on the same day from the crowded resort area Lake Sammamish State Park near Seattle, witnesses told detectives of a slender man named "Ted" who drove a tan or gold Volkswagen Beetle. He would approach women with his arm in a sling and pretend to need assistance. Most of the women he'd asked had felt uneasy around him. Unfortunately, potential suspects named Ted who drove tan Volkswagen Beetles (a very popular car at that time) formed a long list, and detectives in those days had no computers to help sort such information. When the remains of the two missing women were found a few miles from the lake near the skeletal remains of another murdered girl, lead detective Robert Keppel knew he was tracking a dangerous predator.

Yet Bundy had already moved on. He had been accepted into the law school at the University of Utah. As he roamed around Utah and Colorado, several more corpses of young women turned up and several other women went missing. With no central database for communicating across jurisdictions, no one linked these incidents to those in the Pacific Northwest. But then a young woman, Carol DaRonch, reported that on November 8, 1974, a man posing as a police officer had tried to abduct her. He'd smelled of alcohol and acted strangely, so she'd remained guarded when he made her get into his car. When he'd tried to handcuff her, she'd managed to get out of the vehicle and flee.

No one knew who this man was until the following August, when Bundy was arrested on suspicion of burglary. DaRonch identified him as her assailant. Utah authorities processed Bundy for trial and charged mental-health professionals with determining his likelihood of being a future danger. Prison psychologist Al Carlisle interviewed many people who knew him, finding that Bundy had many different "faces." His charm notwithstanding, he was a thief, liar, and con artist, and evidence strongly suggested that he was a killer. Carlisle confirmed that he was likely dangerous.

During this process, a picture of Bundy's early life emerged. Born in a home for unwed mothers on November 24, 1946, as Theodore Robert Cowell, he lived with his mother's parents in Philadelphia as his mother's younger brother. In 1950, his mother took him to Tacoma, Washington, where she married Johnnie Culpepper Bundy, who adopted young Ted.

Bundy would later claim that his home life had been stable, and his mother would describe him as an ideal son. Still, Bundy had shown signs of antisocial behavior at a young age. He was just three when he placed knives around his sleeping aunt as a prank. He also engaged in lies and petty theft, as well as voyeurism. At some point, he'd learned that his "older sister" was actually his mother and that the identity of his real father was unknown. He viewed this deception as a betrayal.

After a rough start in grade school, Bundy was popular in high school and college. Many experts believe it was at the University of Washington where Bundy's anger against women grew sufficiently intense to nurture his murder fantasies. (Possibly this had begun earlier, as he was suspected in the abduction and murder of an eight-year-old girl when he was fourteen, although his involvement was never proven.) Bundy fell in love with a young woman from an upper-class family in 1967, which appealed to his desire for status. However, she thought he lacked direction, so she broke up with him. They reunited in 1973 and become engaged before he inexplicably dumped her—perhaps as revenge. Only a few weeks later, on January 4, 1974, Bundy attacked his first documented victim in Seattle. She survived with serious brain damage.

Over the next five months, Bundy abducted and killed Lynda Ann Healy, Donna Manson, Susan Rancourt, Roberta Kathleen Parks, Brenda Ball, and Georgeann Hawkins in five separate towns. After abducting Janice Ott and Denise Naslund from Lake Sammamish in mid-July, he left the area.

Between October 2 and November 8, four young women disappeared from Utah. Then, between January and June 1975, three were killed or went missing in Colorado, one (who was only twelve years old) vanished in Idaho, and one more was grabbed in Utah. DaRonch's identification of Bundy stopped him temporarily and put him on multiple law-enforcement radars. His second escape got him onto the FBI's Ten Most Wanted Fugitives list. The poster noted his chameleonic persona: he sometimes wore a false mustache or beard, sometimes wore glasses, and could fake a British accent.

Living in Tallahassee as "Chris Hagan," Bundy quickly ran out of resources. He grew agitated and made several uncharacteristically high-risk moves. On January 15, 1978, he entered the Chi Omega sorority house at Florida State University, raping, strangling, or clubbing four girls in their beds. Lisa Levy and Margaret Bowman died, but the other two survived with serious injuries. As Bundy fled with his three-foot club, a resident saw him. In addition, he'd also bitten one of his victims, leaving a distinct, identifiable impression. He ran eight blocks, entered an apartment, and attacked FSU student Cheryl Thomas. She also survived. Bundy left behind a pantyhose mask with strands of his hair.

Three weeks later, on February 8, Bundy grabbed twelve-year-old Kimberly Leach off her school grounds in Lake City, Florida. He raped and strangled her, leaving the body under a collapsed pig shed thirty-five miles away.

MARGARET BOWMAN, A 21-YEAR-OLD FLORIDA STATE UNIVERSITY STUDENT, WAS MURDERED BY TED BUNDY AT THE CHI OMEGA SORORITY HOUSE IN TALLAHASSEE, FLORIDA, ON JANUARY 15, 1978. THIS PHOTO WAS ENTERED AS EVIDENCE IN HIS TRIAL.

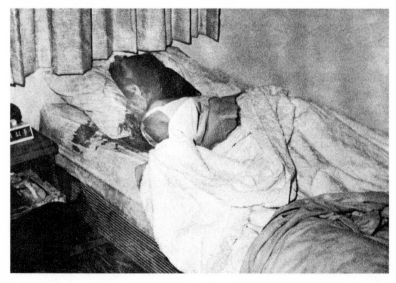

Aware that he could be caught at any time, Bundy decided to flee. He stole an orange Volkswagen Beetle and used it to drive west toward the Alabama state line.

THE CAPTURE

Around 1:00 A.M. on February 15, 1978, patrol officer David Lee pulled Bundy over in Pensacola. He wanted to check on the car, which recently had been reported as stolen. Bundy was initially uncooperative, but finally he exited the car and got down on the ground. Before Lee could cuff him, he kicked Lee's legs out from under him and fled on foot. Lee fired a warning shot and ran after him. He caught up, pulling Bundy to the ground. Bundy tried grabbing Lee's gun, but Lee managed to subdue him and take him in. He heard Bundy say, "I wish you had killed me." Lee didn't realize then who he'd caught.

Bundy initially offered a fake name, Ken Misner, but finally told them who he was. To his surprise, the officers at the jail had never heard of him. David Lee found the FBI's poster, which confirmed that they had captured an infamous fugitive. Bundy began to talk. Between bouts of laughter and tears, he described his escapes and a few minor crimes, but blocked any questions about the Florida murder victims.

The state appointed Dr. Hervey Cleckley, author of *The Mask of Sanity* and an authority on psychopaths, to assess Bundy's competence to stand trial. He found Bundy to be a sociopath but determined that he was competent. For the court, Dr. Emanuel Tanay, an expert on criminality, stated that Bundy had an antisocial personality disorder over which he had no control and which prevented him from fully appreciating his actions. His self-defeating behaviors could interfere with reasonable decision-making and so, in Tanay's opinion, he was *not* competent to stand trial. Dorothy Otnow Lewis, a psychiatrist out of New York, believed that Bundy suffered from a bipolar disorder, which gave him alternating states of depression and energy. The court decided he was competent.

Although his attorneys considered an insanity defense, Bundy refused it and fired them so that he could represent himself. In court, he preened, flirted with girls who flocked to see him, and winked at friends. However, he took such delight in questioning investigators on the stand about the details of his crimes that he estranged the jury.

Two Florida juries convicted Bundy of three murders. He received three death sentences. Yet he had cards to play, starting with legal maneuvers. He appealed on various grounds all the way to the U.S. Supreme Court. During this time, he tried to persuade "scientists" that he was unique and should be kept alive and studied. To add to his notoriety, he revealed his guilt in more crimes, eventually confessing to thirty murders in seven states: Oregon, Washington, Idaho, Utah, Colorado, California, and Florida. (Not all were corroborated by evidence.)

Bundy got married in prison and had a daughter. No matter what he did to appeal his convictions, he could not stave off his ultimate execution. On the morning of January 24, 1989, Bundy died in the electric chair at Raiford Prison in Bradford County, Florida. He was forty-two years old.

THE TAKEAWAY

Name: Theodore Robert Bundy
Country: United States
Born: November 24, 1946
Died: January 24, 1989
Killing Period: 1973 or 1974–1978
Known Victims: 30+
Date of Arrest: February 15, 1978

Bundy discussed his compulsions as a predator with investigators who came to interview him. Among the most revealing interviews were those with Supervisory Special Agent William Hagmaier, from the FBI's budding Behavioral Science Unit. Bundy agreed to work closely with Hagmaier, which gave him an opportunity to prove his worth. Hagmaier maintained a four-year correspondence with Bundy. Detective Robert Keppel, who had launched the Seattle investigation, also collected hours' worth of material in taped interviews. (He also received Bundy's assistance on Seattle's Green River Killer case.)

Bundy's MO, they all learned, had been to first select an appropriate disposal site—somewhere that provided privacy. Then he looked for a victim who matched his sexual preferences. To this woman, he would either fake a need for assistance or portray himself as an authority figure. He would persuade her to accompany him to his car, where he'd hidden a crowbar. Upon reaching the car, he would use the crowbar to strike the woman in the head. Then he would handcuff and place her in the passenger side of the car, from which he'd already removed the seat.

Bundy admitted that he usually drank before an assault. While he most often killed by ligature strangulation from behind during a sexual act, sometimes his victims died when he first bludgeoned them with the crowbar. In some cases, he beheaded the corpse or removed the hands with a hacksaw. He might later return to the murder site, which he considered his "church," to have sex with a decomposing corpse. At one point, he kept the heads of four victims in his apartment. Once they were dead, he told interviewers, they belonged to him. "They are part of you," he stated, "and you are forever one. . . . You feel the last bit of breath leaving their body, you're looking into their eyes. . . . You then possess them, and they shall forever be a part of you."

Bundy would often drive for many miles to find the right set of circumstances for a murder. He even made dry runs, letting go of some women whom he picked up. He described how serial murderers like him have a developmental process, which starts with insecurity and mistakes. Experience gradually boosts their confidence. The predatory urge, he said, is as demanding as an alcoholic's addiction.

Bundy liked to rape his victims in bright moonlight or in the light of his car headlights. He'd buried several and had dumped some in deep water. Occasionally, he would apply makeup to their decomposing faces to make them more appealing. He generally "scripted" his victims to perform certain acts, and even dressed them in clothing he'd brought. He told several interviewers that slasher movies or the salacious covers of true-crime detective magazines had fed his fantasies. He said that during the predatory activity, some malignant part of his personality took over.

Bundy's post-crime behavior was also revealing. He would read newspaper reports about what the police knew and adjust his MO to avoid detection. He steam-cleaned his car, changed the upholstery, tossed victim clothing out the car window, and scattered victim remains; but he apparently was unfamiliar with forensic odontology and the ability to match his teeth to his bite mark (although today that discipline is disputed as a science).

Bundy's charisma and level of confidence helped turn him into America's poster boy for serial murder. He inflated his image for being intelligent and appealing by representing himself in court, as though he were better than any attorney could possibly be. His fame spread, and journalists arrived from all over the world to record his trial.

Over the years, many people have described their interactions with Bundy; collectively, these impressions demonstrate his ability to pose as different things to different people. Interviewers were frustrated to learn that he'd contradict for someone else's report what he'd just told them was the truth. He hedged, deflected, and talked circuitously while sounding completely open and sincere with each person. It was a special talent.

Bundy's chameleonic style presents a unique form of mental flexibility that certain predatory psychopaths possess. It would be useful to develop an objective assessment of this aspect of criminal behavior, for better comprehension and prediction. By making Bundy a "specimen for study," as he'd hoped, we might have used his predatory skills as a tool for analyzing today's cleverest offenders.

To keep his secrets, Bundy had created specific impressions of himself for different people, including that he was open, honest, and easy to know. These skills had helped him to manipulate, as well as to prevent anyone—even close girlfriends—from seeing his violent proclivities. In retrospect, the true-crime author Ann Rule, who had worked closely with Bundy at the Seattle Crisis Clinic, stated that "Ted was never as handsome, brilliant, or charismatic as crime folklore has deemed him. . . . A virtual nonentity before he was suspected of a series of horrific crimes, he somehow became all of those things as the media embraced him."

Bundy's series of murders fostered the development of several new law-enforcement tools. In Washington State, Robert Keppel grew interested in improving solvability factors in homicides. As an investigator for the Office of the Attorney General, he collected data for the Homicide Investigation Tracking System (HITS), which would assist with catching Robert Lee Yates and Green River Killer Gary Ridgway.

More important were changes for the FBI. At a Senate subcommittee meeting for the U.S. Congress during the early 1980s, a group argued for a computerized crime-tracking system. Ann Rule pointed to a large group of serial killers who'd been sufficiently mobile to travel from state to state, including Bundy. In his case, she said, such a system might have saved as many as fifteen lives.

The program was approved. In 1985, under the auspices of the newly formed National Center for the Analysis of Violent Crime (NCAVC), former homicide detective Pierce Brooks became its first director. The Behavioral Science Unit (now the Behavioral Analysis Unit) came under this umbrella. Offenders during Bundy's era had ramped up the FBI's focus on serial killers.

18.

THE CLASSIFIED AD RAPIST

THE CRIMES

Two adolescents discovered a nude female body near I-75, southeast of Tampa, Florida, on May 13, 1984. Responding officers from the Hillsborough County Sheriff's Office believed the woman had been dead for three days. Her body was lying facedown, and her wrists were tied together behind her back. A noose had been wound around her neck three times. Severe facial bruising suggested that her murderer had bludgeoned her prior to death. Worse, he'd broken both her hips in order to pose her at a provocative angle.

The officers cast a set of tire tracks that led to the body, noting that the left rear tire tread had a unique design. They also sent the bindings and items of clothing to the FBI crime lab. The analyst there lifted several red trilobal fibers of similar consistency to automobile carpeting.

The woman's cause of death was strangulation, and she had been raped. A missing-persons report, plus her fingerprints, revealed her identity: Ngeun Thi Long, also known as Lana Long. The twenty-year-old had worked as a dancer at Tampa's Sly Fox Lounge. She was also a drug addict and had no car, so she depended on others for rides. On several levels, she had behaved in a high-risk manner.

Two weeks later, on May 27, the mostly nude body of a female who had been murdered just hours before turned up at a lover's lane near Plant City, north of I-4. She had been bludgeoned, strangled, and bound, with her wrists tied behind her back. Once again, a rope was wound around her neck. Among her wounds were a wide slicing cut to the neck and a blunt-trauma injury over her left ear.

This victim was twenty-two-year-old Michelle Simms, a sex worker and drug addict. She had been raped; the semen stains, when tested, provided information that the killer had type-B blood with an H antigen. Strands of Caucasian hair found on Simms were dissimilar to hers, and a few red fibers were lifted from her body. Tire tracks found in a patch of mud nearby yielded clear patterns. An expert said that the right rear tire was a Goodyear Viva, while the left rear was a Vogue, a pricy product designed for Cadillacs.

On June 8, 1984, the mother of Elizabeth Loudenback, a shy twenty-two-year-old who worked on an assembly line and who had gone for a walk near her home, reported her missing. Loudenback's body was found two weeks later in an orange grove, severely decomposed. She was fully clothed, but her hyoid bone was broken, indicating strangulation. Since there were no ropes involved and she was not a drug addict or sex worker, she was not linked to the other murder victims. At the time, no one noticed the red fibers on her clothes.

There was a lull in these crimes until October 7, when a worker on a ranch north of Hillsborough State Park found a decomposing body shoved under a barbed-wire fence. It appeared to have been there for nearly a week. Female clothing was scattered about, and the autopsy found evidence of rape. The victim had been strangled and shot in the back of the head. Fingerprints identified her as Chanel Devoun Williams, an eighteen-year-old sex worker. The FBI lab found both types of red-carpet fibers on her clothing, a brown Caucasian pubic hair on her sweater, and semen stains that contained both A and H blood-group substances. This conflicted with the Simms case, but both had been sex workers, which could account for differences in the semen that did not negate the case similarities.

In fact, the similarities were sufficient for the FBI's Behavioral Science Unit to devise a behavioral profile for an offender they believed to be a serial killer. With probability analysis based on other serial murders involving rape and brutality, they developed a report that listed the traits and behaviors of the type of person likely to have committed these crimes. With awareness of the usual margin of error, they offered the local police a portrait and suggested they use it to narrow down their list of suspects.

The profilers focused first on victim-related items, or victimology: the killer had chosen women who needed or would be willing to accept a ride, due to personal circumstances or sex work. In need of money, they might have agreed to be transported to an isolated location. They did not seem to know each other, since investigators could find no connection. Their age ranges, along with data on offenders, suggested that their killer was in his mid-to-late twenties, because offenders mostly pick victims near their own age or younger. The fibers intimated that the killer probably owned a flashy car with red floor carpets. The brutality and leash-like ropes showed a need for dominance and a sadistic sexual deviance. It seemed likely that the victims had been randomly selected, since there was no clear pattern. The Caucasian hair strands pointed to a white male. He seemed "organized," because he left little evidence, and organized offenders operate normally in society. He had a macho self-image and probably no more than a high-school education, consistent with other known cases. If he'd ever served in the military, he likely would have joined the Marine Corps, due to the manlier image he could project. He would date subservient women, since he preferred to dominate, but would have no long-term commitments; and he was probably divorced. It was likely that he'd committed other crimes, such as voyeurism, rape, or burglary, because most sexual serial killers tended to evolve from other crimes. Most importantly, he would kill again, because sexual serial killing became addictive. The agents cautioned detectives that other crimes linked to this killer might change their suppositions about his age or degree of organization. Each new repeat crime always added data that potentially changed earlier hypotheses.

Over the next month, from October 14 to November 6, three more bodies turned up. All the victims had been bound, beaten, and strangled. Two bore the red fibers, one had a rope around her neck, one bore strands of Caucasian hair, and all had been involved in high-risk activities, such as drug use, exotic dancing, or sex work.

Despite the accelerated violence and the FBI's assistance, law-enforcement officials were no closer to identifying this man. Then a break in the case came from a courageous young woman.

THE CAPTURE

On the night of November 3, 1984, seventeen-year-old Lisa McVey was biking home from her job when a man drove up and forced her into his car at gunpoint. He told her to remove her clothes and perform oral sex on him. Then he took her to his apartment, where he told her he intended to kill her.

For twenty-seven hours, he repeatedly raped McVey and forced her to perform sex acts on him. What he did not know was that her grandmother's boyfriend sexually abused her on a regular basis at home. McVey had learned how to ensure that he did the least possible amount of damage. She knew that resistance would probably only enrage her current attacker, so she did what she was told and assured him that she liked him.

McVey had remained vigilant for opportunities to identify this man if she ever got free. She'd kept track of the time that passed while in his car and had peeked from under the blindfold to memorize the dashboard. She'd caught glimpses of a stucco building where they'd climbed a set of stairs to his apartment. She'd listened for distinct sounds. Inside, McVey had dropped her barrette into a thick rug and left her fingerprints under the toilet seat so she could prove she'd been there.

Eventually, her abductor softened and started talking with her. She told him she didn't want to go home, because it was rough there. He said he wished he could keep her, but he'd lost interest, so he put McVey in his car. To her surprise, he dropped her off close to her home and urged her to describe a fictional abductor to police. He went out to find another victim.

McVey went to the police, determined to help catch this man. To some officers, she seemed too calm and collected to be credible, but Sergeant Larry Pinkerton sat and listened. McVey described her kidnapper as a white male in his mid-thirties with brown hair, a short mustache, a big nose, a rough face, and small ears. He was slightly overweight and had seemed somewhat feminine. She described his car as dark red or maroon, with a red steering wheel, seats, and carpet. On the dashboard, she'd seen the word "Magnum." She recalled details about the apartment where she'd been raped and tried to help narrow down its location, as well as the location of an ATM where they'd stopped around 3:00 A.M. just before the man had dropped her off.

The information about red carpet in the rapist's car got back to the task force. On a hunch, the sheriff's office sent McVey's rape evidence to the FBI crime lab. The detectives soon learned that the technicians had lifted, from McVey's clothing, the same red fibers that had been found on the murder victims. The place where her rapist had dropped her off gave the task force a general area for where to watch for his car.

Even as McVey told her story to the police, the killer had abducted twenty-one-year-old Kim Marie Swann, another dancer at the Sly Fox Lounge. He strangled her and then drove around with her corpse. He even stopped for gas with her body in the front seat, before he took her to the countryside to dump her. He undressed her, looped a rope around her neck, and forced her legs into a shocking display. The body was found three days later, on November 12. Her jeans bore the telltale red fibers.

Detectives learned that the dashboard in Dodge Magnums bore a "Magnum" insignia, but only for 1978 models. This information yielded a list of owners in the Department of Motor Vehicles records. The list was cross-checked against bank customers in the area where the ATM might have been. Robert ("Bobby") Joe Long, owner of a maroon 1978 Dodge Magnum, had made a withdrawal around 3:00 A.M. on the night that McVey had been released. His home address was nearby, and he fit McVey's description.

When police pulled over a maroon Dodge Magnum on November 15, they found that the car had red carpeting. In addition, it had the right tires to match the track impressions found at two crime scenes. Long let himself be photographed as the cops pretended to be searching for a bank robber. His image was placed in a photo spread. McVey looked it over and picked out Long as her abductor.

Long, who was currently on probation for an aggravated assault in Hillsborough earlier that year, checked all the boxes on the FBI's profile. The task force put surveillance teams on him to ensure that he did not kill again while they prepared arrest and search warrants. They watched him dump items into a trash receptacle and vacuum his car. When he went back inside his apartment, they grabbed the items for potential evidence. As Long exited a movie theater on November 16, officers moved in. They arrested him and searched his home and vehicle.

Fibers in the carpet from Long's car were consistent with the fibers found on the victims, and hair strands picked up inside it were consistent with hair strands from six of the victims. In Long's apartment, detectives located McVey's barrette and fingerprints. They found photos that Long had taken of himself raping women.

During Long's interrogation, investigators learned that the thirty-one-year-old unemployed X-ray technician was divorced and had two children. They asked him about McVey, and he admitted to her abduction and assault. When confronted with the incriminating physical evidence from the murder sites, Long confessed in detail. He added the murder of a missing woman, Vicky Elliott, who'd accepted a ride as she walked to work. He directed investigators to her remains.

Long's transcribed confession ran to forty-five pages. In addition to the murders, he also helped solve a series of rapes from the past several years. His approach had been to scan papers for ads for items for sale—especially bedroom furniture—and to set up appointments when he believed husbands would be away. He would dress to seem clean-cut and trustworthy, and he found that most women let him in. He had practiced this maneuver in Ocala, Miami, and Fort Lauderdale, raping at least fifty women. He'd become known in the media as the Ad Man or the Classified Ad Rapist.

The charges in several counties for abduction, home invasion, rape, and murder piled up for Long. When bound skeletal remains turned up on November 22 and were identified as those of Artis Wick, she was unofficially added to Long's list of victims. He was not charged, but Wick was likely his first kill.

Long faced a lengthy series of trials. Many different attorneys came into and out of his case. His guilt was never in question, but prosecutors were seeking the death penalty, so the proceedings became a parade of experts for the defense who hoped to mitigate his crimes by finding reasonable excuses for them. During the course of his life, Long had

ROBERT JOE LONG WITH HIS ATTORNEY BEFORE BEING SENTENCED TO DEATH FOR A PASCO COUNTY MURDER IN 1989.

sustained numerous blows to the skull from falls and accidents. In addition, he'd been born with an extra X chromosome that had produced abnormal amounts of estrogen during puberty. He'd suffered from blinding headaches and a driving obsession with sex, and had developed an ability to have sex repeatedly. Defense experts said that Long had been unable to control his behavior. One suggested that, as a unique specimen, Long should be studied. Even Dr. John Money, renowned for his work on gender identity, testified about the negative impact of an extra female chromosome, exacerbated by the head injuries, including shame over having breasts as a teenage boy. He said that with Long's fragile ego, the combination had created a Jekyll/Hyde syndrome. (Money's work was later discredited.)

The prosecution countered with psychiatrists who contended that Long had antisocial personality disorder, not a mental illness that undermined his ability to tell right from wrong. He was a liar and he'd known what he was doing when he'd raped and murdered the women.

The jury convicted him. Long received two death sentences and thirty-three life sentences (reached in plea deals). His attorneys challenged the decisions. Owing to police errors, the Florida Supreme Court overturned Long's death-penalty convictions and granted him new trials. Long also got a break when the Department of Justice issued a blistering report in 1997 against the FBI lab's problematic fiber analysis methods. Long's case was among those that came under scrutiny. However, Long's confession and the other physical evidence went against him, so he remained on death row. He appealed on many other issues, including his neurological condition, and it appeared that he might just die an old man in his prison cell. Then on May 23, 2019, thirty-five years after his first known murder, Bobby Joe Long was finally executed by lethal injection at the age of sixty-five.

THE TAKEAWAY

Name: Bobby Joe Long
Country: United States
Date of Birth: October 14, 1953
Date of Death: May 23, 2019
Killing Period: March–November 1984
Known Victims: 10
Date of Arrest: November 16, 1984

The case of Bobby Joe Long presents an example of success through cooperation among numerous jurisdictions. The critical areas, as depicted in an article composed by the head of the Tampa killer task force and the FBI analyst, featured handling the news media, studying evidence, working with a laboratory, and engaging continued commitment from all agencies. Thirty officers had been assigned to the task force from five local, state, and federal agencies. They had worked efficiently to ensure a speedy but careful arrest.

The case also involved a behavioral profile devised during the early days of the BSU's existence. Today it looks primitive, and it did not actually assist in the arrest, but for its time and the FBI's limited database for sexual murders, it was quite accurate. The task force had viewed it as a valuable guide. The analysis revealed a classic sexually compelled serial killer who showed organized and controlled behaviors. Supposedly, according to Long, he was angry at a woman who'd reported him for assault. This had precipitated the murders. Long had been careful about picking up victims without being seen, but he had not been careful about physical or behavioral evidence. He'd used ropes and cordage, indicative of ritual behavior, on seven victims, and all had been easy prey. One or the other type of red fiber was found on all victims except the two badly decomposed bodies that had been exposed to the elements. Long had left semen at three scenes whose analysis yielded a blood type, although it didn't match in one case. The linkage had inspired a focused multi-jurisdictional effort to identify him.

Long was a "power assertive rapist," according to the FBI's classification system, which meant that he was acting out to assert his manhood. Given his childhood issues and the fact that a woman had one-upped him by reporting him, it makes sense that the rapes and murders reassured him of his dominance. He said during his confession that some of the victims had struggled with him, making him angry. McVey had fully cooperated, so she'd failed to fit his notion of women as "bitches."

Thanks to Long's errors, along with sustained police procedure, multiple murder cases were solved.

19.

THE BUNDY WANNABE

THE CRIMES

On February 1, 2012, eighteen-year-old Samantha Koenig prepared to close up Common Grounds, the coffee stand in Anchorage, Alaska where she worked as a barista. She didn't relish going out in the 12-degree weather, but she looked forward to her boyfriend's warm truck when he picked her up.

The last customer ordered an Americano. A surveillance video would show what happened, and his confession added the rest. Samantha chatted a little as she pulled out what she needed for his drink. She had no idea that this "customer" had chosen this stand because it closed later than others. As she handed the cup to him, the man pulled out a gun. "Give me money and turn off the lights," he ordered.

Panicked, Samantha opened the register and grabbed a handful of bills; she shoved the money over the counter. The man told her to come toward him with her hands behind her back. She obeyed. He tied her hands together with zip ties and ordered her onto the floor. Then he forced her outside and into his white Silverado truck. Leaving her bound, he retrieved her cell phone and sent texts "from Samantha" to her boss and her boyfriend: "Had a bad day. Going away for the weekend." He demanded her bank card and PIN number. She said it was in her truck at home.

He drove for longer than she expected and ultimately forced her into a shed. "I have a police scanner," he warned. "If they're alerted, I'll know, and I'll get back here first and kill you." Samantha nodded that she understood. He turned up a radio in the shed to prevent anyone from hearing her scream for help.

When the man went to retrieve the bank card, his activity at her truck attracted attention. Samantha's boyfriend, Duane Tortolani II, came out and saw him. Duane had gone to Common Grounds to pick up Samantha but had found the coffee shop abandoned. Her text had mystified him. Now here was someone wearing a ski mask rummaging in their truck.

Duane ran inside to alert Samantha's father; but when the two came out, the man was gone. He'd returned to the shed to rape and kill his abductee. Samantha never had a chance. He left her body in the shed and flew to New Orleans to go on a two-week cruise.

This man's name was Israel Keyes, and he wanted to be like his dark hero, Ted Bundy (see chapter 17). During the 1970s, Bundy had murdered at least thirty girls and young women in half a dozen states, from the Pacific Northwest to Florida. He'd carefully honed the sort of double life to which Keyes aspired, passing as normal while killing as he pleased. Keyes had studied many of the true-crime books written about Bundy, paying special attention to his idol's errors. Those, he did not want to repeat. He studied other killers as well, and read the books by FBI profilers and crime-scene investigators. He wanted to know what he had to do to avoid detection. Raised as a survivalist, Keyes was good at covering his tracks.

Back in Alaska, Samantha's family and employer realized that something terrible had happened. She hadn't closed Common Grounds up properly: the alarm was off, and money was missing from the register. The police initially thought she'd stolen the money and run off, and so they delayed their investigation. Review of the darkened surveillance video, though, convinced them that the girl had been abducted.

Samantha's father, James Koenig, recalled that they'd seen a man tampering with their truck. He offered a reward, which grew with donations to over $40,000 for information regarding Samantha's whereabouts. But no one had any information about her.

As the search commenced in Alaska, Keyes, now in Texas, robbed the National Bank of Texas in Azle and buried the money in a sealed bucket. Then he returned to Anchorage to prepare for the next stage.

He checked the shed and saw Samantha's body preserved in the cold. Keyes grabbed an edition of the Anchorage *Daily News* from four days earlier, February 13. He posed the corpse for a Polaroid photo and held up the paper to create the ruse that Samantha was still alive (she was not obviously dead in the photo). Keyes photocopied the Polaroid and wrote a ransom note on the back of the photo. He demanded $30,000 for Samantha's return and provided instructions for its delivery via her bank account. Then he went to Connors Bog Dog Park and pinned the note on a board. He used Samantha's phone to text a message about its location to Duane, who turned it over to the police. They retrieved the photo and note.

Keyes dismembered Samantha's remains and placed the parts into bags. These he transported to Matanuska Lake near Wasilla. With a chainsaw, he cut a hole through the ice and pushed the body parts through.

THE COMMON GROUNDS COFFEE STAND IN ANCHORAGE, ALASKA, WHERE SAMANTHA KOENIG WAS ABDUCTED BY ISRAEL KEYES ON FEBRUARY 1, 2012.

James Koenig deposited the ransom Keyes had demanded into Samantha's account. The FBI, now on the case, hoped that her abductor would use her debit card to get it, so they could track him. On February 29, Keyes used Samantha's card to withdraw $500 from an Anchorage ATM, and then $500 from another one. As police swarmed these locations, he left the state.

On March 7, Keyes withdrew $400 from the Western Bank ATM in Willcox, Arizona. He wore a homemade mask and pair of gloves. From there, he drove to New Mexico in a rental car for another withdrawal, and then to Texas.

Authorities retrieved a blurry ATM photo of the 2012 white Ford Focus that Samantha's presumed kidnapper was driving and sent out an alert to several neighboring states. They'd seen a pattern: Samantha's abductor was driving along route I-10. He visited ATMs in Lordsburg, New Mexico, and Humble, Texas. Keyes switched cars at an Avis rental agency and ended up with another white Ford Focus. This was his error.

Instead of insisting on a different car, he accepted one that looked like the car he'd used in Arizona. Keyes made one more withdrawal before he headed for Lufkin, Texas, to attend his sister's wedding.

On March 13, Keyes watched from a balcony at a Quality Inn as a police cruiser stopped near his rental. He tensed, but the officer pulled away. Keyes figured that the cop was checking out a junky van parked next to his car. Alaska news online made no mention that authorities were on his trail. He felt safe.

THE CAPTURE

Corporal Bryan Henry from the Texas Highway Patrol had spotted the white rental parked at the hotel and the Caucasian male watching from the balcony. He'd alerted a law-enforcement network. FBI agents arrived and watched a man get into the white car and drive away. Corporal Henry, back to his regular beat, saw the car again and followed it. When the driver went three miles over the speed limit, Henry signaled for the car to pull over. He saw from the driver's license that the man was Israel Keyes . . . from Alaska.

Keyes was squirming. He'd always planned to kill himself if he were ever in danger of arrest, but his loaded gun was not close to hand.

Texas Ranger Steve Rayburn arrived, along with other law-enforcement personnel, and they searched the car. Inside, they found rolls of cash, a piece of a gray T-shirt cut into a face mask, a map with incriminating highlights, a gun, a stack of ink-stained money from a bank robbery, and Samantha Koenig's cell phone and debit card. They placed Keyes under arrest.

Investigators in Alaska, alerted to the arrest, went to the home Keyes shared with his girlfriend. She was stunned by what they told her. They confiscated the couple's computers, and a digital analyst found Google searches of media coverage of Samantha's abduction. Two investigators from Alaska flew to Texas to tell Keyes he'd been indicted in Alaska. He agreed to be extradited.

Investigators went to work to learn more about Keyes's background. He submitted to intensive psychological evaluations and talked about his background. He was born on January 7, 1978 in Utah, and his friends and family called him Izzy. The second child and first-born son of ten home-schooled children, Keyes had been raised in a Christian Identity community that espoused white supremacy. For his first seven years, he'd lived in a tent. He stole as a kid, and he tortured animals. His parents banned him from home when he espoused atheism. He'd served in the military and had a ten-year-old daughter who lived with him and his girlfriend. He had a small business as a general contractor, Keyes Construction, and he worked for Parks and Recreation, where coworkers found him reliable and polite.

At his arraignment on March 27, 2012, the thirty-four-year-old Keyes pleaded not guilty, even though he seemed to know the game was over. When prosecutors Kevin Feldis and Frank Russo showed Keyes the video surveillance tape from Common Grounds and told him what they had from his home and his computer, Keyes acknowledged it. His body shook and he fervently rubbed the arms of his chair as he admitted to killing Samantha. He told them where to find her remains. On April 2, divers went into the freezing water at Matanuska Lake and recovered them.

Other news stories on Keyes's computer raised concerns that Samantha had not been his first kill. At first, Keyes would not cooperate. He assured detectives, "I am not in this for the glory. I'm not trying to be on TV." He said he could save them "hundreds, if not thousands, of hours investigating." They would find things on his computer, he stated, "but they won't find enough." He wanted to bargain.

Over the next few months, Keyes came into the interrogation room on a regular basis. He revealed that he'd once raped a girl in Oregon. Soon thereafter, he'd enlisted in the Army. Honorably discharged after three years, he'd moved to Neah Bay, Washington, where he'd developed a relationship and had a daughter. When he separated from his girlfriend, he'd fought for custody.

At one point, Keyes admitted that he'd been "two different people" for at least fourteen years, harboring dark proclivities. He had things to confess, but he wanted to get on a fast track for execution. "I want this whole thing wrapped up and over with as soon as possible. I'll give you every single gory detail you want, but that's what I want, because I want my kid to have a chance to grow up. She's in a safe place now. She's not going to see any of this."

Keyes's trial was set for March 2014.

His interrogators told Keyes they couldn't work with him without some concrete information about victims. They wanted times and locations. Keyes offered them the name "Currier." Then with a map, he pointed out Bill and Lorraine Currier's house in Essex, Vermont, as well as an abandoned house where he'd left the bodies. The Curriers had been missing since June 8, 2011. It appeared that they had been forced from their home during the night. Their car was found abandoned, but no trace of them had turned up. Keyes had just solved this mystery.

Keyes had a meticulous MO. He prepared his killing kits from five-gallon buckets purchased from Home Depot. They contained items like Drano (for body disposal), small shovels, a silencer, flares, duct tape, a gun scope, a flashlight, ammunition, and bindings. He left these kits around the country in remote areas, intending to let time pass so as not to be traced via store surveillance while purchasing the items. He confessed that he had buried kits in New York, Vermont, Alaska, and Texas. There might be some in Washington, and perhaps in other western states. Some held cash from bank robberies.

"Why would you do these things?" one officer asked.

Keyes laughed. "It's not so much *why* I did it as why *not*?"

In the spring of 2011, Keyes had donned a fake mustache and a hoodie to rob a bank in Tupper Lake, New York. He'd buried the money in a bucket off a hiking path at the Woodside Natural Area near Essex, Vermont. Then he'd left for a couple of months. Coming back, he'd gotten a room near his buried kit. When he'd gone to dig it up, he'd noticed an abandoned farmhouse. It seemed like a perfect spot to bring victims.

On the night of June 8, Keyes broke into the Curriers' home. He had already scoped it out for the criteria he used to figure out how to enter undetected. Once inside, he'd roused the couple out of bed. He bound their wrists and took them to the abandoned farmhouse three miles away. After he killed them both, he stuffed their bodies into garbage bags. Although he tried not to look up news stories about them on his computer, at times he just couldn't help himself. He knew it was a mistake.

Investigators discovered that a company had demolished the farmhouse and taken the debris to a landfill. Despite special search teams dispatched by the FBI, no one was able to find the Curriers' remains.

The information that Keyes gave out during his forty hours of interviews was vague at best. He liked to grab people in cemeteries, on trailheads, in campgrounds, and in wilderness areas. He committed his first murder soon after his military discharge in 2000, although he also hinted at activities during the late 1990s. Between 2005 and 2006, there were two more murders, both of individuals in Washington State. He also killed a couple. Altogether, he said, he'd murdered eight more people, making eleven. Yet he also hinted that there could be a few more.

Like many serial killers, Keyes described an urge that possessed and compelled him to "do something." It could be a robbery, an arson, or a murder, but it had to be destructive. Only then did he feel better. As his activities received media attention, he'd started to unravel. "I knew that I was getting stupid," he said.

Near the end of July, Keyes learned that word of his interviews had leaked to the press. He was furious. He stopped talking and made a threat: "If things don't go the way I want, then I don't need you guys."

On December 1, 2012, a guard looked into his cell at 10:13 P.M. All Keyes was doing at that time was writing on a legal pad. But earlier, another guard had mistakenly issued him a razor. He used it that night to kill himself. In a suicide note, he wrote, "Okay, talk is over. Words are flaccid and weak. Back it with action or it all comes off cheap. Watch close while I work now, feel the electric shock of my touch, open my trembling flower, or your petals I'll crush."

With no more information to come directly from the killer, the FBI focused on Keyes's paper trail. Agents subpoenaed airlines and car-rental and credit-card companies to piece together his whereabouts over the previous fourteen years. They identified thirty-five trips throughout the U.S., Canada, and Mexico and released video clips of Keyes, hoping to trigger someone's memory. So far, only one more victim has been tentatively identified, because just before he killed himself, Keyes had referred to her photo as someone that he did not yet want to talk about.

THE TAKEAWAY

Name: Israel "Izzy" Keyes
Country: United States
Date of Birth: January 7, 1978
Date of Death: December 2, 2012
Killing Period: Unclear: 2000–2012
Known Victims: 3–4+
Date of Arrest: March 13, 2012

Keyes remains unique among serial killers for his meticulous planning and preparation, as well as the amount of time he could wait before acting on his urge. With no victim type, he killed just to kill, and he was highly painstaking in his plans. He traveled with no predictable pattern, covered his tracks, buried "hit kits" for later, and robbed banks to support his killing ventures. Just as he took a page from the books of organized killers like Bundy, it's likely that Keyes will inspire others like himself who might learn from *his* mistakes.

20.

THE CHESSBOARD KILLER

THE CRIMES

Between 1978 and 1990, someone raped, brutalized, and murdered at least fifty-two women and children in Ukraine. Chief investigator Viktor Burakov had a psychiatrist develop a profile of the killer similar to those that the FBI used. When Andrei Chikatilo was arrested, the profile assisted the police in eliciting his confession. Chikatilo was tried, convicted, and summarily executed.

Around the time of Chikatilo's highly publicized trial in 1992, eighteen-year-old Mikhail Odichuk fell to his death from a window in Moscow. The police questioned those who knew him and deemed it a suicide. But as it turns out, it was actually an experiment. Chikatilo's notoriety had inspired a budding killer to set his life goal: he would beat Chikatilo's record. He liked to play chess. A chessboard has 64 squares. He set this figure as his target. Nearly a decade later, he began killing in earnest.

In 2001, police became aware of missing pensioners in Bitsevsky (or Bitsa) Park, in the southwestern part of Moscow. Several turned up in the drainage system with their heads bashed in. When former cop Nikolai Zakharchenko was found murdered in the park in 2005, officials from the Interior Ministry finally accepted that they might have a serial killer operating in southern Moscow. Other bodies turned up in the woods similarly bludgeoned, sometimes with glass shards stuck into their wounds. Most of the victims had frequented the park, and it would have been easy to lure them into the cover of dense foliage in the 2,700-acre park.

As media caught on, they dubbed the killer the "Bitsa Park Maniac." By the spring of 2006, police had found thirteen bodies in the woods—and a lot more people were missing. They also had three survivors who could describe the attacks: a pregnant woman, a thirteen-year-old boy, and an older man. However, their descriptions of the young man who'd committed the assaults were too vague to help the police find him.

Then someone came across the battered body of Marina Moskalyova in the river. Her head had been beaten in and small wooden spikes had been driven into her eyes. Police found a recent Metro ticket in her pocket. They identified the thirty-six-year-old and learned that she'd worked at a supermarket. Her son gave them a note she'd left, telling him that she was walking with a co-worker, Alexander Pichushkin. She'd included his phone number. When called, Pichushkin said he hadn't seen Moskalyova in two months—a blatant lie, since they worked together.

Police studied surveillance footage from the Metro train stations at Novye Cheryomushki and Konkovo, near the park. They saw Pichushkin on a platform with Moskalyova. He fit the description of the balding, thirtyish man who'd attacked people in the park. This shelf-stocker and grocery-bagger was their best suspect for the murders of the thirteen people found in the Bitsevsky woods. When they learned that he lived near the park with his mother, they prepared to arrest him.

THE CAPTURE

On the evening of June 15, 2006, a team entered Pichushkin's residence to serve their warrant. He went with them peacefully. The male attack survivor identified him as the culprit.

Pichushkin, thirty-two years old, denied his involvement. When police showed him the surveillance footage from the train platform, he agreed to talk. Andrei Suprunenko, the lead investigator, sensed that Pichushkin liked attention. He flattered him and made him feel important, which got him talking even more. Pichushkin was clearly pleased with how long he'd duped the police. They thought he'd killed thirteen people. He had in fact killed over sixty, he said. He took officers to some of the places where he'd buried victims, showing them their remains, but he said he'd dumped most into one of two thirty-foot wells that fed into the drainage system.

Police were shocked to find that this ordinary, irritable alcoholic with few talents and low aspirations might be the country's worst serial killer. Pichushkin claimed he'd wanted to eclipse Chikatilo. "For the record," he said, "I wanted to kill as many people as possible and to beat Chikatilo's record." This odd motivator immediately got him a new moniker: The Chessboard Killer.

Searching his residence, officers found news clippings related to Chikatilo, violent pornography, and a chessboard drawing on which Pichushkin had placed dates on sixty-two squares. This suggested that he'd kept track of his murders as a type of game. He'd often targeted the elderly, he admitted, inviting them to drink with him over his dog's grave in a secluded area of the park. Then he bludgeoned their heads with a hammer or wrench and dumped them into a sewer pit. Some had still been alive but too inebriated to save themselves. Lately, he'd left them where he'd killed them. He said he'd known that killing Marina had been a risk, but he'd been in the mood that night, so he did it. (He also later said he'd purposely made this mistake to get caught.)

Pichushkin recounted his first murder in 1992, when he'd been eighteen. He'd invited Mikhail Odichuk on a "killing expedition." Then he'd pushed the other boy out a window. He was questioned but not charged, and police had closed the case as a suicide. Nine years passed before he tried again in 2001. In two months, he murdered ten people.

Pichushkin started killing people in the park, mostly men. A few had lived in his public-housing building. He generally befriended them at first, playing chess or drinking together. He'd watch them, drink with them, and then get them alone and hit them hard enough for them to understand that they were about to be killed. This had given him a feeling of power. Sometimes he'd shove pieces of empty vodka bottles into the wounds he'd made. He'd always attacked from behind, to avoid getting blood on his clothing. Sometimes, he admitted, he'd ejaculated during a murder.

"A life without murder," he stated, "is a life without food." He believed he'd opened a door for his victims and given them a "new life." In addition, he enjoyed toying with the police. He was amazed that there had been so little investigation.

Pichushkin described his life as difficult. He'd never known his father, who'd left his family when he was one. His mother had placed him in an institution for the disabled, due to his unmanageable personality. After sustaining a head injury when he was four, he'd become an aggressive bully. He admitted that he would hold little kids out a window by one foot to make them understand his power over them. He terrorized children whenever he saw them. He began his string of murders after the death of his dog, which had depressed him.

Pichushkin described his criminal career as a "perpetual orgasm." It had been his goal to kill sixty-four, to match the squares on a chessboard, as was noted above. Later, he said he would have kept killing indefinitely if he hadn't been caught.

At the Serbsky Institute, Pichushkin was subjected to several months of psychiatric evaluations and judged to be "irrecuperable" but competent to stand trial. He was charged with forty-nine murders and three attempted murders. At the brief preliminary hearing on August 13, 2007, he asked to be tried by a jury. Judge Andrei Subarev accepted this request. He also opened the trial to the public. Pichushkin was placed inside a glass cage for its duration. (Chikatilo had been in a cage with bars.)

Pichushkin was angry that the charges against him fell short of Chikatilo's record. He claimed he'd been cheated. He asked the court to add eleven more. However, the police had found no evidence for the additional victims he claimed. Then his defense attorneys asked to have eighteen murders dropped, arguing that there had been mitigating factors for his actions. Pichushkin then asked to have those attorneys removed from the case, as they were not representing his interests.

On October 24, 2007, Pichushkin was convicted of forty-eight murders (not forty-nine) and three attempted murders. Some journalists called him the "silver medal serial killer," which infuriated him. Since capital punishment had been suspended in Russia, he was sentenced to fifteen years of solitary confinement as part of his life sentence.

THE TAKEAWAY
Name: Aleksandr Yuryevich Pichushkin
Country: Russia
Date of Birth: April 9, 1974
Date of Death: NA
Killing Period: 1992, 2001–2006
Known Victims: convicted in 48 cases; claimed 62
Date of Arrest: June 16, 2006

As with many serial killers whose ambition is to surpass the kill records of others, it's difficult to know what to accept about Pichushkin's claims.

He offered several different numbers for his kills—between sixty and sixty-six—but evidence was lacking. Many serial killers have claimed they had more victims than police attribute to them. Their reasons have been mostly self-serving, with four basic motives (explanations below): duping delight; impression management; status enhancement; and delay of execution. Pichushkin would have known about the most famous cases.

Henry Lee Lucas, arrested in the United States in 1983, initially estimated that he'd killed 100 people. Eventually, he raised this figure to more than 500 in twenty-seven different states (and even higher at one point). When lawmen came to Texas to close their open cases, they provided Lucas with outings and better meals than he got in prison. Many also unintentionally fed him details he needed to sound credible. Then he recanted. Just as quickly, he insisted he'd been forced to recant. Then most of his sensational confession was proven to be false. "I set out to break and corrupt any law-enforcement officer I could get," Lucas said. "I think I did a pretty good job." That's an example of duping delight.

H. H. Holmes was an impression manager. He was convicted in Philadelphia in 1896 for killing a partner in an insurance fraud. For $10,000, he proclaimed himself the world's most notorious killer, claiming 100 victims before reducing that number in another narrative to twenty-seven. "The newspaper wanted a sensation," he said. Before stepping into the noose, he admitted to only two murders. The truth was somewhere in between those figures, but he'd enjoyed his spotlight of fame.

For status enhancement, in 1995 Robert Charles Browne initially pleaded guilty to just the 1991 murder in Colorado of Heather Dawn Church. Five years later, he sent cryptic notes to Texas prosecutors: "The score is you[,] 1, the other team, 48." He admitted he'd been killing since 1970, in nine different states. Yet he provided specific information in only seven cases. He briefly "became" America's most prolific serial killer, beating by one the record set at the time by "Green River Killer" Gary Ridgway. However, his confession triggered skepticism.

Investigators could not corroborate any case other than Heather Dawn Church. Browne lost his status.

Regarding Gary Ridgway, when Special Agent Mary Ellen O'Toole from the FBI's Behavioral Analysis Unit interviewed him, he initially confessed to seventy-one before settling on the official toll of forty-eight (now forty-nine). "In my opinion," she said, "many of these people have an egotistical need to control and manipulate, and some like to be bigger and badder than the other guy."

During the 1980s and 1990s, several serial killers gave outrageously high victim counts to enhance their infamy. Larry Eyler, Donald Leroy Evans, Richard Biegenwald, Pee Wee Gaskins, and Paul John Knowles all claimed to have killed many more people than police could link to them. By that time, society had become so fascinated with serial killers that people believed whatever they said. Yet the numbers often were false.

Ted Bundy made several different claims of a victim toll between thirty and more than a hundred. He told Hugh Aynesworth that for every "publicized" murder, there "could be one that was not"; but he assured an attorney that thirty-five was right. He sought to prove his worth as a "scientific specimen" to FBI Supervisory Special Agent William Hagmaier, offering thirty homicides and suggesting he'd need more time than his execution date allowed to confirm the others. He pretended he wanted to help close cases, but he doled out information to serve his own ends.

Pichushkin, an insignificant shelf-stocker, liked attention and wanted to make himself seem larger than life. He definitely committed a number of murders in his quest for infamy, but corroboration is lacking to support his grandiose claims of what that number really was.

With the notoriety attached to serial killers, and with the true-crime narratives that make some into "the world's worst," higher victim tolls are often accepted as fact. However, when the claims are clearly self-serving, caution should be exercised. We certainly want to locate missing victims, but evidence should outweigh confessions.

21.
THE GRINDR KILLER

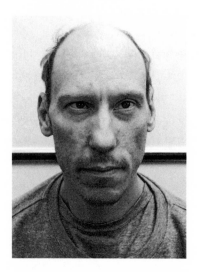

THE CRIMES

The Church of St. Margaret of Antioch in Barking, a working-class sub-urb of East London, dates back to the thirteenth century. Sitting near a ruined abbey, its grounds contain a walled cemetery full of old grave-stones. Barbara Denham walked her border collie there every day. On August 28, 2014, she approached a man slumped against the southwest corner of the wall. His sunglasses were askew, so she thought he was drunk. He didn't move. She leaned toward him and clapped her hands, but he remained still. Denham touched his cheek. Startled by its cold-ness, she withdrew and reported her discovery.

Police arrived and took away the body of Gabriel Kovari. He was just twenty-two. A bottle of gamma-hydroxybutyric acid (GHB), the date-rape drug, was in a nearby bag, along with his ID. The autopsy showed that he'd died from an overdose. People sometimes used this drug, also known as liquid ecstasy, to produce euphoria during sex; but it could be lethal, especially when mixed with sedatives or alcohol. Kovari's death was ruled accidental.

A friend of Kovari's knew he'd been living with a man named Stephen Port in a flat in Barking, not far from the cemetery, but Port told him that Kovari had taken off the night of his death with someone he didn't know and hadn't said where he was going.

A previous roommate of Kovari's, John Pape, searched the Internet for other deaths in the area and came across the case of Anthony Walgate from the year before. He, too, had died from an overdose, and his body had been dumped on the street in the entrance to a block of flats on Cooke Street in Barking. Pape brought this information to the police, but they told him the incidents were unrelated.

Kovari's case took an odd twist on September 20, about three weeks after his body was found. Barbara Denham was again walking her dog along their usual route when, to her surprise, she saw another young man, this one on a blue sheet but leaning against the same wall in the same spot as where Kovari's body had been found. He, too, was dead. When police arrived, they extracted a note from his hand. His name was Daniel Whitworth. The twenty-year-old apparently had known Kovari and blamed himself for Kovari's death.

"I am sorry to everyone," the note said, "mainly my family, but I can't go on anymore, I took the life of my friend Gabriel Kline [sic], we was just having some fun at a mate's place and I got carried away and gave him another shot of G. I didn't notice while we was having sex that he had stopped breathing. I tried everything to get him to breathe again but it was too late, it was an accident, but I blame myself for what happened and I didn't tell my family I went out. I know I would go to prison if I go to the police and I can't do that to my family and at least this way I can at least be with Gabriel again, I hope he will forgive me.

"BTW Please do not blame the guy I was with last night, we only had sex then I left, he knows nothing of what I have done. I have taken what g I have left with sleeping pills so if it does kill me it's what I deserve. Feeling dizey [sic] now as took 10 min ago so hoping you understand my writing. I dropped my phone on way here so should be in the grass somewhere. Sorry to everyone. Love always."

It was signed "Daniel P. W." A small brown bottle next to Whitworth's body contained GHB. The scenario made sense to police: two young men experimenting with drugs to enhance a sexual experience had taken things too far. One had died. The other had grown despondent over this unintended accident. He'd even placed himself in the same position at the same spot as his friend. As he'd claimed, the tox report showed GHB and sleeping pills in his system.

DCI Tony Kirk, a senior police official, told a local paper that the Kovari and Whitworth deaths were "unusual and slightly confusing" but not suspicious. Whatever might have been the identity of "the guy I was with last night," police did not follow up. Having only superficial training in suicide analysis, they might not have realized that mention of another person in a suicide note, especially in a positive light, is a red flag. It often leads to a killer who staged the homicide as a suicide. That seemingly minor "BTW" ("by the way") should have prompted a more thorough investigation.

However, police considered both cases to be closed, despite the protests of both men's relatives and friends, so they did not check into Whitworth's activities prior to his death. They also didn't check whether he was susceptible to depression, or who else might have crossed his path. They did not look for evidence that the two men knew each other. Even a DNA analysis of the bed sheet would have shown that someone else was involved, which might have prevented one more murder. Their slipshod check on Whitworth's handwriting would come back to haunt them.

During an inquest in June 2015, Coroner Nadia Persaud said that the Whitworth case was not a definite suicide. She had found bruises on the victim's neck, on his chest, and under his arms that suggested he'd been dragged. (The other two victims had shown similar evidence of being dragged.) For Persaud, the death was undetermined (an "open verdict") and required more information. She urged investigators to test the sheet found under the body for DNA and the bottle of GHB in his pocket for fingerprints. No one did.

The killer, Stephen Port, had now gotten away with three murders, although he'd had a close call with the first one. On June 17, 2014, he'd found Anthony Walgate, a twenty-three-year-old fashion student, on the male escort website Sleepyboys. He'd offered Walgate £800 for an overnight, meeting him at Barking Station to bring him home. (He did not realize that Walgate had given a friend the details, "In case I get killed.") Walgate had ended up dead. Port had left his body, along with a bottle of GHB to stage the scene as an overdose, just outside his own flat. He'd anonymously called emergency services, pretending to be a good citizen who'd driven by the building and seen a man seemingly in need of medical attention. Police had picked up the body, which had lethal levels of GHB in the blood and urine.

They'd traced Port's call back to him at 62 Cooke Street. He'd told several lies about trying to help Walgate outside, but police had learned about the escort connection. Port admitted that he'd met Walgate for sex but said that Walgate had injected himself with the drugs that he'd brought to their tryst. Walgate had gone to bed wearing his clothes and shoes. When he died, Port moved his body to the street and propped him up against the wall.

As unlikely as this story was, the officers believed it. They hadn't investigated the possibility of a homicide. They'd seized Port's computer but hadn't searched it, not even when Walgate's friends and family had urged them to.

For lying to the police, Port was told to report to court in January for a hearing on perverting the course of justice. While on bail, he'd killed Kovari and Whitworth.

In February 2015, Port pleaded guilty and received an eight-month sentence, but he served just two months. Once out, he reentered the party scene.

In September, Port met Jack Taylor, twenty-five, who worked as a forklift driver. Taylor's body was later found on the other side of the same cemetery wall, near North Street. He'd also died from an overdose. A syringe was in his pocket, needle marks showed on his arm, and white powder turned up in his wallet. Once again, the police chalked it up to an accidental death from abusing drugs. They figured Taylor had entered the churchyard alone to shoot up.

When officials reported the bad news to Taylor's family, they encountered a wall of active resistance that turned the case around.

THE CAPTURE

Taylor's two sisters were outraged at what the officers told them. They were adamant in their insistence that he was against drugs. He would not have taken GHB. When these women discovered that the police had dropped the investigation, they did their own research. It did not take them long to locate news reports about the other three "overdoses" in Barking. Even with no law-enforcement background, they could see that something was clearly wrong.

Although the officers assured Taylor's sisters that there were no suspicious connections, they showed them where Taylor's body had been found. When the women pressed for details about CCTV footage, the officers admitted that there were clear images of Taylor with another man around 2:00 A.M. on the night he died, walking out from Barking Station toward the abbey ruins. However, the police hadn't attempted to identify the man.

The sisters were astonished. Their anger at this negligence spurred investigators to reexamine the footage. This time, they saw that the other man had gone with Taylor into the graveyard. The sisters asked the officers to make the images public. The police initially resisted but eventually got the photos printed in the newspaper. An officer who knew Port identified him as Taylor's acquaintance. By now, no one could dismiss the discovery of four dead bodies in Port's neighborhood as mere coincidence. He was arrested.

Port repeated his story about "helping" Walgate but denied knowing the other men. The evidence went against him. Authorities established solid links between the four murder victims and Port, and a handwriting expert said that Port, not Whitworth, had written the suicide note. He was "the guy I was with." In addition, widespread media coverage brought other men forward who claimed to have been drugged and raped or sexually assaulted in Port's flat. All of them told how Port had spiked their drinks or injected them. All had been ill or dizzy when they left. Some had passed out.

In retrospect, it seemed astonishing that four bodies left in a similar condition so close to one another in just over a year had not prompted a detailed investigation—especially after the coroner expressed her concerns. The cemetery was just a third of a mile from Port's apartment building, where Walgate's body had been left outside. Three of the victims had shown evidence of being dragged into position.

A flurry of news coverage informed the world about this "dating app" serial killer, in part as a cautionary tale. Reporters delved into his background. Forty-year-old Port lived in a one-bedroom flat on Cooke Street and worked as a chef at a bus depot fast-food restaurant. He'd lived in the East London area most of his life; he had come out as gay in the mid-2000s. Those who knew Port were aware that he had a fetish for sex with unconscious teenage males. He used false personas and names like "top fun Joe" and "shy guy" to lure sexual partners via gay Internet dating sites like Grindr, Fitlads, and Gaydar. He would quickly knock out his partners in his apartment with GHB-laced drinks, along with other drugs, so he could rape them. Those who survived realized how naïve and careless they'd been. His MO had been the same from one to the next.

Officials finally tested the bed sheet that had been placed under Whitworth and found Port's DNA all over it, as well as on Whitworth's body and clothing—and even on the "suicide" note and envelope. The paper used for the note was from Port's flat. A search of Port's computer yielded some startling material. After looking at Walgate's profile online, Port had researched "unconscious boys," "drugged and raped," and "guy raped and tortured young nude boy." The police could have had access to this information earlier, but they had not examined Port's computer.

Port insisted that the victims had all injected themselves. He was guilty only of not reporting their deaths and of staging the scenes; he was not a killer. It remained for a jury to decide.

Port went to trial in 2016. During the proceedings, he explained his lies by saying, "The truth sounded like a lie, so I lied to make it sound like the truth."

Port was convicted on November 23 of the four murders, the rapes of three other men who'd been drugged, and four other sexual assaults. Mr. Justice Openshaw sentenced him to life in prison with a whole-life order, which meant no possibility of parole. Port was one of just fifty men in England with a sentence this harsh. Believing he'd been treated unjustly, he launched an appeal to get the charges reduced to manslaughter. As of this writing (2019), the results of that appeal are pending.

THE TAKEAWAY

Name: Stephen Port
Country: England
Date of Birth: February 22, 1975
Date of Death: NA
Killing Period: June 2014–September 2015
Known Victims: 4
Date of Arrest: October 15, 2015

Port's case raised awareness about the dangers of online dating. He himself had rules about personal safety, such as never accepting a drink or food from someone he did not know. The gay community felt especially unsafe in light of what they viewed as police bias and, after the events chronicled in this chapter, the unwillingness of officials to fully investigate Port's crimes. His was one of several cases in which a gay serial killer had acted under the radar, exploiting lack of official concern for the population. Port hadn't even tried to disguise his handwriting on the suicide note for Whitworth.

Key witnesses had not been questioned in any of the incidents. A neighbor in Port's building told a documentary maker that Port had sent suspicious texts to him about Kovari, and inside Port's flat he had seen incriminating white powder and bottles of clear liquid. However, the police had never contacted him.

The families of the victims went public to talk about how badly they'd been treated, and Jack Taylor's sisters made it clear that had they not been so persistent, Port would not have been identified and stopped.

The Independent Police Complaints Commission (now the Independent Office for Police Conduct, or the IOPC) opened an investigation against seventeen officers who had been involved in some stage of the incidents. The result of the investigation was a recommendation that nine of them improve their standard of operation. No wrongdoing was found.

This case highlights the manner in which serial killers exploit expectations. Port was a sexual predator. He'd anticipated drugging and raping those who responded to his solicitations. After Walgate died, Port had known that his activities posed a high risk to his partners, but he'd continued to do them. He'd seen that dumping bodies drew minimal police attention in this area, even after they knew of his association with Walgate. It had been easy to deflect them from investigating.

Specific to the Whitworth incident, research shows that police rely on myths about suicide: e.g., the presence of a suicide note confirms a suicide. However, police officers make incorrect judgments about authentic versus inauthentic suicide notes fifty percent of the time. They rarely consider the possibility of a staged suicide. Police departments could offer better training, or they could consult behavioral experts in suicide analysis. Whitworth's case, especially with the odd marks on his body, justified further examination.

Whitworth's parents claimed that police had given each of them a scrap of the so-called suicide note, asking if it matched their son's handwriting. They said they were not sure, but the police recorded this as a confirmation and did not submit the note for expert analysis. When the couple later saw the complete document, they rejected it as their son's handwriting. They also were astonished that the police had not tried to learn the identity of the "other guy" that the note had mentioned.

A more thorough investigation might have raised some red flags. The note was not in Whitworth's handwriting. He had not been despondent. He had been found propped up in nearly the same posture and place as another dead man, with whom he had no connection. In addition, several studies show that notes written to stage a homicide as a suicide often mention the perpetrator. At the very least, the investigation of a death incident should include an analysis of victim behavior and mental state.

On a positive note, British law enforcement announced that it would delve further into fifty-eight deaths connected to the use of GHB, to check for other factors that might change the death determination.

PART IV

WITNESS REPORTS

Police rely on witnesses to help identify offenders. The various types of witnesses include those who saw something that generated a lead, those who survived a killer and reported it to the police, and accomplices who finally decided to do the right thing.

22.

THE SOAP MAKER OF CORREGGIO

THE CRIMES

The superintendent of *polizei* had no leads in the disappearance of two elderly women in Correggio, in the Po Valley of northern Italy. Tensions were high all over Italy in 1939 as Mussolini dealt with Hitler's takeover of Czechoslovakia and invasion of Poland. People routinely disappeared, but two women in eight months from the same community was suspicious, especially since they'd left most of their personal effects behind.

Fifty-year-old Faustina Setti had vanished first. She'd sent letters to friends to tell them she was now living in Pola, Italy, 150 miles away. A missing-persons check in Pola had turned up no reports of nameless murder victims or women in hospitals.

When Mussolini led the nation to war in 1940, the investigation was shelved. Then Francesca Soavi went missing. She'd told relatives in letters that she was leaving Correggio to take up work in Piacenza, about 55 miles away. She had a job there, set up by a friend (whom she did not name). These letters had all been mailed from Correggio itself. Then, communication had ceased. Police found no trace of Soavi in Piacenza.

Among those whom authorities questioned was Leonarda Cianciulli, a local Correggio shopkeeper who lived in a whitewashed house along the canal from which she sold herbs, baked goods, candles, and soap. This plump, middle-aged woman had a reputation for telling fortunes.

When investigators arrived, Cianciulli offered coffee and cake. She knew the missing women, she said, but she had not heard from them. She proudly told the investigators that her eldest son, Giuseppe, had joined Mussolini's army.

What she did *not* reveal is that she had her own dark secrets. *Very* dark.

Born in 1894, Leonarda was the product of a rape. When young, she had felt unwanted and tried ending her own life on at least two occasions. She wanted her own family so that she could make up for having a poor relationship with her mother, who seemed to resent her. Eventually she eloped with an older man, a registry-office clerk named Raffaele Pansardi, which further alienated her mother, who had picked out a man of better social standing for her. In retaliation, her mother cursed her to a life of unhappiness. Soon, Leonarda had reason to believe that this curse had real power. She had three miscarriages, and ten of her children died at birth or at a young age. Left with only four, Leonarda visited an occult practitioner to find a way to shield her remaining family from the curse. One day, a palm-reader told her that her right hand foretold a prison sentence; her left, incarceration in a criminal asylum.

Shocked, Leonarda consulted another prognosticator, who told her, "You will live to see all your children die." She could not bear this prediction, so she educated herself in the occult to learn how to protect herself.

In 1930, an earthquake destroyed the Cianciulli home, forcing the family to move from Lariano, where they'd been living, to Correggio. Leonarda opened her shop to sell baked goods and charms. Her fierce protection of her children seemed to be working, but then Giuseppe joined the army. Leonarda feared that, once more, she would see one of her children die before her. He was at high risk.

Leonarda knew from what she'd read in her occult books that one paid for a life with another life. To save Giuseppe, she concluded that someone else must die. She had never thought of harming anyone, but she knew she'd have to do it. She soon spotted a good candidate.

Her neighbor Faustina Setti had no family, and she confided to Leonarda that she wanted a change. She'd saved up 30,000 lire, and she offered it all to Leonarda for matchmaking. Leonarda told Faustina that she knew a man in Pola who would be perfect. However, her plan would only work if Faustina did exactly what she was told. She was to keep the arrangement secret, and she should write notes to everyone she knew that she was leaving to find her happiness. She should then send these letters from Pola (to ensure that she did not send them before she left Correggio).

Faustina obeyed. Eager to meet the mystery man, she packed her best dresses, bundled up her correspondences, and took everything to Leonarda's. They sipped a glass of wine to celebrate. But Faustina's glass had been drugged. She went limp and passed out.

With thoughts only for Giuseppe's protection by higher forces, Leonarda picked up a sharp-bladed hatchet and slammed it against Faustina's skull. Faustina jerked twice, then lay still. Leonarda was satisfied. She'd made the necessary sacrifice. In addition, she took the money that Faustina had brought with her for the trip.

Leonarda dragged the corpse into a large closet with an overhead light. She gathered a saw, a boning knife, and a cleaver. With Faustina's body faceup, Leonarda used a mallet to make the saw blade penetrate the skin. She removed the arms and gathered blood from open wounds. She took off the other limbs, cutting off the hands and feet, before removing the head. These she placed into a large iron kettle.

Ready to hand were her soap-making tools: resin, alum, and caustic soda. She boiled these ingredients in the right measure and then dropped the various parts into the mix. Before she tossed in the head, Leonarda held it by the hair. It barely resembled her former friend. She whispered a quick "*grazie*" and then dissolved it. Finally, she added the largest parts, the chest and abdomen.

Leonarda stirred for hours as the body parts melted, holding a cloth over her nose against the noxious fumes. Throughout the night, she thought only of what she was doing for her son, as flesh fell off the bones and the bones eventually disappeared into a brownish sludge. She let the mixture cool until it could be poured into buckets and dumped into a septic tank. She saved the blood, which she'd drained into a basin as she dismembered the body, for a special purpose. This she turned into flour. She let it coagulate before she spread it on flat pans to bake. When it cooled, she ground it into powder and mixed it with eggs, sugar, margarine, milk, and chocolate. She made teacakes to sell out of her shop.

The last step was to mail the letters that Faustina had so painstakingly prepared. The only reason she'd told her to mail them from Pola was to prevent her from sending them too soon. As long as people thought Faustina had gone to Pola, that's all that mattered. When she did not return, they would think something had happened to her there. No one would come looking in Leonarda's house, because she'd told Faustina to keep the plans secret.

There was gossip and concern about Faustina's sudden absence, but the mystery went unsolved. Leonarda sold her teacakes or served them to visitors, with no one the wiser. She even sent several cakes to her son, to double their power, and ate some herself. Giuseppe's letters back to her proved that she'd done the right thing: he remained alive.

When Mussolini went to war, Leonarda wondered if she'd done enough for her son's well-being. Anxious, she looked around for another sacrifice.

During the first week of September, Francesca Soavi came by. They had tea as Francesca described how depressed she was. Thanks to the war conditions, she was running out of money and thought she might lose her home. Leonarda consoled her and told her to return the next day to have her fortune read. Then she formed a plan: she'd spotted her next victim. When Francesca arrived, Leonarda told her about a job at a school for girls in Piacenza and said she could help her to get hired, as long as she strictly performed a specific ritual. The first part was to write letters to friends and family, but to tell them nothing of the plan. When she was settled in Piacenza, she could mail the letters.

Francesca packed her clothes, wrote the letters, collected her meager savings of 3,000 lire, and prepared to leave. On the appointed day, she walked over to Leonarda's house to thank her. Leonarda offered Francesca some celebratory wine. In a repeat of her murder of Faustina, she waited for the drug she'd put in the wine to work; grabbed her hatchet, saw, and cleaver; and once more boiled up a pot of human soup. This time, she kept some of the sludge for making candles and soap. It took a bit of perfume to mask the sour odor, but using the human fat meant there would be less to dispose of. To honor her son, Leonarda lit several of the freshly made candles.

She listened to the worried gossip after Francesca's disappearance. Friends and relatives received the letters but were puzzled by her silence about her plans. Over coffee and "cake," they discussed their concerns with Leonarda, who pretended to share them. Secretly, she gloated at her success in giving her son a double layer of protection. She gave out bars of soap, *gratis*, and reassured her friends that Francesca was probably just fine.

As the war intensified, Leonarda began to panic. She thought she should make another sacrifice. So far, so good; but how long did such protection last? The police had nosed around, but they hadn't suspected her of anything. Besides, the war was keeping them busy.

One of Leonarda's clients, Virginia Cacioppo, had once been a renowned soprano. Now fifty-three, Virginia came to Leonarda just a few weeks after Francesca's disappearance for help in finding employment. She would pay a handsome finder's fee. Like a spider awaiting an unsuspecting bug, Leonarda saw her advantage. The others had been easy because they'd been so vulnerable; this woman would be, too. She told Virginia that she knew of a job for her as the secretary of a wealthy man in Florence. Virginia was delighted. Making her promise to keep their arrangement secret, Leonarda gave her the same instructions on how to prepare.

Virginia agreed to everything. On September 30, she brought 50,000 lire and a handful of valuable gems with her. Leonarda accepted the payment and offered Virginia a glass of wine to see her on her way. Soon, Virginia's butchered remains went into the pot and her blood onto pans for hardening. Leonarda's shop suddenly had an abundance of candles, soap, and cakes.

However, she'd gotten greedy. The police were on the alert: three local women missing in such a short time frame seemed highly suspicious. And there was a witness. Virginia's sister-in-law, who lived nearby, had seen Virginia enter Cianciulli's house with a suitcase. This had seemed strange to her. She knew about the other two women supposedly leaving town, so she'd paid attention. She did not see Virginia come back out. When letters arrived a few days later to Virginia's friends and family, this woman suspected that something was wrong. The pattern was too similar to the others to be coincidence.

Time passed, and no one heard from Virginia again. This was highly uncharacteristic. Virginia's sister-in-law decided to tell what she'd seen to the local police. As impossible as it seemed, she suspected that the soap-making fortune-teller had done something evil.

The superintendent considered the situation: three women from the neighborhood had all disappeared in less than a year, all had written similar letters to friends and family, and all knew Leonarda Cianciulli. Yet she was a popular middle-aged woman. He could think of no motive for murder, let alone how a female could dispose of three bodies. Still, he had to investigate his only lead.

THE CAPTURE

The superintendent brought Leonarda in to the station. At first, she seemed confused, but they reassured her that they just had a few questions about what she might know. When she figured out that she was a suspect, she denied having a hand in the disappearances. The police suggested that her son might have been involved. Ploy or not, it hit a nerve. Everything Leonarda had done, she'd done for him. She had to keep protecting him, so she decided she had no other choice but to confess.

Leonarda provided the full gory details. She described her feats with pride, saying that Giuseppe's survival proved that she'd done the right thing. She was sure that otherwise he would be dead. Those who listened to her talk about how she'd murdered, dismembered, and boiled three adult women were stunned. Some of them remembered with distaste the chocolate cakes she'd served them. They could hardly believe that she'd admitted to eating them herself. This made her not just a murderess but also a cannibal.

At her trial in Reggio Emilia in June 1946, Leonarda's testament, titled "An Embittered Soul's Confessions," provided her official legal statement. A correspondent for *Time* magazine attended the proceedings and described how she had "gripped the witness-stand rail with oddly delicate hands and calmly set the prosecutor right on certain details. Her deep-set dark eyes gleamed with a wild inner pride as she concluded: 'I gave the copper ladle, which I used to skim the fat off the kettles, to my country, which was so badly in need of metal during the last days of the war.'"

She described in cold detail what she'd done with her friends. About Virginia Cacioppo, Italian sources quoted her: "She ended up in the pot, like the other two . . . her flesh was fat and white. When it had melted I added a bottle of cologne, and after a long time on the boil I was able to make some most acceptable creamy soap. I gave bars to neighbors and acquaintances. The cakes, too, were better: that woman was really sweet."

Cianciulli was diagnosed as "manic," which at the time meant that her behavior was at least partly compulsive but not necessarily psychotic. It bordered on delusional, however, given the strength of her superstitious beliefs. Perhaps the insecurity of her youth had created a form of separation anxiety or attachment disorder that made her not just willing to kill for her children but also to be creatively predatory on their behalf.

Despite her bizarre motive, Leonarda was found to be criminally responsible and received a sentence of thirty years in prison. On top of that, she was to serve three years in a criminal asylum in Pozzuoli—exactly as the palm reader had once foreseen in her right and left hands. She was in the asylum when she died from cerebral apoplexy on October 15, 1970, at the age of seventy-six.

THE TAKEAWAY

Name: Leonarda Cianciulli
Country: Italy
Born: April 18, 1894
Died: October 15, 1970
Killing Period: 1939–1940
Known Victims: 3
Date of Arrest: Probably late 1940

The case of Leonarda Cianciulli baffled everyone who heard about it: but, strangely enough, it was an American prison psychiatrist who had insight to offer. Dr. Hervey Cleckley had published a groundbreaking book, *The Mask of Sanity*, about different types of psychopaths. Cleckley had written about how he'd met some charming manipulators who seemed perfectly normal, but who had developed secret lives as con artists, predators, and killers. Among his cases were two females who had shown him how easily they'd duped people into believing that they were innocent of their crimes. Like Leonarda, psychopaths were affable, able to lie easily, self-centered, manipulative, exploitative, and devoid of remorse. They had the ability to plot against a friend or loved one even as they reassured this very person of their love and loyalty. They knew what to say but had no emotional commitment.

At that time, most mental-health professionals viewed psychopaths as male; it would be decades before anyone would study the traits and behaviors of female psychopaths. But Leonarda Cianciulli, the "soap-maker of Correggio," had shown that she was on the same level as remorseless males who committed hideous crimes. In fact, few of them went to the lengths she had gone to in dismembering, cooking, and consuming her victims. Even if she could justify the "sacrifices" for her son's protection, the dismemberments, the making of soap, and the drying of blood for flour made her an extreme criminal deviant. She stands apart from other predatory female psychopathic serial killers in that she killed female friends, cut them up with the weapons generally used by males, and turned them into food and other useful items.

23.

THE SON OF SAM

THE CRIMES

The 1970s jolted Americans with increasing reports of multiple-stranger killers. Right after the Manson murders of 1969, they learned about Juan Corona's murder of twenty-five migrants buried in mass graves in California, the twenty-seven "Candy Man" murders in Texas, Ted Bundy's cross-country killing spree, and the cryptic "BTK" murders in Kansas. Police in New York trapped sex worker killer Arthur Shawcross, and Californians witnessed the simultaneous multiple murders committed by Herbert Mullin and Edward Kemper in Santa Cruz. The FBI responded by developing its Behavioral Science Unit, staffed with "personality profilers" who studied these extreme offenders once they were caught.

New York City came under siege during the mid-1970s, starting with a rash of fires and false alarms. Then a teenage girl was stabbed on Christmas Eve 1975. Her attacker escaped—but he was just warming up.

Around 1:00 A.M. on July 29, 1976, in the Pelham Bay area of the Bronx, Donna Lauria, eighteen, and Jody Valenti, nineteen, sat talking in Valenti's car in front of Lauria's house on Buhre Avenue. As Lauria started to get out of the car, a man approached fast, on foot. He carried a paper bag from which he drew a pistol. He stopped, crouched, and braced his arm. Shooting, he hit Lauria, killing her instantly. Valenti bolted and took a non-fatal shot to the thigh. She heard another shot, which missed. The man hurried away. Valenti told police she did not know the man but described him as white, thirtyish, five-nine, weighing 160 pounds, with curly brown hair. Lauria's father, watching from the house, gave a similar description, adding that he'd seen this man in a compact yellow car. Other local residents had seen the car cruising the neighborhood that evening. No arrests were made.

That fall, a similar shooting occurred in Queens. On October 23, in a residential area of Flushing near Browne Park, Carl Denaro, twenty, sat in a parked car with Rosemary Keenan, who was two years younger. As they talked, the rear window shattered. Denaro drove away in a panic, initially unaware that he'd been shot in the head. While he received medical assistance a short time later, police examined the car. On the floor, they found a .44-caliber bullet. Keenan was unhurt, aside from cuts from flying glass, but her father was a twenty-year veteran of the NYPD. He insisted on an investigation, but nothing turned up to implicate a suspect. The couple had not seen the shooter.

Even with this second incident, New Yorkers were not yet worried and went about their business as usual. Then, on November 27, sixteen-year-old Donna DeMasi and eighteen-year-old Joanne Lomino were sitting on the porch of Lomino's home in Bellerose to chat, after returning home from a late movie. A man in military fatigues approached and asked them for directions. Before they could answer, he lifted a revolver and shot them. When they hit the ground, he shot them several more times. A neighbor rushed out, and the assailant fled. Both girls were rushed to the hospital and survived. The neighbor recalled that the shooter was blond.

At the end of January 1977, a similar incident occurred near the Long Island Rail Road train station in Forest Hills, Queens. Another couple sitting in a car, Christine Freund and her fiancé, John Diel, were preparing to drive to a dance hall when, at 12:40 A.M., gunshots shattered a window in the car. Diel drove away, but it was too late to save Christine: two of the three shots had hit her. Diel suffered superficial injuries. He hadn't seen the shooter, but the bullets were .44 caliber.

Police observed that the targeted women in these shootings almost all had dark brown hair. Composite sketches of the assailant released by the police suggested that at least two different shooters were involved, one blond and one dark-haired.

Five weeks later, on March 8, Virginia Voskerichian, nineteen, was walking home about a block from where Christine Freund had been shot, around 7:30 P.M. An armed man approached her, and she held up the book she was carrying as a shield. The bullet he fired penetrated it, killing her. A neighbor nearly collided with a dark-haired person he'd later describe as a clean-shaven teenager who was fleeing the scene. Another person described a chubby dark-haired man who had been loitering in the area. There were no witnesses to the shooting itself.

Two days later, the police held a press conference on the city's recent spate of shootings. They said the bullets forensically linked two of the incidents. The media dubbed the shooter "the .44 Caliber Killer."

On April 17, around 3:00 A.M., Alexander Esau, twenty, and Valentina Suriani, eighteen, sat in her car where she lived in the Bronx. Someone shot them, killing Suriani. Esau died in the hospital. There were no witness reports but, once again, the bullets were .44 caliber. Police also discovered a handwritten letter near the shooting scene. It was addressed to NYPD Captain Joseph Borrelli.

"I am deeply hurt by your calling me a wemon [sic] hater," the writer said. "I am not. But I am a monster. I am the 'Son of Sam.' I am a little 'brat.' When father Sam gets drunk he gets mean. He beats his family. Sometimes he ties me up to the back of the house. Other times he locks me in the garage. Sam loves to drink blood. 'Go out and kill' commands father Sam. Behind our house some rest. Mostly young—raped and slaughtered—their blood drained—just bones now. Papa Sam keeps me locked in the attic, too. I can't get out but I look out the attic window and watch the world go by. I feel like an outsider. I am on a different wave length then [sic] everybody else—programmed too [sic] kill. However, to stop me you must kill me."

The letter rambled on longer in this whiny manner, making threats and taunting the police. The writer also wished them a "Happy Easter." Police did not initially release the letter, but eventually let some of its contents out. Psychiatrists speculated that the shooter had paranoid schizophrenia and perhaps believed a demon possessed him. On May 30, *New York Daily News* columnist Jimmy Breslin received a bizarre Son of Sam letter that made references to ".44." He urged the shooter to turn himself in.

An atmosphere of terror pervaded New York City, because it seemed that this killer could strike at any time after dark, anywhere, and melt away. Many women with long dark hair cut it short or dyed it a different color, hoping to avoid becoming targets.

The shootings continued, however. On June 26, Sal Lupo, twenty, and Judy Placido, seventeen, sat in Lupo's car in Bayside, Queens. The shooter targeted them. Both survived with serious wounds. They had not seen the shooter, and witness reports conflicted.

A month went by, with the anniversary of the first shooting on everyone's mind. Nothing happened. Two days later, though, on July 31,

Stacy Moskowitz, twenty, was making out in a parked car with Robert Violante, also twenty, when a man approached the passenger side and fired four rounds. Moskowitz died, and Violante lost an eye.

That same night of July 31, traffic police had issued tickets to cars parked in violation of city ordinances. Among them was a yellow 1970 Ford Galaxie, parked near a hydrant. A woman told police on August 3 that she recalled seeing a dark-haired man approach this car on the night of the shooting, get in, and drive away fast. Police checked the tickets and found the name David Berkowitz, from Yonkers, associated with the ticketed car. They recalled that someone had reported seeing a yellow car near the first shootings the year before.

When officers went to Berkowitz's address at 35 Pine Street on August 10, they saw a semiautomatic rifle in plain view in his car. Searching the vehicle, they found crime-scene maps and a handwritten note that looked like the Son of Sam missive. Police were assigned to watch the building. Around 10 P.M., Berkowitz emerged and got into his car.

THE CAPTURE

The officers closed in on Berkowitz and placed him under arrest. He had a .44-caliber Bulldog revolver on his person. In his apartment, 7-E, officers found satanic graffiti on the walls, a scrapbook of news accounts of the crimes, and handwritten diaries that described numerous arsons over the past three years.

Berkowitz, twenty-four, pleaded guilty to eight shooting attacks. He'd killed six and wounded seven. When interrogated, he raised insanity issues by claiming that a former neighbor's black Labrador retriever had commanded him to kill. The neighbor's name was Sam Carr, and he'd been into the occult. Berkowitz claimed that the dog, possessed by an ancient demon, had demanded the blood of pretty young girls.

Despite his claims, three mental-health clinicians found Berkowitz competent to stand trial. His defense attorney still advised him to plead

FOUR OF THE SIX VICTIMS OF DAVID BERKOWITZ, THE "SON OF SAM." FROM LEFT TO RIGHT: VALENTINA SURIANI, CHRISTINE FREUND, VIRGINIA VOSKERICHIAN, AND STACY MOSKOWITZ.

not guilty by reason of insanity, but Berkowitz refused. On May 8, 1978, he accepted responsibility for the shootings and pleaded guilty. One month later, he received six consecutive sentences of 25-years-to-life, one for each murder.

In 1979, FBI Special Agents Robert Ressler and John Douglas interviewed Berkowitz as part of their prison interview program. Berkowitz refused to be tape-recorded but was willing to talk. When he mentioned the possessed dog, Ressler told him to knock it off because they didn't believe him. According to their accounts, he dropped the act.

Their research turned up the fact that Berkowitz had been adopted at a young age and had not adjusted well. He'd tortured the family pets as a child, savoring their slow deaths. When he'd finally located his birth mother, the experience was disappointing. He'd joined the Army and had disliked that experience. He'd contracted a venereal disease from a prostitute. He envied normal relationships but had been unable to have one himself. He acted out his anger at women first by setting fires, and then by stabbing or shooting young girls. Each incident, he admitted, had aroused him.

Berkowitz told the agents that he'd gone out stalking every night, but always waited until the circumstances looked right for getting away with it. Sometimes he revisited the scenes of earlier murders to relive the joy he'd felt. He said he'd followed media accounts of his crimes and had even gotten some ideas from reporters' speculations about where to strike next.

That same year, Berkowitz publicly admitted that his pretense of demonic possession had been a hoax. He merely wanted revenge on the world.

When he tried to sell his story, the New York State Legislature blocked him with the newly enacted "Son of Sam" law that prohibited offenders and their relatives from profiting financially from their crimes. Any money that could be earned potentially by a criminal due to the commission of a crime would first be used to compensate the victims and anyone who had a right to sue.

Berkowitz's case surfaced again some years later in response to cryptic references in one of the "Son of Sam" letters to "other individuals" who'd been involved in the shootings. They were supposedly part of a satanic group called the Process Church of the Final Judgment. Two of the members named were Michael and John Carr, aka "the Joker" and "the Duke of Death." Their father, Sam, was the owner of the so-called possessed dog. Journalist Maury Terry dug up evidence of an alleged conspiracy that connected not just Berkowitz's crimes to this group but also those of the Manson cult. Terry claimed that Berkowitz had acted as part of a consortium of people in a satanic conspiracy and said that the Carr brothers had died violently within two years of Berkowitz's arrest. One had had "666" painted on his hand.

The NYPD reexamined the cases and found nothing to support the claims of a satanic conspiracy.

In 1991, the U.S. Supreme Court struck down the "Son of Sam" law as overinclusive and unconstitutional, but New York revised the prohibition in 1992 to conform to the Constitution. After numerous revisions, New York adopted a new "Son of Sam" law in 2001 that additionally requires that crime victims be notified whenever a person convicted of a crime receives $10,000 or more.

THE TAKEAWAY

Name: born Richard David Falco; adopted and became David Berkowitz
Country: United States
Date of Birth: June 1, 1953
Date of Death: NA
Killing Period: 1976–1977
Known Victims: 6 killed, 7 wounded
Date of Arrest: August 10, 1977

Berkowitz had easily pretended to have a mental illness that he later professed had been fake. Yet some mental-health experts had accepted his claims as proof of a delusional condition. This case shows how easy it can be to find psychiatrists to testify, because clinical psychology and psychiatry are largely interpretive disciplines that generally accept client complaints without requiring evidence. The FBI profilers got Berkowitz to drop the act almost at once. Special Agent Ressler began using the phrase "serial killer" during this case. He thought of the incidents as being like TV serials he'd watched as a child. It became the standard term for referring to multiple killers of this type, distinguishing them from mass murderers.

24.

THE NIGHT STALKER

THE CRIMES

During the 1980s, anxiety over practicing satanists and evil conspiracies mounted in the United States, and narratives told by people in therapy about ritual abuse by secret satanic rings showed strikingly common elements. Some predators, too, adopted a devilish persona.

On April 10, 1984, the body of nine-year-old Mei Leung was found raped, battered, stabbed, and hanging from a pipe in the basement of a San Francisco residential hotel. There were no leads on her assailant, and the case went cold.

That June, seventy-nine-year-old Jennie Vincow was slain in her home in Glassell Park, California, near Los Angeles. Her throat was deeply slashed, and she had been stabbed several times. The killer had engaged in sexual activity with her body post-mortem. The killer left a fingerprint behind, but it did not help police to find him.

In February 1985, sisters Christina and Mary Caldwell, fifty-eight and seventy, respectively, were found stabbed to death in their home on Telegraph Hill in San Francisco. A similar fatal home invasion occurred that March. When Maria Hernandez (also called Angela Barrios on some lists) pulled into her garage in Rosemead, near Los Angeles, a man already inside the garage shot her. The bullet ricocheted off keys in the hand she raised to protect herself, knocking her out but not killing her. Hernandez's housemate, Dayle Okazaki, thirty-four, was not so lucky. The intruder entered their home and shot her in the head, killing her. He fled, but within an hour he pulled Tsai-Lian Yu, thirty, from her car and shot her twice, fatally. The recovering Hernandez described the black-clad Hispanic assailant to police as having curly hair, bulging eyes, and rotted teeth. The media dubbed him the "Valley Intruder" and the "Walk-in Killer."

In March of that year, the Valley Intruder entered a home in Whittier that he had previously burglarized. He saw Vincent Zazzara, sixty-four, asleep on the couch and shot him in the head before entering the bedroom to find Zazzara's wife, Maxine, forty-four. He beat and bound her before ransacking the room for items to steal. Maxine freed herself and grabbed a shotgun. The intruder fatally shot her and carved up her body post-mortem, leaving a "T" on her left breast. He also gouged out her eyes. When police came, they discovered shoeprints in the garden from Avia sneakers. Bullet casings linked this double homicide to the earlier fatal home invasions in nearby towns.

In May, the intruder entered the home of Harold and Jean Wu, sixty-five and fifty-six, respectively, shot and killed Harold, and raped Jean. Later that month, in Monrovia, the killer brutalized eighty-three-year-old Malvial Keller and her invalid sister, eighty-year-old Blanche

Wolfe: he bound and battered both with a hammer, shocked Keller with a live electrical cord, and raped Wolfe. Afterward, he drew a pentagram in lipstick on Wolfe's thigh, and then on the walls of each bedroom. This became part of the killer's MO. Wolfe survived the attack, but Keller died from her injuries.

The next day, the Valley Intruder went to Burbank. He bound Ruth Wilson and her eleven-year-old son and sodomized Wilson before he left. Her description to police of her assailant matched what other witnesses had seen.

People in the affected neighborhoods were terrified that their homes were no longer safe; the killer seemed to get in even when homes were locked. During that summer, he bludgeoned, stabbed, strangled, and shot several more people around the Los Angeles area. In one home, a print from the Avia sneaker was left on the victim's face. Another surviving victim said the smelly man with the rotting teeth had told her to "swear on Satan." He hacked the Kniedings, a couple in Glendale, both in their sixties, with a machete before and after they died. He shot the Petersons in Northridge on August 6, but both survived to give a description.

On August 8, the Valley Intruder killed Ahmed Zia, thirty-one, instantly in his bedroom, then bound and beat his wife, Suu Kyi. After forcing her to reveal where she kept her valuable jewelry, he sodomized her, then tied up her three-year-old son, who had wandered into the room. The intruder left them alive, and Suu Kyi untied her son and sent him to get help.

Media coverage pressuring police to catch the killer now was fierce. No one could predict where he would strike next. Many people bought guns, guard dogs, and stronger locks for their homes.

Ten days after the last home invasion in Los Angeles, the killer appeared to go north to San Francisco. On August 18, 1985, a man entered the home of Peter and Barbara Pan. He shot Peter, sixty-six, in the head before he beat, raped, and shot Barbara, sixty-two. As in many of the Los Angeles incidents, the killer used a strategy of dispatching the males with a quick shot so he could focus unhindered on the females in the home. Once again, he drew a pentagram on the bedroom wall, along with the phrase "Jack the Knife."

Ballistic comparisons and shoeprint impressions confirmed that the Valley Intruder was now in the San Francisco area. When Mayor Diane Feinstein revealed that the killer wore Avia shoes, the police cringed. They knew that if he followed the news, he could easily toss away crucial forensic evidence. He'd also now know that he'd gained a new moniker: The Night Stalker.

Just six days later, he was back in southern California. This time, police caught a break. On August 24, the Night Stalker broke into the Mission Viejo home of thirty-year-old Bill Carns. He shot Carns three times in the head before turning his attention to Carns's fiancée, Inez Erickson. He insisted that she swear allegiance to Satan while beating her with his fists. Then he dragged her to another room to sexually assault her and take what money and jewelry he could find. Before he left, he said, "Tell them the Night Stalker was here." Erickson dragged herself to the window and saw the orange station wagon in which he drove away. She freed herself and got help for Carns, who, miraculously, survived.

Earlier that evening, a thirteen-year-old boy saw the intruder, too, and wrote down the Toyota's license plate number. With the license number and witness descriptions, police located the abandoned Toyota two days later and were able to lift a fingerprint from it. It identified Richard Muñoz Ramirez, a twenty-five-year-old drifter from Texas with arrests for traffic and illegal drug violations. Police released his mug shot from earlier crimes to the media, giving the "Night Stalker" a face. They also discovered that Ramirez was a practicing Satanist whose favorite song was *Night Prowler*.

THE CAPTURE

On August 30, Ramirez's picture was widely publicized in every major California newspaper. That day, he was on a bus to Arizona, so he missed the news. He returned early on August 31, walking right past officers and into a convenience store in East Los Angeles. He noticed a group of elderly Mexican women looking at him and saying, "El Matador" (the Killer). Then he saw his face on the front page of the newspaper. He fled across the Santa Ana Freeway and tried to carjack a woman, but bystanders chased him away. A mob pursued him as he hopped over fences and tried to force other drivers to let him into their cars. Police went into action, sending a helicopter to track him. Ramirez's pursuers finally caught him and grabbed and beat him with a metal bar. The police arrived in time to save him.

Sergeant George Thomas recorded Ramirez saying, "Of course I did it. So what? Shoot me. I deserve to die." Then he hummed the *Night Prowler* tune. He told someone else that he was a minion of Satan sent to commit his dirty work.

At a preliminary hearing, Ramirez maintained this theme. He praised Satan and flashed a pentagram tattooed on the palm of his hand. He was charged with thirteen murders and thirty-one other felonies related to his crime spree. Court-appointed lawyers warned him that he could get the death sentence. "I'll be in hell, then," he retorted, "with Satan."

Ramirez disliked his two public defenders, so the Ramirez family retained Daniel and Arturo Hernandez (not related). They had never before tried a death-penalty case, and their method was to introduce an exhausting round of delays, from appeals to out-of-town interviews and absences from court. Ramirez sat through most of his hearings, slouching in his chair, drumming his fingers on the table, and bobbing his head as if listening to rock music. He seemed oblivious to the seriousness of the charges.

In March, San Francisco authorities had tentatively linked Ramirez to four homicides, a rape, and ten burglaries, but since they had no physical evidence in most of those crimes, they'd narrowed their focus to the murder of Peter Pan and the attempted murder of his wife.

Impatient with defense motions for delays, Los Angeles County prosecutor Phil Halpin finalized his case and filed the charges. He claimed he had nearly a thousand potential witnesses and hundreds of thousands of pages of statements, reports, and photographs. He projected a two-year trial, admitting that it was one of the "most complicated criminal cases" he'd seen.

On July 21, 1988, jury selection began. Three weeks into it, the *Los Angeles Times* reported that jail employees had overheard a plan by Ramirez to shoot and kill the prosecutor with a gun that someone was going to slip him in the courtroom. The court installed a metal detector.

The trial began with Halpin's two-hour opening statement on January 30, 1989. He intended to introduce at least four hundred exhibits, including fingerprints, ballistics evidence, and shoe impressions. On that same day, the *Times* reported that Ramirez had referred to himself as a "super criminal," claiming he loved to kill and had murdered twenty people. "I love all that blood," a sheriff's deputy claimed he said.

On April 14, after interviewing 137 witnesses and presenting 521 exhibits, the prosecution rested its case. It was soon evident that the defense strategy would be to discredit the eight eyewitnesses—including the assault survivors. This risked alienating the jury. Another hurdle the defense team faced was the linkage via pentagrams. Ramirez had even drawn one in his cell. This behavioral evidence was nearly as unique as his fingerprint.

The defense team claimed that each item of the prosecution's evidence was inconclusive or defective. In a surprise move, they had Ramirez's father provide an alibi for his son by saying he had been in El Paso during two of the attacks. The defense attorneys also found testimony to the effect that police officers had covertly alerted witnesses to Ramirez's position in the lineup after his arrest.

Psychologist Elizabeth Loftus, an expert in eyewitness testimony from the University of Washington, testified that the stress of assault might have affected the witnesses' ability to accurately recall details. She also pointed out that errors are more likely when the attacker and victim are of different races. Yet she conceded under cross-examination that those victims who'd had more than a fleeting exposure to Ramirez were more likely to be accurate.

Rebuttal witnesses for the prosecution contradicted Ramirez's father by showing that Ramirez was in fact in Los Angeles, having dental work done, at the time that his father placed him in El Paso. A comparison of Ramirez's teeth to the dentist's charts left no doubt, although Ramirez had used an alias when getting this work done.

After nearly a year, the jury started deliberations with 8,000 pages of trial transcripts and 655 exhibits to consider. Ramirez had flirted with a responsive female juror, hoping to trigger a hung jury. On September 20, almost two months after they'd begun, the jury announced that they'd reached a unanimous decision. On each count, they'd voted guilty and affirmed nineteen "special circumstances" that made Ramirez eligible for the death penalty. He seemed shocked that his "special" juror had turned on him. (She mouthed, "I'm sorry" to him.)

On October 3, 1989, the jury announced that they'd voted for death for Ramirez. He smiled. "Big deal," he said. "Death always went with the territory." As he was led in shackles back to the county jail, he added, for reporters, "I'll see you in Disneyland."

On November 9, Ramirez was officially sentenced to death nineteen times. He chatted with his attorneys throughout. Afterward, he added to his dark image with his rather incomprehensible speech to the court, which went, in part: "You do not understand me. I do not expect you to. You are not capable of it. I am beyond your experience. I am beyond good and evil. Legions of the night, night breed, repeat not the errors of night prowler and show no mercy. I will be avenged. Lucifer dwells within us all." As he was led away to eventually join the 262 inmates already on death row in San Quentin, he flashed his two-fingered devil symbol.

In 2009, DNA analysis results implicated Ramirez in the 1984 murder of the child Mei Leung, adding one more killing to his toll.

Ramirez married Doreen Lioy while in prison and died from B-cell lymphoma on June 7, 2013, at the age of fifty-three.

THE TAKEAWAY

Name: Ricardo Leyva Muñoz Ramirez
Country: United States
Date of Birth: February 29, 1960
Date of Death: June 7, 2013
Killing Period: April 10, 1984–August 24, 1985
Known Victims: 14; 5 attempted murders
Date of Arrest: August 31, 1985

Ramirez was born in El Paso, Texas, in 1960, the youngest of five children. He was a quiet boy, with hard-working parents, but his father had a temper and sometimes beat the kids. An abusive parent can often be a bad model for a child, especially a boy watching his father. Add to this some alleged abuse from a male teacher, and Richard had two role models who'd demonstrated how to use others for their own frustrated ends.

Most significant was the impact of his cousin, Mike Ramirez, who'd fought in Vietnam as a Green Beret. Mike liked to show twelve-year-old Richard his Polaroid photos of the butchered dead and of himself raping and murdering Vietnamese women. Mike said that killing made him feel like a god. Together, they smoked marijuana and talked about this brutality. When certain images become associated with physical excitement and intrigue during early sexual development, as they seem to have done for Ramirez, they can become eroticized. Fantasies that joined sex with a violent death seem to have yielded feelings of power for the nascent Night Stalker.

Young Richard also witnessed a murder: One day, Mike got into a fight with his wife. In front of Richard, he drew a revolver and shot her. He ordered Richard to leave. When Richard reentered the house with his father after the body had been removed, he smelled the blood and felt a connection with the dead that he later said bordered on the mystical.

When he moved to California at the age of eighteen, Ramirez was attracted to the Church of Satan because it appealed to various aspects of his temperament: it was religious, dark, and violent. Being a Satanist erased the feelings of insecurity and weakness he'd felt as a boy. It also played into his sense of being a marginalized loner.

Ramirez's Night Stalker's persona developed early, rising out of his abuse, his feminine appearance, and his yearning for power. Death and blood fascinated him. Burglary came easy, and soon he used his home-invasion skills for feeding his need to inflict pain on women. Media reports and a sinister nickname, the Night Stalker, only enhanced his belief that he was Satan's special agent.

25.

THE MAN-EATER

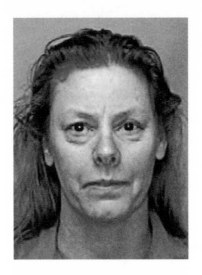

THE CRIMES

In December 1989, an abandoned car with bloodstained seats was found not far from the city of Ormond Beach in Volusia County, Florida. Papers indicated that the car belonged to a Clearwater electronics shop owner, Richard Mallory, who was known to pick up prostitutes, and there were indications that the fifty-one-year-old had enjoyed some drinks in the car with a companion, but as of now he was missing. Within two weeks, Mallory's corpse was found in the woods, under a rug. He'd been shot four times in the chest with a .22-caliber weapon. Personal items and money were missing.

In May 1990, a truck registered to David Spears, a forty-three-year-old construction worker from Winter Garden, Florida, was found along a Florida highway in Marion County. He was missing. His nude corpse was discovered on June 1 about sixty miles away, north of Tampa. He'd been shot six times in the chest with a .22. A single strand of blond hair found at the scene indicated that he'd been with a woman.

Five days later, another male corpse was found in Pasco County, also shot with a .22. The pathologist removed nine bullets. This victim was Charles Carskaddon, forty-one, a part-time rodeo worker. His killer had abandoned his car about sixty miles away in Marion County.

In June, Peter Siems, a sixty-five-year-old missionary, left Jupiter, Florida, to travel to New Jersey. He didn't make it. His wrecked silver Sunbird was found in Orange Springs, Marion County on July 4. A witness had seen two women leave the car and remove the license plates. They'd run into the woods. Siems remained missing. Police lifted a palm print from the car's door handle and distributed composite sketches of suspects drawn from witness accounts.

Sausage salesman Tony Burress went missing on July 30. His body was found in the woods along State Road 19 in Marion County on August 4. He'd been shot twice. Then the corpse of Florida state child abuse investigator Charles Humphrey, fifty-six, was found in the woods not far away on September 12. He was also a former police chief and major in the Air Force. He'd been shot six times in the head and torso, and his car was found a week later in Suwanee County. About $300 of his money was missing.

Two months later, sixty-year-old security guard Walter Jeno Antonio also went missing. His nude body turned up on a remote unfinished road in Dixie County on November 18. His car was found in Brevard County. He'd been shot in the back four times.

Since the bodies all were found in different counties, no links were established initially between the murders, even though the victims' cars mostly were abandoned in Marion County. Finally, police spotted the pattern and a task force was formed with representatives from each county involved. The composite pictures were publicized and leads came in.

Police followed what they knew from the Siems case, although Siems himself remained missing. Witnesses identified two women leaving the scene of the Sunbird's crash as Tyria Moore and her companion, "Lee." Police had found items in a pawnshop related to some of the victims, which yielded fingerprints that matched those they'd found in some of the cars. One set belonged to Aileen Wuornos, who had a record in Florida for numerous crimes. She was "Lee." It was just a matter of locating her, which wasn't difficult. She liked to hang out in The Last Resort, a biker bar. Police found her there and arrested her on a parole violation. They used a key in her possession to enter a storage space, where they found items belonging to some of the victims.

THE CAPTURE

Other detectives located Wuornos's girlfriend, Tyria Moore, in Scranton, Pennsylvania, and threatened her with prosecution as an accomplice unless she cooperated. She said Wuornos was the killer and agreed to try to get a confession from her on tape. With police guidance, she made calls to Wuornos, pleading for help to clear her name, since she had not participated in any murders. On January 16, 1991, Wuornos finally said what the police were waiting for. She had killed seven men. She described how she'd wrestled with Mallory before she shot him, and said, "I just kept shooting him." After describing what she'd done with the others, Wuornos said she'd confessed because she wanted to "get right with God."

She revealed where she'd tossed the murder weapon, but she did not know exactly where Siems's body was. She'd dumped it somewhere in Georgia. When Wuornos learned that one man she'd killed had been a missionary, she reportedly professed remorse, but she still insisted that all of her murders had been committed in self-defense. She'd been hitchhiking, and they'd picked her up and propositioned her. When they'd gotten violent, she'd shot them.

During her interviews, Wuornos offered many different narratives about why she'd killed the men. It was never clear from evidence which story to believe. She said she'd planned to kill at least twelve men, which sounded predatory, but then she would insist she'd only been defending herself.

On January 14, 1992, Wuornos went on trial for Mallory's murder. She claimed that Mallory had tied her to the steering wheel, tortured her, and sodomized her. After she shot him in self-defense, she'd covered him with a carpet to protect him from birds.

The prosecutor did not believe her. He thought she'd lured men with the possibility of sex, and then killed them for their money and possessions. His star witness was Tyria Moore, who'd known about the murders but had told detectives nothing about rape or self-defense. She didn't corroborate Wuornos's account.

AILEEN WUORMOS WAS ARRESTED AT THE LAST RESORT, A BIKER BAR IN PORT ORANGE, FLORIDA, IN 1991 FOR THE SERIAL MURDERS OF SEVEN MEN.

"I'm the victim as far as I'm concerned!" Wuornos shouted.

The defense psychologist, Elizabeth McMahon, backed her up, explaining that her background had made her paranoid about men, as well as highly reactive.

According to the story Wuornos told to psychologists, her mother had abandoned her as an infant, and her schizophrenic father had been imprisoned for the rape of a seven-year-old. Suspected of murder, he'd hanged himself in his cell. Aileen and her brother had been forced to live with her maternal grandparents (who she had believed were her parents until she was eleven), and her grandfather had been an abusive alcoholic. He'd frequently beaten her and called her a whore. When a friend of his (she said) impregnated her in Troy, Michigan, when she was fourteen, she'd been forced to have the baby boy and give it up for adoption. Soon thereafter, she'd dropped out of school. When her grandmother died, her grandfather had kicked her out, so she'd started turning tricks to survive.

As a girl, Wuornos had developed an explosive temper. When she was nine, she'd set the family home on fire. She also became a thief. Her IQ during adolescence tested at 81, significantly below average. She'd started drinking at twelve and had frequently run away. She'd attempted suicide six times between the ages of fourteen and twenty-two. She'd collected arrests in three states for a wide variety of crimes, and had gone through many short-term relationships. She'd given and received plenty of abuse.

At the age of seventeen, Wuornos had hitchhiked to Denver, and then to Florida. When she was twenty, she'd married a sixty-nine-year-old man, remaining married just over a month. She'd indulged in alcohol and overspent her husband's money. When she grew violent, he obtained a restraining order and then a divorce. She'd continued to commit crimes, and served time for armed robbery.

Then she met Tyria Moore, and they'd become sexually involved. Wuornos had continued to sell herself to men to make money. She also acquired a gun. After killing Mallory, she'd waited five months before killing her next victim. The defense psychologist believed that Mallory had done something significant to her that had triggered the killing spree. Binding and sodomizing her was a credible narrative.

Wuornos's MO had been to stand by the side of the road, looking for a ride. Once picked up, she'd offer sexual services, then suggest a secluded place. She'd get the man to undress, making him vulnerable. She might have initiated minimal sexual contact before grabbing her gun to shoot him. Sometimes she yelled, "I knew you were going to rape me!" She'd take the man's money and his car, abandoning it elsewhere before joining Moore for a beer.

The jury wasn't impressed with the sob story of this "exit-to-exit" hooker who cleared $200 a day, which wasn't bad money in 1990. They thought Wuornos had given them little reason to feel sorry for her. She'd had a rough life, yes, but that was no reason to kill. It seemed more likely that she'd killed the men just to steal from them, and perhaps to retaliate just because they were men.

On January 28, 1992, the jury recommended the death penalty. Wuornos called them the "scumbags of America." She got the death sentence.

In March, Wuornos pleaded no contest to three more of the murders and received three more death sentences, yet she still insisted that Mallory had violently raped her. Another plea in June got her a fifth death sentence. Evidence that Mallory had been convicted for sex offenses offered hope of a retrial, but it didn't work out; so in February 1993, Wuornos pleaded guilty to the murder of Walter Jeno Antonio, her final victim. She was not charged for Siems's murder, because his body was never found.

In a 2001 petition to Florida's Supreme Court, Wuornos said she wanted to dismiss her legal counsel and terminate all appeals. "I killed those men," she wrote, "robbed them as cold as ice. And I'd do it again, too. There's no chance in keeping me alive or anything, because I'd kill again. I have hate crawling through my system . . . I'm competent, sane, and I'm trying to tell the truth." Nevertheless, she also expressed that she felt railroaded. Her story changed with her moods.

Forensic psychiatrist Wade Myers, an expert on homicide, interviewed Wuornos shortly before she was scheduled for execution. With Drs. Reid Meloy and Erik Gooch, he evaluated Wuornos's testimony and her Department of Corrections case files with the twenty-item Psychopathy Checklist-Revised (PCL-R), the instrument used to diagnose someone as a psychopath. They knew that male psychopathy appeared in about 1 percent of males but was found to a lesser extent in females. Even then, it rarely showed as violent or predatory aggression.

Wuornos received a score of 32, placing her in the checklist's psychopathic range of 30 to 40, and in the 97th percentile for American female offenders. She also met the criteria from the *Diagnostic and Statistical Manual-IV-TR* for antisocial and borderline personality disorders. She showed emotional instability, behavioral unpredictability, aggressiveness, and rage. She'd blamed others and felt no remorse for her treatment of her victims (aside from a passing regret over the missionary). Her childhood traumas had likely exacerbated her psychopathic temperament, raising the probability of violent criminal behavior. She denied gaining sexual satisfaction from murder, but seemed to have achieved a sense of power and symbolic payback against males. Despite her statements, the experts thought her crimes had been gratifying and possibly erotic. Thus, they categorized her as a sexually motivated serial killer.

Wuornos was executed in the electric chair on October 9, 2002, at the Broward Correctional Institution.

THE TAKEAWAY

Name: Aileen Carol Wuornos
Country: United States
Date of Birth: February 29, 1956
Date of Death: October 9, 2002
Killing Period: 1989–1990
Known Victims: 7
Date of Arrest: January 1, 1991

When the study of serial killers became more formalized during the 1980s, it was assumed that such criminal acts were largely a male phenomenon. Females account for only 10–12 percent of serial killers. Predatory female serial killers outside of a healthcare setting who target strangers for self-empowerment are among the rarest types. Most kill for money, with poison as the most common method. Wuornos was therefore somewhat unique. Some criminologists call her a greed killer; others say she was a sexual predator. She appears to have been both.

Female serial offenders differ from their male counterparts in having a more complex crime pattern. They have more motives and go unsuspected for longer periods before arrest. For them, murder is not generally addictive. They're often stealthy and show an ability to camouflage their actions in crafty ways.

Although Wuornos has been called America's first female serial killer, that's not quite accurate. However, she is among the few females who have acted like a true predator, targeting strangers by exploiting their expectations and by using a gun to kill them. Her abusive background probably contributed to her violence. Her male victims were symbolic, presenting an opportunity for her to retaliate against the wrongs she believed had been perpetrated on her by men throughout her life.

26.

THE MILWAUKEE MONSTER

THE CRIMES

Young males began disappearing in Milwaukee, Wisconsin, between 1987 and 1991. A local man was enticing them, usually with an offer of money, before drugging them to kill them. The person responsible had gotten his start a decade earlier in a small town in Ohio. Getting away with his first murder had emboldened him to do it again.

Jeffrey Dahmer had long fantasized about having power over an attractive male. After killing several men in the basement apartment of his grandmother's house in West Allis, Wisconsin (a suburb of Milwaukee), where he was living, Dahmer got his own place, number 213 at the Oxford Apartments in Milwaukee. Here in this one-bedroom apartment, he killed again; but soon he began to experiment. Having learned that corpses decompose quickly, he thought it might be better to keep his victims alive in a zombie-like state, depriving them of all memory of their lives and homes. He knew this would require damaging their frontal lobes. When they fell unconscious from the drug-laced drinks he served them, Dahmer drilled holes into their skulls to inject boiling water or acid into their brains. Not surprisingly, these experiments failed in the end, but some of his victims remained alive for a few days.

In May 1991, for example, Konerak Sinthasomphone, fourteen, was at a local mall when Dahmer enticed him into his apartment to pose for photos, drugged him, and drilled a hole for acid injection. Konerak seemed docile, so at 1:30 A.M. Dahmer left to get a beer. Konerak, dazed, went out naked into the street. Three women encountered him just as Dahmer returned. They saw that the boy struggled against Dahmer, so they tried to get the police to intervene. When Dahmer persuaded them that Konerak was his lover, the police let him take the boy back home, despite the fact that he was clearly underage. They even went inside, but failed to check on the odor in the apartment (which came from the decomposing corpse of another victim). After the police left, Dahmer strangled Konerak, cut him up, and placed his remains in a vat of acid.

Konerak was one of seventeen boys and men that Dahmer murdered. He fried and tasted the muscles of one, took photographs of most in post-mortem poses, and designed an altar to be made from their skulls and bones.

Most of his victims were in their teens and twenties, but Tracy Edwards was thirty-two—around the same age as Dahmer (who was thirty-one). Dahmer later said that he met Edwards near the local mall on July 22, 1991, and offered money in exchange for taking photos of him. Edwards said that Dahmer had invited him and his friends to a party. In any event, Edwards went to apartment 213 at 924 North 25th Street alone that night. Dahmer was showing one of the movies in the *Exorcist* series, and they watched it together for a while. At some point, Dahmer got a large butcher knife and threatened Edwards with it. Edwards tried to keep him calm. Dahmer slapped a handcuff on him and pulled a skull from a cabinet, telling Edwards that he would end up there too. He also said he'd eat Edwards's heart and organs. Edwards managed to fight off Dahmer and flee the apartment.

THE CAPTURE

It was near the end of the afternoon shift for two patrol officers in Milwaukee as they were driving through the crime-ridden area when they first saw Tracy Edwards. As he approached them, they saw a pair of handcuffs dangling from one wrist. He needed a key, he said. He'd been with a "weird dude" who'd threatened to kill him. They thought Edwards was high on something, but he insisted that they check it out. Inside, he said, they'd find a knife, photos of dismembered men, and a homicidal lunatic. The cops asked him to show them where this incident had occurred, so he led them back to the three-story Oxford Apartments.

The police knocked on the door of Apartment 213 and Dahmer answered. He looked and smelled as if he'd been drinking, but he seemed calm and unintimidating. They asked for the key to the handcuffs on Edwards and hoped to get the incident resolved. Dahmer said the key was in his bedroom, but Edwards warned the officers that Dahmer had a knife in there. Officer Rolf Mueller went into the bedroom alone while his partner detained Dahmer. When Mueller saw Polaroid photos of skulls and dismembered men in an open drawer, he placed Dahmer under arrest. After initial resistance, Dahmer surrendered. When Mueller found a head in the refrigerator, he knew they had a serious problem. He called in backup and a crime-scene unit to search the one-bedroom apartment. The smell alone told him they were in for a long night. Another team took Dahmer to headquarters.

A detailed search revealed severed heads and human hearts in the kitchen, painted or bleached skulls in a closet, and an arm muscle wrapped in a plastic bag. An entire male torso took up most of the stand-alone freezer, along with some heads and a bag of frozen organs. Dahmer had assembled two human skeletons and collected a scalp and several preserved hands and penises. He'd been in the process of dissolving more torsos in barrels of acid. Police collected seventy-four Polaroid pictures that showed dismembered men. In cupboards and drawers, they turned up chloroform, bleach, electric saws, an electric drill, rope, and formaldehyde. They would eventually find extensive dried bloodstains under the carpet.

Investigators found the remains of what they estimated to be eleven different men. They could hardly believe that Wisconsin had yet another serial killer who dismembered people and kept their body parts. Ed Gein's two murders had horrified the state in the 1950s, but he had not been nearly as prolific a killer as Dahmer. No other American serial killer they'd heard of had kept body parts to this degree.

Two officers had been in the apartment just weeks earlier to check on a complaint, but they'd apparently decided that the noxious odor of decomposition that often permeated the building was from the neighborhood trash buildup. Neighbors had grumbled about this smell for years, along with the sound of a power saw in this apartment. However, the landlord and police had ignored them.

As Dahmer was taken to headquarters, he confessed that officers would find the remains of numerous men. He knew he'd been caught dead to rights with bodies, so there was no getting out of it. Although serial killers who confess quickly have different motives, from bragging to getting full "credit" for everything they've done, they rarely do it to clear their conscience. Sometimes they just enjoy the attention they get from law enforcement. As soon as he arrived at the police station, Dahmer provided details about victims and what he'd done to them.

He smoked cigarettes, drank coffee, and talked easily for six hours. He didn't recall all the names, but he knew the dates and circumstances for each incident. He admitted to some experiments with cannibalism, but he had not enjoyed it. He said he'd killed these men because he'd wanted to be with them, to bond. Keeping the skulls had been his way of keeping them close.

His complete confession would eventually fill 160 pages. He'd been just eighteen in 1978 when he killed for the first time. When his estranged parents abandoned the family home in Medina, Ohio, in 1978 to go their separate ways, Dahmer had brought home a hitchhiker, nineteen-year-old Steve Hicks. They hung out and drank beer. But when Hicks wanted to leave, Dahmer bludgeoned him with a barbell. According to his account, seeing the man unconscious had given him the same rush as the pornographic pictures in gay magazines that had teased him for years, so he strangled Hicks to make sure he was dead. Dahmer wanted to keep the body. In the isolation of his house in the woods, he had the complete control that he'd long envisioned. Recalling how he'd enjoyed cutting up roadkill when young, he worked on the body in the same way, feeling aroused as he removed the head and limbs. Dahmer had buried most of the pieces in the back yard and smashed some of the bones with a sledgehammer.

Years passed before he tried something like that again. In his confession, he said that in the months leading up to his arrest, he'd been consumed by the need to kill. He claimed that he'd designed an altar to be made from skulls and bones, which he hoped to build after he'd killed enough men to make it into a medium for channeling supernatural powers. He offered a drawing to illustrate what he'd had in mind. He usually lured victims from local gay bars, he said, with the promise to pay them for posing for photos. They came willingly to his lair. Once back in his apartment, he'd typically given them a drink spiked with drugs that knocked them out.

Dahmer became like a specimen. Everyone wanted to know how someone could develop such predilections. Fantasy was one thing, and being aroused by the dead was not unique to him; but acting it out repeatedly was another matter. His childhood came under scrutiny. The older of two brothers, Dahmer had been shy and awkward. It was natural for him to fantasize about ways to gain status and feel more powerful. Being gay made things hard for him, but he found ways to secretly indulge his appreciation for the male body. Pornography appealed to him, and he imagined having an unconscious nude male under his complete control. It did not help that his parents' marriage had gone sour and the home was filled with tension and rancor. Young Jeffrey found solace in alcohol, letting his father believe that his drunken stupors were just self-indulgent daydreaming.

When his parents left the family home in 1978 to go their separate ways, Dahmer gained the opportunity to act out his fantasies. That's when he spotted Steve Hicks.

Years later, while living with his grandmother, Dahmer attended the funeral of a young man and made plans to dig up the corpse. This time, he thought, he could have a body without hurting anyone. Thwarted in this effort, he picked up men in bars or at the mall. He killed one man, Steven Tuomi, in a hotel room in 1987, but later claimed he had no memory of the incident, aside from heavy drinking; he only knew that when he woke up, Tuomi was dead. Then Dahmer brought men home to the apartment in his grandmother's basement. After killing and dismembering them, he packaged the parts in plastic for dumping into the trash. He used her sledgehammer to crush the bones. Twice his grandmother complained to his father about the odor in the garbage, but Jeffrey had always convinced Lionel that the smell came from his experiments with chicken parts from a grocery store.

"I allowed myself to believe Jeff," Lionel later mused in *A Father's Story*, "to accept all his answers regardless of how implausible they might seem. . . . More than anything, I allowed myself to believe that there was a line in Jeff, a line he wouldn't cross. . . . My life became an exercise in avoidance and denial."

It's easy to blame parents when such cases turn up, but most parents prefer the most benign explanation for their child's odd or aberrant behavior as just a phase. They hope the child will eventually outgrow it and become a normal adult. Understandably, they see what they want to see. At one point, when Jeffrey was charged with child molestation, Lionel believed Jeffrey's lie that he'd "touched" the boy by accident. He fell into a habit of accepting his son's version of events.

Finally, Jeffrey persuaded his father to help him get his own apartment. There, he was able to operate freely, without the threat of discovery. He killed several men before he started thinking about how he might keep them alive as mindless companions that would obey him without question. He wanted a sex slave who would never leave him. Although he was careless at times, allowing victims to get out and outsiders who might notice the smell of the decaying bodies to come in, he became skilled at deflection and deception.

Because Dahmer pleaded guilty, there was only a sentencing hearing in which his attorneys attempted to show that his deviance amounted to insanity—that he did not understand that his acts were wrong or that he could not control his compulsions. Tracy Edwards, still traumatized, testified. He described how Dahmer had offered him a drink and had then seemed to change into someone else—a terrifying monster determined to kill him. Edwards struggled to put his ordeal into words.

Dahmer's father, helpless with grief and horror, suggested that a neighbor had molested Dahmer when he was eight, but Dahmer denied it. He could achieve an erection, he claimed, only if his sexual partner was immobile, and he'd found the heat arising from a dismembered body highly pleasurable. He said he'd consumed some body parts so the victims could return to life through him. He'd had sex with the bodies and enjoyed

THE MILWAUKEE POLICE LOADING A REFRIGERATOR IN WHICH JEFFREY DAHMER STORED THE REMAINS OF SOME OF HIS VICTIMS.

having them close, and when he finally disposed of them, he felt he'd lost something. Alcohol had helped him to block out any sense of this being evil or wrong. "If I knew the true, real reasons why all this started, before it ever did," Dahmer said, "I probably wouldn't have done any of it."

On February 15, 1992, Dahmer was found guilty of fifteen counts of first-degree murder and sentenced to fifteen life terms. In May, in Ohio, he received one more sentence for the murder of Steve Hicks. The remains of a seventeenth victim, Steven Tuomi, were never found. Dahmer's memory of this murder was blank, although he recalled drinking with Tuomi and waking up to find him dead. Since Dahmer could not be linked to the still-missing man, let alone to his murder, no charges could be brought.

During his incarceration in the Columbia Correctional Institute, Dahmer found religion and asked to be baptized. He debated biblical passages with a minister who was eager to be his friend, and he manipulated prison groupies who corresponded with him.

On November 28, 1994, inmate Christopher Scarver entered the shower area that Dahmer and another inmate were cleaning and used the bar from a barbell (similar to what Dahmer had used on Steve Hicks) to bash in Dahmer's skull. He died quickly right afterward.

At the autopsy, Dahmer's brain was removed and kept locked up at the University of Wisconsin Medical School. Several researchers who requested tissue samples for analysis were blocked by the requirement for a court order. Joyce Flint, Dahmer's mother, had hoped to donate his brain to science, but Jeffrey had asked to be cremated, so Lionel blocked the request, and the brain was cremated.

THE TAKEAWAY
Name: Jeffrey Lionel Dahmer
Country: United States
Born: May 21, 1960
Died: November 28, 1994
Killing Period: 1978–1991
Known Victims: 17
Date of Arrest: July 22, 1991

Dahmer pleaded guilty, and his attorney conceded that he'd killed all these men. The attorney used Dahmer's unspeakable acts to insist that he be found insane and sent to a forensic hospital. The sentencing hearing became a battle of mental-health experts.

For the defense, experts offered psychiatric diagnoses that ranged from borderline personality disorder to schizotypal disorder to necrophilia. Dahmer had developed a distorted sense of reality since childhood, one said, which in turn had influenced his poor judgment about right and wrong.

The prosecution experts agreed that he was disturbed but not that he was psychotic. Some thought he'd disliked being gay, so killing gay men was a form of purging this part of himself. Dr. Park Dietz, a forensic psychiatrist from UCLA, stated that Dahmer was not suffering from any known mental illness but that he had a paraphilia, or addiction to a sexual deviance. He believed that Dahmer had been conditioned toward sexual excitement over corpses by fantasies that arose from his mutilation of animals. Yet, since Dahmer had been so strategic in his lies to police whenever he came close to being caught, he certainly understood that his actions were wrong and had legal consequences. By legal standards, therefore, he was sane.

Later, former FBI special agent Robert Ressler, one of the founding members of the FBI's Behavioral Science Unit, interviewed Dahmer in prison to learn more about his MO and motives. He'd found the experience unsettling. "When you get pure unadulterated repetitive homicide with no particular motive in mind and nothing that would make it understandable as a gain," he opined, "that indicates that you have something above and beyond rational motivation. You just have evil incentive and evil tendencies. I've had the feeling in interviews with these people that there's something beyond what we can comprehend.... It was evident that Dahmer knew what he was doing and knew it was wrong, and yet at the same time he had this element of fantasy that drove him to dismember his victims and experiment with them by putting acid into their brains. He went way beyond the realm of what a person could understand."

As an American serial killer, Dahmer was shockingly unique. By 1991, serial killers had been grabbing headlines for over two decades. The cases were starting to run together in terms of their similar motives, victims, and approach; but Dahmer showed that there was more to learn about this type of criminal mind. Even thirty years later, his name evokes horror and disgust. Although he experimented only briefly with tasting human flesh, he's remembered as a cannibal. When people think of American serial killers, Dahmer often appears in the top five, if not even the top three, with Ted Bundy and John Wayne Gacy.

27.

LA MATAVIEJITAS

THE CRIMES

The murders began in 2002. Maria de la Luz González Anaya, sixty-four, was discovered near the end of November, fatally strangled in her home in Mexico City. She'd also been beaten. There were no leads to who might have held such a deadly grudge against her.

On March 2, 2003, eighty-four-year-old Guillermina Leon Oropeza was found strangled in the same manner. A thin but deep impression around her neck showed the mark of a ligature, which was missing from the crime scene. Six more women were killed in the area over the next seven months, all of them over the age of sixty. In 2004, the killer (or killers) appeared to have targeted another fourteen victims. The following year, there were eighteen more. The oldest victim was ninety-two. Her face had been badly beaten before she was asphyxiated with her own scarf.

The victim type was an elderly woman who lived alone. Sometimes she was strangled with something from inside the home, like a telephone cord or a pair of stockings, but often the fatal ligature had been removed from the scene. The strangulation mark looked as though a slender rope or thin rubber tube had been used. The targeted homes did not appear to have been ransacked, but relatives of the deceased might report a piece of jewelry or a religious charm missing. Even with growing alarm in media reports, these women seemed always to open their doors to this individual. Police thought the killer might be posing as an authority figure. For a while, officials publicly played down the serial-killer angle, but soon it was too obvious to ignore.

Sometimes there were witnesses. Someone had reported seeing a broad-shouldered figure with a stocky build wearing a red dress in the vicinity. Police looked at the transvestite community for suspects, questioning nearly fifty people, which raised outrage before they acknowledged that it could also be a man posing as a woman.

The killer got a nickname, *La Mataviejitas*—the Little Old Lady Killer. The police collected fingerprints from some of the scenes but were unable to match them to prints in the forensic database. They released two separate sketches based on eyewitness reports of a suspect, and even made a plaster bust. They also provided a written description: five-foot-six, male, blond, and mid-forties. The killer dressed as a woman, they said, and had delineated eyebrows, as though wearing makeup.

A psychological analysis was created based on a database of killers from Spain and France who'd similarly victimized the elderly. The best case for a rough comparison was that of "Monster of Montmartre" Thierry Paulin, who'd murdered elderly women in Paris between 1984 and 1987.

Paulin was a mixed-race gay man who dyed his hair blond. Abandoned by his father as a child, he'd been raised by his neglectful paternal grandmother. He'd sensed that no one really wanted him. In 1982, Paulin was arrested for robbing a woman at knifepoint, but he received a suspended sentence. He began dressing in drag to perform at a nightclub, where he met a lover willing to commit crimes with him. In 1984, Paulin killed several women, beating some before robbing them. He singled out the most vulnerable. When he learned that he was HIV-positive, his murders accelerated. With stolen credit cards, Paulin funded lavish parties. One victim recovered from her attack and gave police a description that assisted with Paulin's arrest. He confessed to killing twenty-one women, nine of them with his partner. He died in prison before his trial.

The Paulin case gave police in Mexico City ideas about what they were looking for. They thought *La Mataviejitas* was an intelligent homosexual with identity issues who dressed in drag. He resented elderly women due to childhood abuse from a caregiver. These speculations notwithstanding, the police got no closer to stopping the killer.

Late in 2005, eighty-two-year-old Carmen Camila Gonzalez Miguel was murdered. Her son was a noted criminologist. One report, which police later denied, indicated that at some point officials launched *Operación Parques y Jardines* (Operation Parks and Gardens), employing elderly women to walk around parks and shopping malls as bait. Police stepped up patrols and posted flyers to raise awareness.

When the murders seemed to stop after a recent escalation, police wondered if *La Mataviejitas* had committed suicide. They checked the fingerprints on the bodies of unknown males in the morgue, but no matches were found to the fingerprints taken from the crime scenes.

By 2006, officials had linked more than forty murders, based on a common *modus operandi*. It was difficult to find anything in common among the victims, other than gender and advanced age, although three had owned a print of an eighteenth-century oil painting, "Boy in a Red Waistcoat," by French artist Jean-Baptiste Greuze. Painted around 1775, it features a sprightly young boy with a head full of dark curls. These prints could be found in numerous outlets, including online, so attempts to trace the sales to a particular store or gallery proved impossible.

On January 25, just three days after they'd arrested a serial killer of gay men, Raúl Osiel Marroquín, police got the break they'd been hoping for. But still, *La Mataviejitas* caught them by surprise.

THE CAPTURE

Ana Maria de los Reyes Alfaro lived in the Venustiano Carranza borough. She was eighty-four. Although she lived alone, she rented rooms out to help with expenses. Around noon, she answered the door to a social worker offering free services. Reyes Alfaro invited her in and ended up dead. Her lodger, however, had seen a stranger leave the house. When he discovered Reyes Alfaro's body in the living room, he phoned the police with a description. A passing patrol officer responded. He found a woman dressed as the lodger had described.

Her name was Juana Barraza. Her close-cropped dyed blond hair and muscular middle-aged body gave her some rather masculine features. In her possession were pension forms, a stethoscope, and a card that falsely identified her as a social worker. The stethoscope matched the bruises on the victim's throat, which resembled the marks on many of the earlier victims. In Barraza's home, investigators found files full of newspaper clippings about the murders, as well as objects that had belonged to some of the victims. They couldn't deny it; their killer was a woman.

Barraza said she had not killed anyone, but her fingerprints at the scene implicated her in this incident as well as in ten other murders. She did not know Reyes Alfaro, she claimed, so she couldn't explain why she'd been in the house. Even when she finally confessed in a court hearing in February, she said, "I only killed one little old lady. Not the others. It just isn't right to pin the others on me." Asked why she had killed Reyes Alfaro, she simply said, "I got angry." She demonstrated for police how she'd done it.

Prosecutors planned to charge Barraza with twenty-seven murders, but for a solid case with this many incidents they knew they needed a full confession. She refused to offer one. They looked into her background to determine her motive.

Barraza was born to an alcoholic thirteen-year-old sex worker, Justa Samperio, on December 27, 1957, in the poverty-stricken village of Epazoyucan, in the state of Hidalgo, north of Mexico City. Samperio left her philandering husband three months after the birth. When young Juana was twelve, her mother reportedly traded her to an older man for a few beers. This man repeatedly raped the girl. She got pregnant and miscarried twice. Although Barraza was thought to be a good mother to the four children she later had with a succession of husbands, she never forgave her own mother for allowing her to be neglected and abused. Just as criminologists had theorized, Barraza blamed her mistreatment of older women on her mother's treatment of her as a child.

Hardly able to read or write, Barraza had become a shoplifter and petty thief to support her children. Then she began breaking into homes to take whatever pawnable items she could find. In 1996, with a friend, Barraza had posed as a nurse. They selected their victims from among elderly people who lived alone. Presenting their services at the door, they'd force their way in and rob the women. Eventually Barraza turned to murder.

Journalists soon learned about her unusual hobby, which added spice to her story. She'd been a *luchador*, a masked wrestler in the sport of *lucha libre*. The contenders adopted cartoonish names and costumes before they clashed in the ring as *técnicos* (good guys who played by the rules) or *rudos* (bad guys who defied the rules). Barraza had claimed on a television interview a few days before her arrest to be a *rudo* "to the core." Mostly, however, she was an event organizer. As *La Dama del Silencio*, or The Silent Lady, she'd dressed in a butterfly mask, a frizzy orange wig, and striped pink tights. She said she'd chosen her stage name because she liked to keep to herself. At her best, she could bench-press up to 200 pounds, but she was a poor wrestler and injury had often sidelined her. Her immersion in this form of aggression had done nothing to lessen her resentment. As she neared fifty, her anger from childhood still simmered.

Barraza went on trial in 2008, with the prosecutor claiming she was responsible for at least forty murders. The prosecutor described to a judge how Barraza had gained her elderly victims' trust by pretending to want to assist with their groceries and laundry. She'd also posed as a nurse or social worker, offering free services. She carried a stethoscope to abet the impression—before using it as a murder weapon.

Although members of the public are barred from courtroom proceedings in Mexico, the police often parade defendants outside in front of the press, which runs its own trial. They posed Barraza with the plastic bust made from witness reports during the investigation, as though the similarity to her proved her guilt. Detectives also released her video interrogation and the photos they'd taken of her recreating the murder of Reyes Alfaro for them.

Barraza's defense attorney faced a tsunami of accusations against his client. He'd attempted to get her declared mentally unfit for trial, but the mental-health experts had found that she'd been fully aware of her actions during the murders and assaults, and that she did not suffer from any serious mental defect. Criminologist Miguel Ontiveros blamed Barraza's anger against elderly women on her mother, who'd abandoned her to sexual abuse and a difficult life. Ontiveros said that Barraza's early experiences had severely distorted her perspective.

Undermining this defense, however, was evidence that Barraza's relationship with her children had been stable and free of the abusive behaviors that are often associated with the parenting style of formerly abused children. Barraza did have an altar in her home dedicated to the scythe-wielding cult figure Santa Muerte, or Saint Death, but no one could link it to a delusional belief that human sacrifice empowered her.

Barraza insisted that she was not the only one behind the killings. She told the press that the crimes were extortion murders, and that a ring of people was involved. She thought it was unfair that the police had targeted her. However, only *her* fingerprints had been lifted from the victims' homes. One report suggested that the police thought a cab driver had partnered with her, but no cab driver was ever identified or arrested.

Some sources say that Barraza never budged from her admission to one murder, but others claim she added three more. On March 31, she was found guilty of eleven murders and five counts of aggravated assault and was sentenced to 759 years in prison. She would be a hundred years old before she was eligible for parole. Barraza showed little reaction, except to say, "May God forgive you and not forget me."

Juana Barraza became Mexico's only known solo female serial killer.

THE TAKEAWAY

Name: Juana Dayanara Barraza Samperio
Country: Mexico
Born: December 27, 1957
Died: NA
Killing Period: 2002–2006
Known victims: 11+, estimated 40–48
Date of Arrest: January 25, 2006

Investigators often assume that serial murder is exclusive to male offenders. Despite media coverage of female killers, stereotypes persist. Barraza is large and broad-shouldered, with short hair, so even when witnesses caught a glimpse of her in a dress, bias skewed toward a male cross-dresser.

"Women are seldom viewed by the public as killers," says criminologist Eric Hickey. "Because those women who kill do so primarily in domestic conflicts, there is even less reason to suspect women to be multiple killers." Female *solo* serial killers account for about 10–12 percent of serial killers, although they show up on 40–50 percent of *team* serial killers. Over 90 percent of known female serial killers are Caucasian, with an average killing period of seven years. Poisoning and strangulation account for 42 percent of their methods of killing. About 93 percent kill only adults, with the average age of capture around forty-seven.

Some authorities called Barraza a psychopath because she appeared to have no remorse for the crimes she committed or the pain she caused. She invented a ruse, posing as a social-welfare official to intentionally deceive her prey and make them more vulnerable. When caught, she blamed the victims for making her mad enough to attack them. "When I saw them, I felt much anger," she said, "and more when they acted uppity or believed that because of their money, they could humiliate me."

Psychopaths exist across cultures and ethnic groups, at a frequency of about 1 percent of the population for males and 0.3–0.7 percent for females. Some female psychopathic offenders show symptoms from other conditions, such as borderline personality disorder (BPD), which is characterized by emotional instability, impulsive behavior, and unstable relationships. BPD shows similar affective disturbances as psychopathy, especially reactive aggression. These disorders also have neurological and cognitive similarities, which suggests that they share a common vulnerability to an unstable disposition. Although Barraza wasn't tested neurologically, her attitudes and behaviors showed the cold calculation typical of psychopathic predators, as well as reactive aggression toward those whom she had beaten or sexually assaulted.

PART V

SELF-SURRENDER

It happens rarely, but occasionally a serial killer initiates his or her own arrest. Sometimes they've been caught for some unrelated crime and they just start confessing (even falsely confessing). Other times, they feel cornered. A few have expressed remorse and a desire to stop. It's a myth that all serial killers *want* to be caught, but there are some cases where that holds true.

28.

THE CANDY MAN'S APPRENTICE

THE CRIMES

In the early 1970s, the Heights in northwest Houston had fallen on hard times. Sometimes a boy would disappear from the area. When this happened, police made little effort to investigate and often dismissed the missing kids as runaways. Few people noticed a slender teen with a thin mustache and wavy brown hair who drove a white Ford Econoline van a bit too slowly through the streets. Elmer Wayne Henley didn't much care what happened to the kids he lured into his vehicle. He'd later say he thought only of the "candy" he'd get from his boss, Dean Corll.

Everyone knew Corll as the "Candy Man." He'd once made real candy, but now he gave out drugs and booze to teenage boys who came to his parties . . . or who were forced to. Corll employed Henley and another teen, David Owen Brooks, as his procurers. *They* brought the "guests."

For nearly three years, teenage boys fed Corll's appetite for rape, torture, and murder. Donald and Jerry Waldrop, fifteen and thirteen, respectively, were the sons of a builder working near Corll's apartment. Both vanished at the same time. Another missing boy had worked with Corll at his mother's candy company. Yet another was the son of a police officer. Ranging in age from thirteen to twenty, Corll's victims sometimes were strangers and sometimes friends. Corll had a kit full of tools to use on his favorites.

Born on Christmas Eve in 1939, Corll had worked for his mother in her candy company, which was near an elementary school. He hung out with the boy students. In 1967, he met Brooks, an insecure sixth-grader. Corll gave Brooks money whenever he asked and worked him up to performing sexual acts. When the candy company closed in 1968, Corll found work as an electrician. He asked Brooks to bring other teens to his parties.

Corll's earliest known murder victim, college student Jeffrey Konen, was thumbing a ride in September 1970 when Corll picked him up. After killing him, Corll wanted to kill again. He offered Brooks $200 (a lot of money in 1970) for any boy he'd bring over, telling him it was for a sex-trafficking ring. In December, Brooks brought James Glass and Danny Yates. Corll handcuffed them to a three-by-eight-foot plywood board to rape and torture before he strangled them. The next month, he killed the Waldrop brothers, Donald and Jerry, together, as mentioned above. Over the next six months, Corll tortured and murdered six more boys. He kept one of them alive for repeated abuse for four terrible days.

To keep Brooks quiet, Corll bought him a Corvette in early 1971.

One day in the winter of 1971, Brooks brought Corll fifteen-year-old Henley, who'd dropped out of school around that same time. Brooks might have intended him to be a victim, but Corll recognized something else in Henley: the kid was smart.

Henley was a petty juvenile delinquent who came from an abusive home and seemed to

DEAN ALLEN CORLL, KNOWN AS THE "CANDY MAN," CONVINCED ELMER HANLEY TO JOIN HIM IN THE MURDERS OF TEENAGE BOYS. THIS PHOTO SHOWS CORLL HOLDING A STUFFED DOG AT HOME.

attract trouble. In need of money, he was easy to groom. Corll told Henley the lie about the white slavery ring and offered to pay him for each boy he brought. Henley agreed. Although he'd later say Corll had paid him only once, he continued to work for pocket money, drugs, and alcohol.

Corll taught Henley the "handcuff trick": he'd show a boy how he could put them on and take them off of himself, urging the boy to do the same. But once the boy was cuffed, he was trapped. Corll would then bind him with rope and gag him with adhesive tape. Or he would just give the boy alcohol until he passed out. He tied most of them to the torture board.

Henley learned about the abductions and murders of several of his childhood friends, including Gregory Malley Winkle and David Hilligiest, for whom he helped to search. Their deaths didn't affect him. He and Brooks grabbed several more boys and turned them over to Corll.

The Candy Man liked to use a double-headed dildo to make his victims scream when he forced it into their rectums. Then he might insert a glass rod into their penis and break it. He also used an electric motor with a bare wire to shock their genitals, and pliers to pluck out pubic hair. Once, he bit off a boy's genitals. Another time, he tied two boys to the board and ordered them to fight to the death: whoever survived would be let go. When both were exhausted after considerable pummeling, he'd shot one and asphyxiated the other. Henley would later say he could take up to half an hour to fatally strangle someone.

The year 1973 began with the murder of Joseph Lyles in Corll's place on Wirt Road. He then moved to 2020 Lamar Drive in Pasadena, Texas, a city within the Houston metropolitan area. From June to August, the killings escalated. Billy Lawrence was abducted for three days of torture. Less than two weeks later, a twenty-year-old hitchhiker named Raymond Blackburn was likewise abducted and strangled. Next, Corll raped and shot fifteen-year-old Homer Garcia. Then came the murders of Michael Baulch, Charles Cobble, and Marty Jones. Brooks stopped working for Corll that July to marry his pregnant fiancé, so Corll used Henley to step up his spree. On August 3, Henley grabbed thirteen-year-old James Dreymala off his bike and took him to Corll's slaughterhouse.

Henley and Brooks not only lured and helped kill the victims but also helped with victim disposal. They transported the bodies to one of three sites outside Houston. Nineteen victims were wrapped in plastic and distributed strategically beneath the dirt floor of a boathouse shed in southwestern Houston. The others they buried either at High Island Beach or at the Corll family's property at Lake Sam Rayburn.

Although Corll looked for another boathouse that summer for future burials, he also told his mother he thought he was going crazy and might kill himself. Then, in August, Henley threw a wrench into the works.

He liked a fifteen-year-old girl named Rhonda Williams, whose missing fiancé he'd once delivered to Corll. He wanted to help Williams when she decided to leave her abusive home, so he invited her to stay at Lamar Street. In Henley's car, Williams met nineteen-year-old Timothy

Kerley, also on his way to the Candy Man's house. When they arrived, Corll yelled at Henley for bringing a girl. Henley shrugged it off. Steamed, Corll watched as the kids got high. When they passed out, he bound and gagged all three, including Henley.

Henley came to and felt the handcuffs. Shocked, he realized he was in the position that usually ended in assault and murder. He begged Corll to let him go.

Corll kicked Williams in the ribs before dragging Henley to the kitchen. There, he aimed a .22-caliber pistol at his stomach. Henley begged again and promised to help kill Kerley and Williams.

Corll relented and removed the handcuffs. Then he dragged the other two into the bedroom. He placed the torture board between them and tied Kerley on one side, forcing him flat on his stomach. He then tied Williams to the board on her back. He opened his toolbox and ordered Henley to rape Williams. Placing the .22 on a table, Corll began to sodomize Kerley. The stunned boy screamed and begged him to stop.

Henley cut Williams' clothing with a large knife. He hesitated. With her eyes, she begged him to help her. Henley saw the gun on the table. He knew he could just shoot her and end it. Or . . . he could shoot Corll.

Henley grabbed the gun and shouted at Corll to stop.

Annoyed, Corll stood and approached Henley. "Kill me, Wayne," he challenged. "You won't do it."

Henley pulled the trigger and shot Corll in the forehead, but Corll kept moving toward him. Henley shot again, putting two bullets into Corll's left shoulder. Corll staggered, turned, and headed into the hallway. Henley shot three more times, hitting him in the back. Corll finally fell and went still.

In shock, Henley released the other two captives. Kerley and Williams insisted that they call the cops. They had no idea that Henley had secrets he needed to keep: he, too, was a serial killer. He was the Candy Man's chief apprentice. He had two options: kill these two, or surrender.

THE CAPTURE

At 8:24 A.M. on August 8, Henley told a police dispatcher that he'd shot a man. Then he went outside, placed the pistol on the driveway, and sat on the porch step. He started to cry. That's how two officers found him when they arrived—just a scared skinny kid.

Inside, the officers found Corll's naked, blood-spattered body sprawled on the floor, facing the wall. In a bedroom, they saw plastic sheets on the floor, a large hunting knife, a length of rope, a toolbox, and a board rigged with manacles and ropes.

At the police station, Henley tried to pretend he'd had no part in the murders. It was all Corll's doing. He told a horrific tale, providing names of recent victims, and offered to take police to the graves. Several detectives took him to the boathouse.

Handcuffed, Henley guided them to number 11. They got the owner to open it. The dirt floor was lumpy, so the officers retrieved shovels. It wasn't long before they hit a layer of lime over a thick piece of plastic. As they moved dirt away, they saw the body of a blond teenage boy.

More diggers arrived. They pulled out more plastic-wrapped bodies, some of which were still bound or had ligatures around their throats. A few had been shot, and one had been buried sitting up. Henley broke down. He admitted bringing these boys to Corll.

David Brooks and his father came to the Houston police station. Brooks said he'd known Corll for six years but denied being present at any murders. When cops got him alone, he admitted learning that Corll had killed two teens in 1970. Brooks spotted Henley and started to sweat. Henley told him he was confessing.

Henley accompanied another police team to Lake Sam Rayburn, over a hundred miles away. The first grave contained Billy Lawrence. They found three more bodies. The victims had been severely beaten around the head and face.

On August 9, police placed Brooks under arrest. He admitted to his involvement in the procurement, body transport, and burial of Corll's victims. He'd lured James Glass and Danny Yates in December 1970, he said, but he'd thought it was for a sex ring. He also named Mark Scott and Billy Baulch as victims.

Brooks and Henley both went to the beach at High Island to help the police find bodies. They exhumed just four, but Henley insisted there were two more. Officers did find an arm bone and pelvis that belonged to none of the sets of remains they'd exhumed, but they stopped digging.

Seventeen bodies were removed from the floor of the boathouse, along with a container of genitalia. Henley insisted two more victims were buried in there. The police were apparently satisfied to stop at twenty-seven, the largest serial murder toll thus far in U.S. history. To the Houston Police Department, this was embarrassing.

During the grand jury investigation, Rhonda Williams, Timothy Kerley, and Billy Ridinger all testified. Corll had tortured Ridinger, intending to kill him, but Brooks had asked Corll to release him. Ridinger's account confirmed the truth of what Henley had described. Henley was indicted for six murders and Brooks for four. The murder of Dean Corll was deemed self-defense.

The remains of twenty-one of Corll's murder victims had been identified by December 17, 1973, when the Honorable William M. Hatten, Judge of the District Court of Harris County, commenced pretrial hearings. Truman Capote, author of the bestselling nonfiction novel *In Cold Blood*, considered writing about the case, but he took one look at Henley and backed out. Reportedly, he decided there was nothing new in this story and that Henley was just a two-bit offender. The tale could not live up to his hope for another masterpiece.

Henley's trial commenced in mid-1974. The prosecution team offered 82 pieces of evidence. After 92 minutes, the jury found Henley guilty. He received six 99-year sentences.

In 1975, David Brooks was tried for the 1973 murder of Billy Lawrence. He was convicted and given a 99-year sentence.

In an interview with James Conaway before his sentencing, Henley mused on killing his mentor: "He'd have been proud of the way I did it." He also said he felt no real remorse. "That's something I've tried to build in me. I don't really feel about it, you know."

THE TAKEAWAY

Name: Elmer Wayne Henley
Date of Birth: May 9, 1956
Date of Death: NA
Killing Period: 1972–1973
Known Victims: 7 (including Corll)
Date of Arrest: August 8, 1973

Predators like Corll who seek accomplices look for kids with low self-esteem, family troubles, uncertainty about their sexuality, frustration about parents or teachers, and other issues common to the difficult transitions of adolescence. Brooks and Henley were scrawny high-school dropouts with few life options and low ambition. Both were from broken homes, and both had difficult fathers (as did Corll). Henley had been physically abused. The two were prime targets, although Henley seemed to adapt easily to a life of crime.

Pedophilic predators might offer a "mentoring" relationship so they can establish a sense of intimacy. They groom their targets with money, gifts, praise, and promises. They provide a home away from home; they become the adult who "understands." Corll's various apartments had served as hangouts, and he was always ready to help. Little by little, he reeled in his partners, getting them to procure victims for him. Once they did, they were psychologically and morally implicated, and Corll had leverage over them.

Corll's greatest ally, it turned out, were the authorities who had declined to look for missing boys from this seedy district. It was a highly mobile time, certainly, but these boys and their families were too casually dismissed. Even the victim-identification process was sketchy.

In 1983, another body was found on a beach in Jefferson County, not far from High Island: seventeen-year-old Joseph Lyles. Corll might have killed and buried this young man on his own, making him Corll's twenty-eighth victim.

Henley insisted that Mark Scott, missing since April 20, 1972, had been buried on High Island Beach, but law enforcement had identified the fifteenth set of remains from the boathouse as his. Henley said they were wrong. It would be 2010 before a DNA analysis on a bone sliver from those remains proved Henley right.

In 1985, the remains of Willard Branch, the son of a police officer, were identified. He'd been emasculated.

In 2008, one of the unidentified boathouse victims was confirmed to be Randy Harvey, only fifteen when he disappeared in 1971 while riding his bicycle.

In April 2011, anthropologist Sharon Derrick tested the DNA of three unknown victims and looked at old missing-persons reports. She identified the fifteenth body from the boathouse, mistakenly thought to be Mark Scott, as seventeen-year-old Steven Sickman, who'd disappeared on July 19, 1972.

Investigative reporter Barbara Gibson, working with Sharon Derrick, found that numerous details in an autopsy report for Michael Baulch failed to match Henley's account. The leg bones also seemed too long for his recorded height. Michael had disappeared on his way to get a haircut a year after Henley and Brooks had abducted his older brother, Billy. Henley had said that Baulch was buried at Lake Sam Rayburn, not the boathouse. Derrick confirmed this, and the Baulch brothers were finally buried together.

Derrick located a report for Roy Bunton, a teenager missing since 1971. He'd been tall. The shape of Bunton's teeth matched the long-legged remains originally misidentified as Michael Baulch.

From prison, Henley says there are still missing victims, and he's likely right. Mark Scott, who Henley said was buried at High Island Beach, might never be found, due to flooding in 2008 from Hurricane Ike. Corll's favorite digging spots prior to meeting Brooks and Henley have never been explored, despite witness reports that Corll was in these places with rolls of clear plastic. Even the boathouse shed was never exhaustively excavated. A photo discovered in 2012 suggested that there may have been a twenty-ninth victim.

Police were criticized for ending their search once the U.S. record of twenty-five victims (attributed to Juan Corona in 1970) had been surpassed. In fact, at least forty-two boys and young men had vanished from the Houston area since 1970. The police never considered that Corll might have killed others that Henley and Brooks didn't know about. Brooks indicated that Corll had killed a nine-year-old neighbor boy prior to September 1970.

How boys like Henley could have been groomed into becoming sadistic accomplices has yet to be deeply explored. Greed and need fail to fully explain.

29.

THE COED KILLER

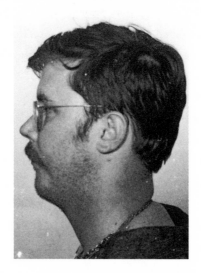

THE CRIMES

On May 7, 1972, Mary Ann Pesce and Anita Luchessa, both eighteen, hitchhiked from Fresno State College in California to meet some friends at Stanford University in Palo Alto. They felt safe. Hitchhiking was a common form of traveling for college students during the early 1970s. But the young women never arrived. Months later, on August 15, Pesce's skull was discovered in a remote area on Loma Prieta Mountain in Santa Cruz County. Police knew that if she'd been murdered, it was likely that Luchessa was dead too. But no more remains turned up.

On September 15, the mother of ballet student Aiko Koo reported her missing. The family had no car, and she knew that her fifteen-year-old

260

daughter had started hitchhiking. She'd had to get to a ballet class the evening before, so her mother had urged the girl to take the bus. She feared that Aiko had thumbed a ride instead. She remained missing.

A man was found dead along a Santa Cruz road in mid-October, killed with a baseball bat. Ten days later, a Cabrillo College coed went missing.

The University of California at Santa Cruz and Cabrillo College warned girls not to hitchhike, but the 1970s was a time of freedom and liberation, when young women felt invincible. And then nineteen-year-old Cynthia Ann Schall vanished on January 9, 1973, after she'd hitched a ride to get to class. A patrol officer near Big Sur came across a pair of severed arms. A week later, a female torso, badly mutilated, floated into a Santa Cruz lagoon. Soon, a surfer found a dismembered left hand, and someone else reported a female pelvis. The remains all turned out to be from Schall. She'd been sawn into pieces. Her head and right hand were still missing.

On February 5, Rosalind Thorpe, twenty-three, and Alice Liu, twenty-one, disappeared. Both depended on the bus or rides they could get from others. Students formed search teams, but they found nothing that revealed where the missing women were. Before this date, a priest was stabbed to death in a local church and five people were shot and stabbed inside two Santa Cruz homes (including two children). Then four young men camping illegally in a state park near Santa Cruz were shot and killed.

In mid-February, a road crew came across two decomposing headless female corpses, one of them fully nude. The hands had been removed from the nude body. One turned out to be the remains of Thorpe, and the other Liu.

When twenty-five-year-old Herbert Mullin was arrested that same month for shooting a man in his yard, he confessed to thirteen murders since October 13, starting with the baseball-bat assault and including the priest, the two mass murder incidents, and the Cabrillo College coed. However, he refused to admit to the other murders of college girls. Authorities could hardly believe they might have another killer in the area preying on young women. District Attorney Peter Chang said that Santa Cruz had become the murder capital of the world. By month's end, the heads of Thorpe and Liu were found in Pacifica. The media tagged the killer with several gruesome nicknames, among them "the Chopper" and "the Butcher." They finally settled on "the Coed Killer." Was it Mullin, they wondered, or someone else?

The police discussed the cases in the Jury Room, a bar near City Hall in Santa Cruz. Among them was "Big Ed" Kemper, whose dream to be a cop was denied at the time at both local and state police departments, due to his six-foot-nine height. He pretended to be a security guard so he could seem like one of the guys. They let him hang around. Listening to them talk, he learned the details of their investigations.

The murders seemed to stop with Mullin's arrest, so police figured he'd been lying and that he was the local killer. Still, they acknowledged significant differences between most of Mullin's murders and the dismemberments of the coeds. Mullin had disemboweled one female, mostly out of curiosity, but he hadn't repeated this act for any of his other kills. He seemed too psychotic to have succeeded at picking up hitchhikers, especially with all the warnings. He would have seemed dangerous. Whoever was killing these girls, that person didn't scare them.

At 4:00 A.M. on April 24, the Santa Cruz police received a stunning surprise. Big Ed Kemper was calling from a phone booth in Colorado. He claimed *he* was the Coed Killer. "I can show you," he said, "where I hid the pieces of their bodies."

THE CAPTURE

Kemper said he'd just murdered his mother and her best friend, and that the bodies could be found at his mother's house. He wanted someone to pick him up so he could turn himself in and tell them everything. Someone at the station accidentally cut off his call, but he eventually called back.

The officers went to Kemper's home and found the dismembered remains of Clarnell Kemper Strandberg and Sara Hallett in a closet. Strandberg's head had been removed. A bed was soaked in blood, and a bloodstained hammer and a saber lay nearby. Still stunned, the police removed the evidence and impounded Kemper's car.

Colorado police sent officers to arrest Kemper, who'd remained at the phone booth. Once in custody and back in California, the 280-pound killer showed police where he'd buried the remains and then talked for hours. He described in detail what he'd done to each of his victims, usually dismembering them with the ornamental saber from his home. He'd killed six girls, sometimes two at a time, in addition to his mother and her friend. Then he showed detectives where he'd buried or tossed parts of victims who'd not yet been found. One head was in the yard outside his mother's apartment. Kemper described cutting off the heads and having sex with them. He'd been playing a game, he told them.

"I'm picking up young women," he said, "and I'm going a little bit farther each time. It's a daring kind of thing. . . . We go to a vulnerable place, where there aren't people watching, where I could act out and I say, 'No, I can't.' . . . And this craving, this awful raging eating feeling inside, this fantastic passion. It was overwhelming me. It was like drugs. It was like alcohol."

According to his confession, he'd had bizarre sexual fantasies about females for years. He'd gotten ideas for murder from crime novels, which had shown him how to relax his targets with the impression that they were safe. Sometimes he'd picked up girls and let them go, acting only when he felt his "little zapples." He estimated that he'd picked up 150 female hitchhikers. He added that he'd fatally shot his grandparents when he was fifteen and "mad at the world." (He'd turned himself in to the sheriff that time as well.)

Detectives asked for his background. Born on December 18, 1948, Edmund E. Kemper III had two sisters, one older and one younger. He'd been close to his father before his parents' divorce in 1957, when he was nine. At that time, his mother had taken him and his sisters to live in Montana. She had placed his troubled older sister in the basement for a while, to keep her under control. Then it was Edmund's turn. The basement room had terrified him. Worse, his mother had verbally attacked him, undermining his sense of worth. When he grew old enough to date (after he got out of juvenile detention for killing his grandparents), she'd told him he wasn't worthy of college girls. This had sent him out looking for them, to kill them.

When he picked up Pesce and Luchessa, he initially decided to rape them, but then realized he should eliminate witnesses. Once they entered his Ford, he drove to a dirt road he'd already scouted. Handcuffing Pesce to the back seat, he locked Luchessa into the trunk of the car. He tried to smother Pesce but failed, so he stabbed her. As she died, Kemper had held her to absorb the experience. He'd killed Luchessa quickly. Wrapping the bodies in blankets, he'd placed both in the trunk of his car and taken them to his mother's home in Aptos, California. There he'd posed and photographed them. Then he'd removed their arms and heads, engaging in sexual acts with the severed parts. After keeping them overnight, he buried the parts the next day in the mountains.

Kemper told detectives that murder made him feel invincible. On the day after he killed Aiko Koo and placed her head in the trunk of his car, he'd appeared before two psychiatrists who'd examined him to decide whether his juvenile records should be sealed. They found him to be "normal" and "safe." They thought he'd shown an excellent response to the five years of treatment.

He buried Koo's head and hands above the town of Boulder Creek, California, then purchased a .22-caliber pistol. When he killed Cynthia Schall, he brought the body home to dismember. He buried her head outside, with the face turned toward his bedroom window. After an argument with his mother, he killed two more girls and dumped their remains in separate counties.

Kemper thought his mother had found the items he'd removed from victims, so he decided to kill her. That evening, she had come home slightly drunk and gone to bed. They'd argued a little. He waited until she was asleep and then entered her room with a clawhammer. After killing her, he removed her head and placed it on the living-room mantel. He'd thrown darts at it. Finally, he removed the larynx and stuffed it down the garbage disposal before placing the body in a closet. Afterward, he'd penned a note: "Appx. 5:15 A.M. Saturday. No need for her to suffer anymore at the hands of this horrible 'murderous butcher.' It was quick, sleep, the way I wanted it."

He invited Clarnell's friend, Sara Hallett, to come over, and he killed her too. Then he packed Hallett's car with guns and ammunition and went to the Jury Room for a few drinks. Finally, he left. In Nevada, he rented a car and drove to Colorado.

Kemper was indicted on May 7, 1973, on eight separate counts of first-degree murder. Jim Jackson, Santa Cruz County's chief public defender, pleaded insanity on Kemper's behalf. He used Kemper's juvenile evaluation after he'd murdered his grandparents. One psychiatrist had diagnosed Kemper with paranoid schizophrenia. Even after five years of treatment, psychiatrists had advised that Kemper not be returned to Clarnell's care. Since he had no other means of support, he'd moved back in with her anyway. The stage had been set for him to continue to act out violently.

Kemper's trial began on October 23, 1973, and three psychiatrists testified that they found him to have been aware of his actions and aware that they were wrong. Thus, he was sane. Dr. Joel Fort had looked at Kemper's juvenile records and stated that there had been no reason to have diagnosed schizophrenia. Kemper had not been delusional: he'd just been troubled. Fort testified that even if Kemper had cannibalized pieces of his victims during his murders, this wouldn't make him insane. He'd shown evidence of premeditation and had acknowledged that he'd known he should eliminate witnesses.

Kemper himself took the stand. He described his mental state while killing and tried to convince the jury of his instability. He stated that two beings inhabited his body, and when "the killer" took over, it was "kind of like blacking out." Kemper compared the experience to the time he'd shot his grandparents; he claimed he'd blacked out during this incident as well. However, by this time, the jury realized that he'd studied the psychiatric manuals and knew how to malinger. His history of lying had caught up to him.

On November 8, after five hours of deliberation, the jury found Kemper to have been sane during his murders. He was a cold-hearted killer. Although Kemper had requested the death penalty, the U.S. Supreme Court had placed a moratorium on capital punishment from 1967 to 1972, inspiring states that enforced capital punishment to rewrite their laws. So, during the transition period, Kemper received life in prison.

THE TAKEAWAY

Name: Edmund Emil Kemper III
Country: United States
Date of Birth: December 18, 1948
Date of Death: NA
Killing Period: 1964, 1972–1973
Known Victims: 10
Date of Arrest: April 24, 1973

Kemper called the police himself. Once he was on the run, he realized that he had no resources, so he decided to turn around. This decision reflects his basic inability to support himself. Despite hating his mother, he was dependent on her. But experts determined that there were complex reasons for his murders and for his surrender to the police.

Psychiatrist Donald Lunde read the trial transcripts, Kemper's psychological testing, his background profile, and his confession, and decided that long-term anger and violent fantasies had influenced his sexual aggression. An ambivalent relationship with the mother is common among sexual sadists, Lunde had discovered. Kemper's relationship seemed to have been highly volatile.

"In rare individuals," Lunde wrote, "for reasons that are not well understood, sexual and violent aggressive impulses merge early in the child's development, ultimately finding expression in violent sexual assaults, and in the most extreme cases, sadistic murders or sex murders."

Kemper's psychological testing prior to the coed killings had shown his propensity for sadistic violence, and these results should have been predictive. Kemper was found to be volatile and immature, with depression and latent hostility. He was lonely, lacking in confidence, and unable to deal adequately with conflict. Despite his intelligence, he lacked the emotional ability to mature into a self-supporting human being. Beautiful women made him physically ill.

Kemper told Lunde about his intense urge to kill females. While he apparently did hope for a real relationship one day, he thought he could get close to women only by having sex with their corpses. Blaming his mother as the sole source for his sense of inadequacy, he'd blocked himself from detaching from her and becoming a man in his own right. She'd belittled him but had not beaten or tortured him. He'd simply never taken personal responsibility for his own actions—that is, until he turned himself in to authorities.

30.
THE ANGEL OF DEATH

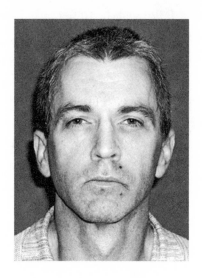

THE CRIMES

On the evening shift for June 15, 2003, at Somerset Medical Center (SMC) in Somerville, New Jersey, someone ordered the heart medication digoxin for a patient for whom it had not been prescribed. The computerized care system showed that the drug was removed from stock. Then the order was canceled—but the drug was not returned. Around the same time, someone accessed the records of Jin Kyung Han, a forty-year-old cancer patient. The next morning, she went into cardiac seizure. Her doctor stabilized her. After checking her blood work, he asked why she'd been given digoxin against his orders.

About two weeks later, Reverend Florian Gall died from an over-dose of digoxin. Errors were expected in hospitals, but these incidents looked suspicious, especially with the two insulin overdose deaths that had occurred the month before. SMC's administrators sent reports and samples to the New Jersey Poison Control Center and launched an inter-nal investigation. Forty-three-year-old male nurse Charles Cullen had ordered digoxin, but he'd requested it for patients under his own care. State laws prevented SMC from learning if Cullen had caused trouble at other facilities where he'd worked. A seemingly quiet man with a mil-itary background, all reports said that he acted compassionately toward patients. But the investigation did not turn up the fact that he'd been present at other worrisome incidents.

In 1988, Jersey City Municipal Judge John Yengo, seventy-two, came to the St. Barnabas Medical Center in Livingston, New Jersey, to be treated for a side effect of his heart medication, a rare type of allergic reaction. He died on November 6, 1988. His daughter was surprised by how quickly he had succumbed. At the same facility, several nurses suspected Cullen of putting insulin into the IV bags, and many patients developed inexplica-ble hypoglycemia. When an investigation commenced, Cullen left.

In Phillipsburg, New Jersey, at the end of August 1993, 91-year-old Helen Dean had recovered from surgery for colon cancer. Her son, Larry Dean, recalled a thin male nurse entering the room and ordering him to leave. He did so. When he returned, Helen was upset. "He stuck me!" she exclaimed. She knew she was not supposed to receive medication that morning. She pointed out the injection mark. Larry reported the incident, but no one seemed concerned. The next day, Helen died. Larry felt certain that the nurse who injected her had murdered her, but an investigation turned up no evidence. Cullen was questioned, but he denied everything. He was given an indefinite paid leave. His suicide attempt shortly there-after didn't help his cause; but in the end, no evidence implicated him.

Cullen moved on to find work at Hunterdon Hospital in Flemington, New Jersey. Here, he made so many "medication errors" that his supervisors wrote him up. Between January and July 1996, five patients died. After being chastised, Cullen resigned.

His next hospital fired him in short order for incompetence.

In May 1998, Francis Henry was hospitalized for spinal injuries from a car accident at the Liberty Nursing and Rehabilitation Center in Allentown, Pennsylvania. Nurse Kimberly Pepe was in charge of his case, and when he died, it turned out that he'd received an unauthorized and highly lethal dose of insulin. Administrators confronted Pepe and she denied mishandling his care. Nevertheless, she was fired. Pepe filed a discrimination claim with the Equal Employment Opportunity Commission, pointing out that Nurse Charles Cullen had been in the room as well. Although the hospital would later claim that it had not investigated Cullen at the time, he was fired that same year for an issue related to medication delivery schedules. Again, he moved on.

In 1999, Northampton County Coroner Zachary Lysek told officials that he thought there was an "angel of death" at Easton Hospital in Easton, Pennsylvania. He'd examined the suspicious demise of seventy-eight-year-old Ottomar Schramm, who succumbed to a fatal dose of digoxin. His condition had not warranted receiving this medication, and his daughter told Lysek about a nurse who'd come in with a syringe. While Lysek could not prove where Schramm had received the injection, since he'd come from a nursing home, he believed someone had administered the digoxin with malignant intent. Believing this death to be a homicide, based on eyewitness reports from one of Schramm's relatives, Lysek requested an internal investigation, but it was inconclusive.

Cullen went next to the burn unit at Lehigh Valley Hospital in Allentown. Patients were expected to die here. A twenty-two-year-old young man, Matthew Mattern, might have survived, but his injuries were severe and his chances slim. Digoxin in his IV ended his life.

Other patients died as well, before Cullen took a job down the road in Bethlehem at St. Luke's Hospital.

In 2002, Coroner Lysek heard from a nurse at St. Luke's about the suspicious behavior of a male nurse working there, Charles Cullen. Seven St. Luke's nurses had done their own detective work and were prepared to go to the state police. That June, they had found opened and unopened packages of drugs improperly placed in a trash bin, and had seen Cullen leaving the rooms of patients who'd soon expired. There had also been spikes in Code Blues (an emergency in which a patient is in cardiopulmonary arrest) on his shifts. The nurses believed he was killing patients.

When Cullen was confronted, he resigned. The state hired a forensic pathologist to make a comprehensive investigation; but after reviewing sixty-seven cases, he said he'd found no proof of criminal activity that would support prosecution. Hospital administrators did notify the Pennsylvania Board of Nursing. By then, Cullen was already at work at SMC in New Jersey.

In July 2003, toxicologist Steven Marcus, director of the New Jersey Poison Control Center, warned SMC about a poisoner on their staff. Hospital officials complained to the state's health department that Marcus had rushed to judgment. Yet he insisted that someone start a forensic investigation.

SMC found that Cullen was the common factor in four suspicious cases, each of which involved poisoning with either a high level of insulin or digoxin. Cullen had even accessed the records of one, the Reverend Florian Gall, after his death, although Gall had not been his patient. Then several more "unexplained fatal incidents" occurred between July and October; so after thirteen months on the job, Cullen was fired. Somerset County Prosecutor Wayne Forrest launched a formal investigation. The detectives assigned to the case, Timothy Braun and Daniel Baldwin, looked at records from nine institutions and identified a pattern. They picked Gall as a New Jersey victim for whom they could make a formal charge. They exhumed his body, which confirmed their suspicions. Further investigation linked the overdose to Cullen.

THE CAPTURE

On the evening of December 12, 2003, Cullen was arrested after he left a restaurant, and was charged with the murder of Florian Gall and the attempted murder of Jin Kyung Han. At his arraignment, Cullen said "I don't intend to contest the charges. I plan to plead guilty."

The judge did not want Cullen to enter a plea just yet. His response was to rescind Cullen's request for a public defender. His bail was set at $1 million, and he was taken to Somerset County jail.

But on December 14, Cullen had already dropped a bombshell to the two detectives that went well beyond the charges. Over the past sixteen years in ten different institutions, he admitted, he'd intentionally overdosed up to forty patients. Over the course of seven hours, he told Braun and Baldwin that he'd intended to kill these people. It had been easy, he said, to go from one healthcare facility to the next, and to experiment with different substances. No one ever checked. He blamed the administrators at these places for letting him get away with it.

At first, he claimed, he'd killed patients to end their suffering; but as the cases were opened, it became clear that many of his victims had not been suffering. Quite to the contrary, some had been recovering. In addition, Cullen had committed malicious mischief just to see what he could get away with. He'd thrown out expensive drugs and put insulin into IV bags stored in a closet to see what would happen. He was no mercy killer: he was a prankster who felt contempt for both colleagues and patients.

Cullen expected to get the death penalty, but in a quick turnabout he accepted the services of public defender Johnnie Mask, who said that Cullen would offer the names of his victims in exchange for taking the death penalty off the table. Both states' officials agreed. Cullen admitted to twenty-nine murders (twenty-two in New Jersey and seven in Pennsylvania) and six attempted murders (three in each state). He had committed his final murder just ten days before he was terminated at SMC.

In May 2005, newspapers published Cullen's advice for healthcare institutions about how to make it more difficult for people like him to kill. In short, he said, there should be protocols for accountability for staff and for drug-handling procedures. Among them would be installing surveillance cameras and using swipe cards and bar codes, along with keeping a daily count of all lethal medications. He also said there should be a national database for updating employment history of healthcare workers. Institutions should pass information along to one another, and hospitals should pay attention to the mental health of their employees. Poor performance such as his should be reported to the state board of nursing.

Cullen's life history showed a parallel between his murders and times when he'd been depressed or failing at something. In 1993, his wife had filed for a restraining order against him, based on her fear that he might endanger her and their two children. She said he'd spiked people's drinks with lighter fluid, forgotten his daughters at a babysitter's house for a week, and showed extreme cruelty to the family pets. His wife suspected that he'd poisoned a neighbor's dog. Shortly after being served with divorce papers, he'd stalked a colleague and broken into her house. On several occasions, he'd tried to kill himself. During this time, he'd killed three elderly female patients in New Jersey, including Helen Dean. Murder made him feel better.

Cullen was the youngest of nine brothers and sisters who grew up in a working-class neighborhood in West Orange, New Jersey. His father was a bus driver, his mother a homemaker. Cullen's father died when he was seven months old, and his mother was killed in a fatal car accident while he was in high school. Two of his siblings had also died young.

In 1978, he dropped out of high school and enlisted in the Navy, serving on a nuclear submarine. When he was discharged in 1984, he attended the Mountainside Hospital School of Nursing. By 1988, he was working at the first of many hospitals where he would stay only a short while. He got married and had two daughters, but soon was divorced. He began killing people during his first year as a nurse.

Cullen went to court in Somerville, New Jersey, on March 2, 2006 to receive eleven life sentences, while relatives of his victims battered him with name-calling and descriptions of their pain. He sat with his eyes closed. In the court in Pennsylvania, he made a scene and had to be gagged with a spit mask.

In mid-March of that year, Cullen was sent to the New Jersey State Prison in Trenton, to serve his life sentences.

THE TAKEAWAY

Name: Charles Cullen
Country: United States
Born: February 22, 1960
Died: NA
Killing Period: 1987 or 1988–2003
Known Victims: 29+ killed, 6 attempted
Date of Arrest: December 12, 2003

Healthcare providers know how to use subtle murder methods like smothering and overdoses, and they have access to drugs that can poison patients undetected. Unless some specific behavior prompts suspicion, they might well be able to effectively hide their crimes. They tend to select patients who cannot speak for themselves or who are expected to die.

Once a patient has died, he or she is generally either embalmed or cremated and, in either case, evidence can be lost. Even an extensive investigation at a hospital where Cullen actually did kill a number of people had failed to find any clear criminal activity. District attorneys need a strong case, and sometimes they can acquire only circumstantial evidence or witness reports that will not support a conviction.

Cullen is not alone. Male registered nurses are disproportionately represented among caretakers who kill. They represent only 5 to 7 percent of nurses in the United States but are responsible for about one-third of the healthcare serial murder cases.

Nurses who kill learn how to exploit the atmosphere of trust in the hospital community and to hasten deaths that may go unnoticed. When caught, many have taken the easiest path and said their motives were about mercy, but few cases have supported that claim. It appeared more likely that, similar to others in his position, Cullen killed because something he derived from the act fulfilled a psychological need.

In addition, laws that prohibit sending warnings to future employers protect these killers. SMC administrators said they did not know that Cullen had been investigated elsewhere. When they'd checked his credentials, they learned nothing that would have prevented them from hiring him. It was at SMC where Cullen might have been most active, killing twelve to fifteen patients in just over a year.

At St. Luke's, Cullen had worked just over 20 percent of the total hours available in critical care, but he was present for over 56 percent of the deaths that occurred there. Yet hospital administrators had found themselves in a Catch-22: if they didn't warn, they could be sued; and if they did, they could be sued.

Often, these killers have been allowed to drift from one hospital to another, fired under a cloud of suspicion but rarely brought to justice until incriminating evidence reaches shocking levels. While there's no distinct psychological type, there are red flags: secretive behavior, unmotivated lying, association with missing medications, a preference for the night shift, spikes in unexpected deaths on their shift, presence in rooms where patients died unexpectedly, and spotty past work records can be troublesome signals. Cullen had all of these.

One of Cullen's tricks was to get medications by opening patients' drawers or closets, because no one tracked the drugs. When electronic drug tracking was put into place, he learned how to manipulate computer records. When administrators checked deaths from one medication, he experimented with others. He left "tracks," but no one noticed until he made a mistake.

After Cullen, officials in Pennsylvania and New Jersey put more protective policies into place. State regulators strengthened nursing standards, with new rules and harsher penalties. They also introduced the Safe Health Care Reporting Act, which would expand the current National Practitioner Data Bank to include all licensed healthcare workers, not just physicians. Legislation was considered to protect hospitals from lawsuits should they have solid reasons to offer a negative evaluation of a former employee. In April 2004, New Jersey Governor James McGreevey signed a law that requires all healthcare facilities in the state to document and report serious medical errors.

Perhaps the wake-up call from this case will deter some potential angels of death. Hospitals must acknowledge their existence and train their personnel to spot them, document their movements, and take appropriate action.

SUMMARY

The history of serial murder parallels the history of criminal investigation, helping to document and demonstrate new ideas and technologies. Although some flukes happen, such as killers making mistakes or surrendering before investigators can identify them, forensic innovation and solid police work most often bring killers to ground and get them locked up.

SOURCES

1. THE MAD CARPENTER

Baring-Gould, Sabine. *The Book of Were-wolves*. Blackmask Online, 2002, first
   published 1865.

Masters, R. E. L., and Eduard Lea. *Perverse Crimes in History*. New York: Julian Press,
   1963.

Thorwald, J. *The Century of the Detective*. New York: Harcourt, Brace & World, 1964.

Von Krafft-Ebing, R. *Psychopathia Sexualis with Especial Reference to the Antipathic
   Sexual Instinct*. Rev. Ed. Philadelphia: Physician and Surgeons, 1928.

2. THE FOOTPAD KILLER

Jeffreys, A. J., V. Wilson, and S. L. Thein. "Individual-Specific 'Fingerprints' of Human
   DNA." *Nature*, 316 (July 4, 1985): 76–79.

Scheck, Barry, Peter Neufeld, and Jim Dwyer. *Actual Innocence*. New York: Random
   House, 2000.

Wambaugh, Joseph. *The Blooding: The True Story of the Narborough Village Murders*.
   New York: William Morrow, 1989.

3. THE CLEAN-CUT KILLER

DeNevi, D., and J. H. Campbell. *Into the Minds of Madmen: How the FBI Behavioral
   Science Unit Revolutionized Crime Investigation*. Amherst, NY: Prometheus
   Books, 2004.

Francis, Greg, director. "Dark Woods." *FBI Files*. 11(5). May 27, 2003.

Hale, R. "The Role of Humiliation and Embarrassment in Serial Murder." *Psychology: A
   Journal of Human Behavior*. 31, no. 2 (1994): pp. 17–23.

McGraw, Carol. "A Question of Life and Death." *Orange County Register,* February 18,
   1996.

Michaud, Stephen. "The FBI's New Psych Squad." *New York Times*, October 26, 1986.

Mullany, P. J. *Matador of Murder: An FBI Agent's Journey in Understanding the Criminal Mind.* CreateSpace, 2015.

Sullivan, Tim. "Personal Items Belonging to 1974 Murder Victim Found in Manhattan." *Bozeman Daily Chronicle*, October 12, 2005.

Teten, Howard. Personal interview, 2010.

"Vanished: The Power of Forgiveness." *ABC News 20/20*, July 19, 2000.

4. THE VIENNA COURIER

"Forensic Psychiatric Aspects of the Case of Jack Unterweger," *Forensische Psychiatrie und Psychotherapie*, Expenditure 4.

"Killer Abroad." *The FBI Files*, Season 2:14, Discovery Network, 2000.

Leake, John. *Entering Hades: The Double Life of a Serial Killer*. New York: Farrar, Straus and Giroux, 2007.

McCrary, Gregg, and Katherine Ramsland. *The Unknown Darkness: Profiling the Predators Among Us*. New York: Morrow, 2003.

Unterweger, Jack. *Fegefeuer, oder die Reise ins Zuchthaus*. Augsburg: Maro Vlg., 1983.

5. BTK

Cohen, Sharon. "Computer Disk and DNA Led to BTK Suspect." Associated Press, March 3, 2005.

Jones, K. C. "Surveillance Technology Helps Catch Serial Killer." *Information Week*, January 5, 2007.

Nixon, Ron, and Dan Browning. "Computers Leave a High-tech Trail of Crime Clues." *Minneapolis Star Tribune*, March 31, 2005.

Ramsland, Katherine. *Confession of a Serial Killer: The Untold Story of Dennis Rader, the BTK Killer.* Lebanon, N.H.: University Press of New England, 2016.

Simons, Erica B. "Forensic Computer Investigation Brings Notorious Serial Killer BTK to Justice." *The Forensic Examiner*, 14, no. 4 (Winter 2005): 55–57.

Wenzl, Roy, Tim Potter, L. Kelly, and Hurst Lavinia. *Bind, Torture, Kill: The Inside Story of the Serial Killer Next Door.* New York: HarperCollins, 2007.

6. THE GOLDEN STATE KILLER

Crompton, Larry. *Sudden Terror*. Bloomington, IN: Author House, 2010.

Gartrell, Nate. "Retired Cold Case Investigator Tracked the Golden State Killer to His Door." *The Mercury News*, April 26, 2018.

Hare, Breeanna, and Christo Taoushiana. "What We Know About the Golden State Serial Killer Case, One Year After Suspect Was Arrested." *CNN.com*, April 24, 2019. https://www.cnn.com/2019/04/24/us/golden-state-killer-one-year-later/index.html

"Interactive Map: Follow the Route of the East Area Rapist a.k.a. the Golden State Killer." April 25, 2018. *KTVU.com*. https://www.ktvu.com/news/interactive-map-follow-the-route-of-the-east-area-rapist-aka-golden-state-killer

Lillis, Ryan, Dale Kasler, Anita Chabria, and Sam Stanton. "East Area Rapist: GEDmatch provided DNA Link to Investigators." *Sacramento Bee*, April 28, 2018.

McNamara, Michelle. *I'll be Gone in the Dark: One Woman's Obsessive Search for the Golden State Killer.* New York: Harper, 2018.

Shapiro, Emily, and Whit Johnston. "How DNA from Family Members Helped Solve the 'Golden State Killer' Case: DA." *ABCNews.com*, April 28, 2018.

Stirling, Steven. "How a N.J. Pathologist May Have Helped Solve the 'Golden State Killer' Case." *nj.com*, April 26, 2018. https://www.nj.com/data/2018/04/how_a_nj_pathologist_may_have_helped_solve_the_gol.html

7. THE CANNIBAL KILLER

"Albert Fish Pays Penalty at Sing Sing." *New York Times*, January 17, 1936.

Borowski, John, editor. *Albert Fish: In His Own Words: The Shocking Confessions of the Child Killing Cannibal.* Chicago: Waterfront Productions, 2014.

Borowski, John, producer. "Albert Fish." Waterfront Productions, 2007.

"Fish is Sentenced. Admits New Crimes; Death in Electric Chair Fixed for Week of April 29, 1935. Move to Set Aside Verdict." *New York Times,* March 26, 1935.

"Fish Held Sane by Three Experts. Defense Alienists Say Budd Girl's Murderer Was and Is Mentally Irresponsible." *New York Times,* May 21, 1935.

Schechter, Harold. *Deranged: The Shocking True Story of America's Most Fiendish Killer.* New York: Pocket, 1990.

Stone, Michael H., and Brucato, Gary. *The New Evil: Understanding the Emergence of Modern Violent Crime.* New York: Prometheus Books, 2019.

Wertham, Frederic. *The Show of Violence.* New York: Doubleday & Co., 1949.

8. THE KILLER CLOWN

Amirante, Sam. *John Wayne Gacy: Defending a Monster: The True Story of the Lawyer Who Defended One of the Most Evil Serial Killers in History.* New York: Skyhorse, 2011.

Cahill, Tim. *Buried Dreams: Inside the Mind of Serial Killer John Wayne Gacy.* New York: Bantam, 1986.

Cohen, Sharon. "Doctor Hunts for Motive in Brain of a Serial Killer." Associated Press, May 8, 2004.

Hickey, Eric. *Serial Murderers and Their Victims,* 6th ed. Belmont, CA: Wadsworth, 2013.

Morrison, Helen, and Harold Goldberg. *My Life Among Serial Killers.* New York: William Morrow, 2004.

Ressler, Robert K., and Tom Schachtman. *I Have Lived in the Monster: Inside the Minds of the World's Most Notorious Serial Killers.* New York: St. Martin's Press, 1997.

Sullivan, Terry, and Peter Maiken. *Killer Clown: The John Wayne Gacy Murders.* New York: Grosset & Dunlap, 1983.

9. THE *DATING GAME* KILLER

Gardner, David. "Rodney Alcala Sentenced to Death for Murders of Four Women and Girl, 12." *The Daily Mail,* April 1, 2010.

Hays, Tom. "Rodney Alcala, California Killer Sentenced to Death, Admits to Killing Two New York City Women." *Huffington Post,* December 14, 2012.

Keshishyan, Gayanne, producer. "Rodney Alcala's Killing Game." *48 Hours Mystery,* CBS, September 25, 2010.

Pelisek, C. "Rodney Alcala's Final Revenge." *LA Weekly,* February 10, 2010.

Perelman, Marina. "New Case Linked to *Dating Game* Killer." NBCbayarea.com, March 8, 2011.

Ramsland, Katherine, and Mark Safarik. "Rodney Alcala: The *Dating Game* Killer." *Serial Killer Quarterly,* Fall 2015.

Safarik, Mark. Criminal Investigative Analysis Report. December 2012.

Sands, Stella. *The Dating Game Killer.* New York: St. Martin's, 2011.

Secret, Mosi. "Forty Years On, Detective Sees Light Shed on Killing." *New York Times,* February 5, 2011.

Wellborn, Larry. "Questions Surround Alcala in 1977 Slaying in New York." *Orange County Register,* July 18, 2010.

Weller, Sheila. "A Cold Case of Cold-Blooded Murder." *New York Times,* January 13, 2013.

10. THE SLAVE MASTER

Douglas, John, and Stephen Singular. *Anyone You Want Me to Be: A True Story of Sex and Death on the Internet.* New York: Scribner, 2003.

Glatt, John. *Internet Slave Master.* New York: St. Martin's Press, 2001.

Harris, Chris. "Her Mom was Murdered by a Serial Killer—and Then She was Adopted by the Serial Killer's Brother." *People,* October 2, 2019. https://people.com/crime/heather-tiffany-robinson-adopted-by-brother-serial-killer/

Hickey, E. *Sex Crimes and Paraphilias.* Upper Saddle River, NJ: Prentice Hall, 2006.

Richmond, T. "More Internet Predators are Challenging Agents." *Chicago Tribune,* March 21, 2009.

State of Kansas vs. John E. Robinson, Sr. 90.196 (2015).

11. THE ABC KILLER

Hodgskiss, Brin. "Lessons from Serial Murder in South Africa." *Journal of Investigative Psychology and Offender Profiling,* 1, no. 1 (2004): 67–94.

Labushangne, G. N. "Offender Profiling in South Africa: Its Definition and Context." *Acta Criminologica: Southern Africa Journal of Criminology,* 16, no. 4 (2003): 67–74.

Pistorius, Micki. *Catch Me a Killer: A Profiler's True Story.* South Africa: Penguin, 2000.

Ramsland, Katherine. *The Human Predator: A Historical Chronicle of Serial Murder and Forensic Investigation.* New York: Berkley, 2005.

Ressler, Robert K., and Tom Shachtman. *I Have Lived in the Monster: Inside the Minds of the World's Most Notorious Serial Killers.* New York: St. Martin's Press, 1997.

"Still No End to the Serial Killings." *Mail and Guardian,* September 22, 1995. https://mg.co.za/article/1995-09-22-still-no-end-to-the-serial-killings

von Nekerk, Philip. "A Time to Kill." *Maxim*, October 2000. maximonline.com.

12. THE HANGING PRO

"Aki, Kaori. "Serial Killers: A Cross-Cultural Study Between Japan and the United States." Unpublished master's thesis. California State University, Fresno, 2003.

All Nine Victims of Zama Serial Killer Identified, Including Three High School Girls." *Japan Times,* November 10, 2017. https://www.japantimes.co.jp/news/2017/11/10/national/crime-legal/police-id-nine-dismembered-corpses-found-mans-zama-flat-including-girl-15/#.XXZEqyV7nUo

Hickey, Eric W. *Serial Murderers and Their Victims.* 6th ed. Belmont, CA: Wadsworth, 2013.

"Japanese Suicide Websites targeted after 'House of Horrors.'" BBC.com, November 10, 2017. https://www.bbc.com/news/world-asia-41941426

Motoko, Rich. "Japan Serial Killer Takahiro Shiraishi." *The New York Times,* November 1, 2017. https://www.nytimes.com/2017/11/01/world/asia/japan-serial-killer-takahiro-shiraishi.html

Rowe, Aaron. "Japanese Websites Make Suicide a Breeze." *Wired,* June 2008. https://www.wired.com/2008/06/japanese-websit/

Sim, Walter. "Inside the Mind of the Japanese Serial Killer who Killed 9 People." *Straitstimes,* November 5, 2017. https://www.straitstimes.com/asia/east-asia/inside-the-mind-of-a-serial-killer

"Suicide Website Killer Lived Out His Fantasies." *Japan Today,* August 24, 2005.

Vankin, Jonathan. "Takahiro Shiraishi: Severed Heads Buried in Cat Litter Found in 'Horror Movie' Home of Suspected Serial Killer." *Inquisitr,* October 31, 2017. Inquisitr.com/4590858/takiro-shiraishi-severed-heads-serial-killer

Yamaguchi, Mari. "Japan Serial Killer Behind the Murder of Nine People Offered Suicide Pact to Women." *The Independent,* November 1, 2017. https://www.independent.co.uk/news/world/asia/japan-serial-killer-suicide-pact-women-murder-nine-victims-takahiro-shiraishi-zama-a8030751.html

13. THE GRUDGE COLLECTOR

Awes, Maria, Andy Awes, and Diana Sperazza, producers. *Serial Killer: Devil Unchained.* ID Network, August 2019.

Burns, Michael. "Mom of accused serial killer Todd Kohlhepp: He 'is not a monster.'" *Greenville News,* November 11, 2016.

Carlson, Adam. "Survivor of Suspected Serial Killer Opens Up About Horrific Captivity: 'I Was Numb, I Couldn't Think.'" People.com, February 14, 2017. https://people.com/crime/kala-brown-update-on-dr-phil/

Gross, Daniel. "Missing feet, more killings. Serial killer Todd Kohlhepp drops clues, makes claims on TV show." *Greenville News,* August 6, 2019.

Zarinksy, Susan, executive producer. "Buried Truths," *48 Hours.* CBS, November 12, 2016. https://www.cbs.com/shows/48_hours/video/XOqMI2Kt33EDrJZHWgZSJWqRQdC7HiKS/buried-truth/

14. THE CHOKE-AND-STROKE KILLER

Chamberlin, Bob. "How an Alleged Serial Killer Went Unnoticed for 40 Years." *Rolling Stone,* November 30, 2018.

"Convicted Killer Linked to 90 Murders." fbi.gov, November 27, 2018. https://www.fbi.gov/news/stories/vicap-links-murders-to-prolific-serial-killer-112718

Crisp, Lacey. "In His Own Words: Serial Killer Samuel Little Confesses to Killing Woman, Dumping Her Body in Grove City." 10.tv.com, September 23, 2019.

Gerber, Marisa. "LA Serial Killer Gets 3 Life Terms, Screams, 'I Didn't Do It!'" *Los Angeles Times,* September 25, 2014.

Lauren, Jillian. "The Serial Killer and the Less Dead." *The Cut,* December 24, 2018.

Myers, Wade, Heng Choon Chan, Timothy Y. Mariano, Mark Safarik, and Vernon Geberth. "Sexual Homicide by Older Male Offenders." *Journal of Forensic Science,* 62, No. 4 (2017): 940–946.

Wilber, Del Quentin. "A Texas Ranger got a Prolific Serial Killer to Talk: This is How." *Los Angeles Times,* September 26, 2019.

———. "The Inside Story: How Police and the FBI Found One of the Country's Worst Serial Killers." *Los Angeles Times,* December 14, 2018.

15. THE CHICAGO SCAMMER

Borowski, John, producer. "The H. H. Holmes case." Waterfront Productions, 2003.

Boswell, Charles, and Lewis Thompson. *The Girls in Nightmare House.* New York: Fawcett Gold Medal, 1955.

Boucher, Anthony. *The Quality of Murder.* New York: E. E. Dutton, 1962.

Franke, David. *The Torture Doctor.* New York: Hawthorn Books, 1975.

Geyer, Frank. *The Holmes-Pitezel Case: A History of the Greatest Crime of the Century.* Salem, Massachusetts: Publisher's Union, 1896.

Holmes, H. H. *Holmes' Own Story.* Burk & McFetridge, 1895.

———. Confession. *Philadelphia Inquirer,* April 12, 1896.

Larson, Erik. *The Devil in the White City.* New York: Crown, 2003.

Schechter, Harold. *Depraved: The Shocking True Story of America's First Serial Killer.* New York: Pocket, 1994.

16. THE MOORS MURDERERS

Brady, Ian. *The Gates of Janus: Serial Killing and its Analysis.* Washington: Feral House, 2001.

Davis, Carol Ann. *Women Who Kill.* London: Allison & Busby, 2001.

Hickey, Eric W. *Serial Murderers and Their Victims,* 6th ed. Belmont, CA: Wadsworth, 2013.

"Ian Brady: A Fight to Die," *BBC News,* October 3, 2000.

Lee, Carol Ann. *One of Your Own: The Life and Death of Myra Hindley.* London: Mainstream, 2010, revised 2012.

McVeigh, Karen. "Death at 60 for the Woman Who Came to Personify Evil." *The Scotsman,* November 16, 2002.

"Myra Hindley Loses Murder Appeal." *The Times,* October 18, 1966.

Ramsland, Katherine. "Partners in Crime." *Psychology Today,* 47, no. 4 (August 2014): 62–69.

Smith, David. *Evil Relations: The Man Who Bore Witness Against the Moors Murderers.* London: Mainstream, 2011, 2012.

Warren, Janet, and Robert R. Hazelwood. "Relational Patterns Associated with Sexual Sadism: A Study of Twenty Wives and Girlfriends." *Journal of Family Violence,* 17, no. 1 (March 2002): 75–89.

Williams, Emlynn. *Beyond Belief: The Moors Murderers.* London: Pan Books, 1969.

17. THE CROSS-COUNTRY CHAMELEON

Carlisle, Al C. *Violent Mind: The 1976 Psychological Assessment of Ted Bundy.* Encino, CA: Genius Book Publishing, 2017.

Dekle, George R. Sr. *The Last Murder: The Investigation, Prosecution, and Execution of Ted Bundy.* Santa Barbara, CA: Praeger, 2011.

Dobson, J. *Life on the Edge.* Dallas: Word Publishing, 1995.

Kendall, Elizabeth. *My Phantom Prince: My Life with Ted Bundy.* Seattle: Madrona, 1981.

Keppel, Robert. *The Riverman: Ted Bundy and I Hunt for the Green River Killer.* New York: Simon & Schuster, 2005.

Larsen, Richard W. *Bundy: The Deliberate Stranger.* Englewood Cliffs, NJ: Prentice Hall, 1980.

Michaud, S. G., and H. Aynesworth. *The Only Living Witness.* New York: Signet, 1983.

Nelson, Polly. *Defending the Devil: My Story as Ted Bundy's Last Lawyer.* New York: William Morrow, 1994.

Rule, Ann. *The Stranger Beside Me.* New York: W. W. Norton, 1980.

Sullivan, Kevin. *The Bundy Murders: A Comprehensive History.* Jefferson, NC: McFarland & Company, 2009.

18. THE CLASSIFIED AD RAPIST

Douglas, John, Ann Burgess, Allen Burgess, and Robert K. Ressler. *Crime Classification Manual.* San Francisco: Jossey-Bass, 1992.

Egger, Steve A. *Killers Among Us.* Upper Saddle River, NJ: Prentice Hall, 1998.

Flowers, Anna. *Bound to Die: The Shocking True Story of Bobby Joe Long, America's Most Savage Serial Killer.* New York: Pinnacle, 1995.

Robert Joe Long v. State of Florida. June 30, 1988.

Terry, Gary, and Malone, Michael. "The 'Bobby Joe' Long Serial Murder Case: A study in cooperation." *FBI Law Enforcement Bulletin,* 56, No. 12 (December 1987): 7–13.

Ward, Bernie. *Bobby Joe: In the Mind of a Monster.* Boca Raton: Cool Hand Communications, 1995.

Wellman, Joy, Lisa McVey, and Susan Replogle. *Smoldering Embers: The True Story of a Serial Murderer and Three Courageous Women.* Far Hills, NJ: New Horizon Press, 1997.

19. THE BUNDY WANNABE

Anderson, Ben. "Vermont Authorities Point to Suspected Serial Killer Israel Keyes in 2011 Double Murder." *Alaska Dispatch,* December 3, 2012.

Callahan, Maureen. *American Predator: The Hunt for the Most Meticulous Serial Killer of the Twenty-first Century.* New York: Viking, 2019.

Demer, Lisa. "Israel Keyes Dead in Apparent Suicide; Suspected in Lower 48 Deaths." *Anchorage Daily News,* December 2, 2012.

D'Oro, Rachel. "Alaska Barista Slay Suspect Linked to NY Killing, 6 Others." *NBC New York,* December 3, 2012.

D'Oro, Rachel, and Wilson Ring. "Israel Keyes, Admitted Alaska Serial Killer Found Dead, Linked to 7 Slayings." *Huffington Post,* December 3, 2012.

"FBI: Israel Keyes a 'Force of Pure Evil Working at Random.'" KING5.com, December 3, 2012.

Gorra, Charlie. "Israel Keyes Stashed 'Murder Kit' in Essex Before Murders." WPTZ.com, December 7, 2012.

Grant, Jason. "A Son's Torment: Believing a Serial Killer Strangled His Mother, South Hackensack Man Tries to Adjust." *Newark Star Ledger,* December 11, 2013.

Johnson, Kirk. "A Killer Ends Half-told Tale of his Crimes." *New York Times,* December 7, 2012.

Kaneski, Molly. "Acting at Random: A Study of Israel Keyes." May 19, 2013, Israelkeyes.blogspot.com

Keyes, Israel. "Audio Tapes Reveal Serial Killer Israel Keyes' Wish to be Executed." *Alaska Dispatch,* April 9, 2013. http://www.alaskadispatch.com/article/20130409/audio-tapes-reveal-serial-killer-israel-keyes-wish-be-executed

Pearce, Matt. "Attacks by Suspected Serial Killer Israel Keyes followed a pattern." *Los Angeles Times,* December 5, 2012.

Peters, Justin. "Was Israel Keyes the Most Meticulous Serial Killer of Modern Times?" Slate.com/blogs/crime, December 10, 2012.

Silverman, Adam. "When the Killing Ended: The Capture of Israel Keyes." *Burlington Free Press,* May 11, 2013.

20. THE CHESSBOARD KILLER

"Another Chikatilo Who Killed 66 People Arrested in Moscow." *Pravda Report,* June 19, 2006. http://www.pravdareport.com/hotspots/82185-serial_killer/

"Chessboard Killer Gets Life." Inthenews.co.uk, October 29, 2007.

Chivers, C. J. "Man Accused of Killing 49 Goes on Trial in Moscow." *New York Times,* September 14, 2007.

Levine, Yasha. "Interview with a Russian Serial Killer." *The Exile,* March 13, 2008.

Savodnik, Peter. "The Chessboard Killer." *Gentleman's Quarterly,* May 1, 2009. https://www.gq.com/story/alexander-pichushkin-serial-killer-russia

"TV Confession by Moscow Man Who Says He Killed 61 People." *The Guardian,* July 14, 2006. https://www.theguardian.com/world/2006/jul/14/russia.nickpatonwalsh

21. THE GRINDR KILLER

De Simone, Daniel. "How did Police Miss Serial Killer Stephen Port?" *BBC News,* November 24, 2015. https://www.bbc.com/news/magazine-38045742

Ferguson, C. E. "Staged Crime Scenes: Literature and Types." In W. Petherick (ed.), *Serial Crime: Theoretical and Practical Issues in Behavioral Profiling,* 3rd ed. (pp. 141–164). Boston: Andersen, 2014.

Ferguson, C. E., and W. Petherick. "Getting Away with Murder: An Examination of Detected Homicides Staged as Suicides." *Homicide Studies,* Vol. 20, No. 1 (2016): 3–24.

Glanfield, Emma. "Dogwalker Tells How She Found Two Alleged Victims of Gay Serial Killer Both Sitting up in Same Spot against Churchyard Wall." *Daily Mail,* October 20, 2015. https://www.dailymail.co.uk/news/article-3281114/Dogwalker-tells-TWO-alleged-victims-gay-serial-killer-sitting-spot-against-churchyard-wall.html

Sanford, Daniel, and Daniel De Simone. "Stephen Port Case: Coroner Raised Concerns about Police Investigation." *BBC News,* November 24, 2016.

Snook, B., and J. Mercer. "Modelling Police Officers' Judgments of the Veracity of Suicide Notes." *Canadian Journal of Criminology and Criminal Justice.* 52, no. 1 (2010): 79–95.

"Stephen Port Trial: Police Took Fake Suicide Note at Face Value." *The Guardian,* October 16, 2016. https://www.theguardian.com/uk-news/2016/oct/06/stephen-port-trial-police-took-fake-suicide-note-daniel-whitworth-face-value-court-told

22. THE SOAP MAKER OF CORREGGIO

Cleckley, Hervey. *The Mask of Sanity: An Attempt to Clarify Some Issues about the So-called Psychopathic Personality.* 5th edition. St. Louis: C. V. Mosby, 1976 (1941).

"The Correggio Soap-maker." *Museo Criminologico Catalog.* Rome, 2003, pp. 23–25.

"Foreign News: A Copper Ladle." *Time,* June 24, 1946. http://www.time.com/time/magazine/article/0,9171,852845,00.html

23. THE SON OF SAM

Abrahamson, David. *Confessions of Son of Sam.* New York: Columbia University Press, 1985.

Ewing, Charles Patrick. *Insanity: Murder, Madness and the Law.* New York: Oxford University Press, 2008.

Gibson, Dirk C. *Clues from Killers: Serial Murder and Crime Scene Messages.* Westport, CT: Praeger, 2010.

Klausner, Lawrence D. *Son of Sam: Based on the Authorized Transcription of the Tapes, Official Documents and Diaries of David Berkowitz.* New York: McGraw-Hill, 1980.

McFadden, Robert. ".44 Caliber Killer Wounds 12th and 13th Victims; He Strikes in Brooklyn for First Time." *New York Times,* August 1, 1977.

Perlmutter, Emanuel. ".44 Caliber Killer Wounds Two in Car Parked on Queens Street." *New York Times,* June 27, 1977.

Ressler, Robert K, and Tom Shachtman. *Whoever Fights Monsters: My Twenty Years Tracking Serial Killers for the FBI.* New York: St. Martin's Press, 1992.

Terry, Maury. *The Ultimate Evil.* New York: Doubleday, 1987.

"2 Witnesses Describe Man Fleeing Scene of Shooting as Police Press Efforts to Find the .44-caliber Killer." *New York Times,* June 28, 1977, p. 1.

24. THE NIGHT STALKER

Carlo, Philip. *The Night Stalker: The Life and Crimes of Richard Ramirez.* Liverpool, NY: Pinnacle, 2006 reprint edition.

Chen, Edwin. "Ramirez Guilty on All Night Stalker Murder Charges." *Los Angeles Times,* September 21, 1989.

Freed, David. "Night Stalker Suspect Tied to '84 Killing: Fingerprint on Screen where Glassell Park Woman, 79, Was Slain." *Los Angeles Times,* September 5, 1985.

Montaldo, Richard. "Profile of Serial Rapist and Killer Richard Ramirez, the Night Stalker." ThoughtCo. May 30, 2019. https://www.thoughtco.com/richard-ramirez-the-night-stalker-profile-973174

Ramsland, Katherine. "The Night Stalker: Satan and Ramirez, Perfect Together." CourtTV. Atlanta: Turner Entertainment Networks, 2004.

Stone, Michael H., and Gary Brucato. *The New Evil: Understanding the Emergence of Modern Violent Crime.* Amherst, NY: Prometheus, 2019.

Van Derbeken, Jaxon. "Night Stalker Tied to Slaying of S. F. Girl." *San Francisco Chronicle,* October 23, 2009.

Winton, Richard. "Night Stalker Richard Ramirez Died of Complications from Lymphoma." *Los Angeles Times,* June 7, 2013.

25. THE MAN-EATER

Hare, Robert. *Without Conscience: The Disturbing World of the Psychopaths Among Us.* New York: Guilford, 1999.

Manner, Terry. *Deadlier than the Male: Stories of Female Serial Killers.* London: Pan Books, 1995.

Myers, W., E. Gooch, and J. R. Meloy. "The Role of Psychopathy and Sexuality in a Female Serial Killer." *Journal of Forensic Sciences,* 50, no. 3 (2005): 652–657.

Ramsland, Katherine. "Heart of Darkness." *Psychology Today,* 52, no. 4 (August 2019): 82–90.

Russell, Sue. *Lethal Intent: The Shocking True Story of America's Most Notorious Female Serial Killer.* New York: Pinnacle, 1993.

Scott-Snyder, Stephanie. *When Women Offend: Crime and the Female Perpetrator.* San Diego: Cognella, 2019.

Wuornos, A. C. *Dear Dawn: Aileen Wuornos in Her Own Words, 1991–2001.* Berkeley: Soft Skulls Press, 2012.

Wuornos v. State of Florida. 19 Fla. Law W. S 455 (September 22, 1994).

26. THE MILWAUKEE MONSTER

Berlin, Fred S. "Jeffrey Dahmer: Was he ill? Was he impaired? Insanity revisited." *American Journal of Forensic Psychology,* 15 (1994): 5–29.

Borowski, John, editor. *Dahmer's Confession: The Milwaukee Cannibal's Arrest Statements.* Chicago: Waterfront Productions, 2017.

Dahmer, Lionel. *A Father's Story.* New York: William Morrow, 1994.

Jentzen, J., G. Palermo, L. T. Johnson, K. C. Ho, K. A. Stormo, and John Teggatz. "Destructive Hostility: the Jeffrey Dahmer Case, A Psychiatric and Forensic Study of a Serial Killer." *The American Journal of Forensic Medicine,* 15, no. 4 (1994): 283–294.

Masters, B. *The Shrine of Jeffrey Dahmer.* London: Hodder, 1993.

Ressler, R. K., and T. Shachtman. *I Have Lived in the Monster: Inside the Minds of the World's Most Notorious Serial Killers.* New York: St. Martin's, 1997.

27. LA MATAVIEJITAS

Hickey, Eric. *Serial Murderers and Their Victims.* 6th ed. Belmont, CA: Wadsworth, 2013.

"Life for Mexico's Old Lady Killer." BBC, April 1, 2008.

McMahon, Joe. "The Female Luchador who was also Mexico's Notorious 'Old Lady Killer.'" Melmagazine.com, August 22, 2019. https://melmagazine.com/en-us/story/the-female-luchador-who-was-also-mexicos-notorious-old-lady-killer

"Mexico Police Hunt Serial Killer." BBC News, October 11, 2005.

Ramsland, Katherine. "Hearts of Darkness." *Psychology Today,* 52, no. 4 (August 2019): 82–90.

Tuckman, Jo. "The Lady Killer." *The Guardian,* May 19, 2006.

———. "'Old Lady Killer' Set to Strike Again." *The Guardian,* November 21, 2005.

Watson, Julie. "Police Nab Two in Serial Killings Case." Associated Press, January 26, 2006.

Webster, Paul. "Paris Mass Murder Suspect Admits All." *The Guardian,* December 4, 1987.

28. THE CANDY MAN'S APPRENTICE

"Behavior: The Mind of the Mass Murderer." *Time,* August 27, 1973.

Conaway, James. "The Last Kid on the Block." *Texas Monthly,* April 1976.

Elmer Wayne Henley v. State of Texas, 1978, 644 SW2d 950.

Hollandsworth, Skip. "The Lost Boys." *Texas Monthly,* April 2011.

Oberg, Ted. "The Texas Following: Under a Serial Killer's Spell." ABC13, February 4, 2013.

———. "DNA Test Confirms Serial Killer Victim's Body Misidentified." ABC13, November 30, 2011.

———— "Surviving a Serial Killer." ABC13, August 8, 2008.

Olsen, Jack. *The Man with the Candy: The Story of the Houston Mass Murders.* New York: Simon & Schuster, 1974.

Olsen, Lise. "After Decades, Another Serial Killer Victim Identified." *Houston Chronicle,* December 1, 2011.

Reilly, Jill. "Could There Be Even More? 29th Victim of Candy Man 'Revealed' after Photo of a Terrified Handcuffed Young Boy Discovered." *Daily Mail,* February 9, 2012.

29. THE COED KILLER

Cheney, Margaret. *The Co-ed Killer.* New York: Walker, 1976.

Damio, Ward. *Urge to Kill.* New York: Pinnacle, 1974.

Douglas, John. *Mind Hunter: Inside the FBI's Elite Serial Crime Unit.* New York: Pocket Books, 1995.

Lunde, Donald T. *Murder and Madness.* San Francisco: San Francisco Book Co., 1976.

Ressler, Robert K., and Tom Shachtman. *Whoever Fights Monsters: My Twenty Years Tracking Serial Killers for the FBI.* New York: St. Martin's Press, 1993.

Stephens, Hugh. "I'll Show You Where I Buried the Pieces of Their Bodies." *Inside Detective,* August 1973.

Yamanaka, Sharon. "Serial Murders in Santa Cruz County." santacruzpl.org/history/crime.

30. ANGEL OF DEATH

Alexander, Max. "Killer on Call." *Reader's Digest,* November 2004.

Assad, M. "Cullen Gives Tips for Stopping Killings." *The Morning Call,* May 21, 2005.

Campbell, C. "AG Uses One Killer to Catch Others." *Newark Star Ledger,* November 21, 2004.

Dunbar, Carol N. "Nurses Who Kill: Picking up the Pieces After the Charles Cullen Arrest." *Forensic Nurse,* March 2004.

Graeber, Charles. *The Good Nurse: A True Story of Medicine, Madness, and Murder.* New York: Twelve, 2013.

Hepp, R. "Coroner Had Gut Feeling about an 'Angel of Death.'" *Newark Star Ledger,*
October 3, 2004.

———. "Nurse's Lawyer Seeks to Bar Death Penalty." *Newark Star Ledger,*
December 18, 2003.

"In His Own Words." *Newark Star Ledger,* September 12, 2004.

Kraus, S. "Seven Nurses had Warned about Killer." *Morning Call,* July 10, 2005.

Ramsland, Katherine. *Inside the Minds of Healthcare Serial Killers: Why They Kill.*
Westport, CT: Praeger, 2007.

Ramsland, Katherine, and Dana DeVito. "Nurses Who Kill." *Nursing Malpractice,*
3rd Ed. Tucson: Lawyers and Judges Press, 2007; updated 2011, pp. 909–923.

Yorker, Beatrice Crofts, Kenneth W. Kizer, Paula Lampe, R. Forrest, Jacquetta M.
Lannan, and Donna A. Russell. "Serial Murder by Healthcare Professionals."
Journal of Forensic Sciences, 51, no. 6 (2006): 1362–1371.

IMAGE CREDITS

Abraham Lincoln Presidential Library and Museum: 136

Alamy: Everett Collection Inc.: 205; Historic Collection: 78, 213; History and Art Collection: 196; Keystone Press: 141 right; PA Images: 141 left, 230; SPUTNIK: 179; Dan Sullivan/Tampa Bay Times/Zuma Wire: 167; Tribune archive photo/TNS: 75; UTCon Collection: 260; Zuma Press Inc.: 48, 160

AP Images: 210, 250; Murray Becker: 58; Florida Department of Corrections: 222; Handout: 95; Travis Heying/The Wichita Eagle: 36; Home News Tribune: 268; Houston Chronicle: 252; Kansas Department of Corrections: 87; Kyodo: 109; Joe Picciolo: 237; Pool: 154; Seventh Circuit Solicitor's Office: 120; Spartanburg County Sheriff's Office: 112; The Yomiuri Shimbun: 104; Ronald Zak: 27

Billings Gazette/UPI: 18

FBI: 51, 122, 170, 173

Getty Images: David Deolarte/AFP: 240; Acey Harper/The LIFE Images Collection: 225; iStock/Getty Images Plus: ffikretow: throughout (vertical fingerprint), Marek Trawczynski: throughout (horizontal fingerprint); NY Daily News: 64

Redux Pictures: Metropolitan Police: 186

Science Source: Neville Chadwick: 10

Courtesy of Wikimedia Commons: 3, 132

INDEX

ABOUT THE AUTHOR

Dr. Katherine Ramsland teaches forensic psychology and criminology at DeSales University in Pennsylvania, where she is an assistant provost. She has published more than 1,000 articles and 68 books, including *The Mind of a Murderer*, *Spree Killers*, *Inside the Minds of Serial Killers*, and *Confession of a Serial Killer: The Untold Story of Dennis Rader, The BTK Killer*. Dr. Ramsland has appeared on more than 200 crime documentaries and news magazine shows, is an executive producer for *Murder House Flip*, and has consulted for *CSI*, *Bones*, and *The Alienist*. She currently pens the "Shadow-boxing" blog at *Psychology Today* and teaches seminars on extreme offenders to homicide groups.